The International Politics of Judicial Intervention

This volume considers the most recent demands for justice within the international system, examining how such aspirations often conflict with norms of state sovereignty and non-intervention.

From an interdisciplinary approach that combines issues of international relations with international law, this book addresses issues neglected in both disciplines concerning the establishment of a more just international order and its political implications. Through detailed examples drawn from key developments in international law, the author explores how new norms develop within international society, and how these norms generate both resistance and compliance from state actors. Case studies include:

- Pinochet and the House of Lords
- the Congo versus Belgium at the International Court of Justice
- the establishment of the *ad hoc* war crimes tribunal for the Former Yugoslavia
- the creation of the International Criminal Court and US opposition.

The International Politics of Judicial Intervention will be of interest to students and scholars of International Relations, Human Rights and International Law.

Andrea Birdsall is a Lecturer in International Relations at the University of Strathclyde.

The New International Relations
Edited by Richard Little,
University of Bristol,
Iver B. Neumann,
Norwegian Institute of International Affairs (NUPI), Norway
and Jutta Weldes,
University of Bristol.

The field of international relations has changed dramatically in recent years. This new series will cover the major issues that have emerged and reflect the latest academic thinking in this particular dynamic area.

The International Politics of Judicial Intervention

Creating a more *just* order

Andrea Birdsall

Routledge
Taylor & Francis Group

LONDON AND NEW YORK

First published 2009
by Routledge
2 Park Square, Milton Park, Abingdon, Oxon OX14 4RN

Simultaneously published in the USA and Canada
by Routledge
711 Third Avenue, New York, NY 10017

Routledge is an imprint of the Taylor & Francis Group, an informa business

First issued in paperback 2011

Typeset in Times New Roman by Pindar NZ, Auckland, New Zealand

British Library Cataloguing in Publication Data
A catalogue record for this book is available from the British Library

Library of Congress Cataloging-in-Publication Data
Birdsall, Andrea.
The international politics of judicial intervention creating a more just
order / Andrea Birdsall.
    p. cm.
  Includes bibliographical references and index.
   ISBN 978-0-415-46392-8 (hardback : alk. paper) —
ISBN 978-0-203-88848-3 (ebook : alk. paper) 1. Jurisdiction
(International law) 2. Conflict of laws—Jurisdiction. 3. Judicial assistance.
4. Judicial process. I. Title.
  KZ4017.B57 2008
  341.4—dc22   2008019911

ISBN 13: 978-0-415-50258-0 (pbk)
ISBN 13: 978-0-415-46392-8 (hbk)
ISBN 13: 978-0-203-88848-3 (ebk)

Contents

Illustrations

Figures

Tables

Acknowledgements

This book was written as part of my PhD at the University of Edinburgh and a different version of chapter five, entitled 'Creating a More 'Just' Order: the International War Crimes Tribunal for the Former Yugoslavia' was published in *Cooperation & Conflict*, vol. 42 (4), 2007.

I would like to thank my supervisors Dr. Roland Dannreuther and Prof. Emilios Christodoulidis for their advice and support during my studies. I am also very grateful to Prof. John Peterson and Prof. Russell Keat who have offered valuable comments and suggestions at different stages of this research project. My biggest thanks go to my mother, Cornelia Orth, whose support and generosity enabled me to return to university to follow my ambition of studying for a PhD. A special thanks to Kate Bilton who was there for me from the start and has read numerous versions of different chapters and has made useful comments throughout. Thanks also to Caroline Bouchard and Claire Duncanson for their support and for being great office mates and friends.

Thanks to all my family and friends for their support and encouragement. To my grandparents Gerda and Hans Kaiser who always kept me up-to-date with newspaper articles from Germany, and my sisters Karin Menden and Sabine Schellenberg who sent continuous encouragement from the 'homeland'. Thanks also to Anne Bielefeld, Constanze Driesdow, and Ulla Neugebauer for their friendship and moral support over all these years. Finally, a big thank you to Gareth who has always believed in me and who has supported me all the way.

Thanks to all of you for ongoing encouragement that it can be done.

Andrea Birdsall

Abbreviations

ASPA	American Servicemembers' Protection Act
CAR	Central African Republic
DRC	Democratic Republic of the Congo
ECOSOC	Economic and Social Council
HRC	Human Rights Committee
ICC	International Criminal Court
ICISS	International Commission on Intervention and State Sovereignty
ICJ	International Court of Justice
ICTR	International Criminal Tribunal for Rwanda
ICTY	International Criminal Tribunal for the Former Yugoslavia
ILC	International Law Commission
IMET	International Military Education and Training
IMT	International Military Tribunal
LRA	Lord's Resistance Army
NATO	North Atlantic Treaty Organization
PrepCom	Preparatory Committee
SFRY	Socialist Federal Republic of Yugoslavia
SOFAs	Status of Force Agreements
UDHR	Universal Declaration of Human Rights
UN	United Nations
UNPROFOR	United Nations Protection Force

Series editor's preface

Western liberals are predisposed to see the promotion of human rights as an inherently good and worthwhile endeavour. No reasonable person, they argue, could question the virtue of establishing the 1948 Universal Declaration of Human Rights (UDHR) because by promoting human rights across the globe, attention has been focused on ways to identify and restrain evil people who hold positions of authority in the international community. As we move into the twenty-first century, however, Western liberals are now acutely conscious of problems with this assessment of human rights. On the one hand, it is acknowledged that there are ubiquitous violations of human rights around the world and yet the international community has only very occasionally attempted to deal with the perpetrators of these violations. On the other hand, it is also recognised that during the second half of the twentieth century an increasing number of governments began to express profound scepticism about the UDHR. It was argued that there is nothing universal about these human rights; on the contrary, the declaration is now often seen to be very much a product of the Western world, and rides roughshod over deeply held and long-established values in other parts of the world.

During most of the cold war, the question of human rights was only studied on the margins of international relations and the main theoretical perspectives failed to throw much light on the subject in part because they were focused on the behaviour of states rather than individuals and in part because they focused on the task of explaining the persistence of conflict and the difficulty of generating cooperation in the anarchic international arena. On the margins of the field, however, members of the English School began at this time to open up a debate, which impinged on the issue of human rights, and that has helped to move the school much closer to the centre of the field in the post-cold war era. Although the English School is best known for developing the idea of an international society, the first generation of theorists were also very preoccupied with the distinction between order and justice as well as the consequences for the future of the growing number of states joining the international society that did not share the cultural values of the original European members.

Retrospectively, it has become increasingly apparent that this first generation of theorists were operating within a very Eurocentric view of the world. Nevertheless, the terms of the debate generated within the English School during the cold war still have considerable resonance at the start of the twenty-first century. The issues raised by questions of order and justice as well as cultural divergence are captured, albeit in very different ways, by the distinction drawn between pluralists and solidarists. According to English School theorists, pluralists argue that while the state is the main provider of both order and justice, order must take precedence over justice because without order there can be no justice. From this perspective, international order presupposes a need to preserve the state system itself, and so all states are required to acknowledge each other's sovereignty and thereby subscribe to a non-intervention norm. Such a norm necessarily precludes any international defence of human rights. This injunction, however, is of little concern to pluralists who do not accept that there is any universal agreement, at least at this point in time, about fundamental values.

Solidarists, by contrast, subscribe to the tenets of natural law and do presuppose the existence of universal values and they accept, moreover, that we all have a moral responsibility to ensure that these values are secured. As a consequence, they are deeply suspicious of the argument that order can take precedence over justice. Indeed, from the solidarist perspective, there can be no order without justice. In the international context, it follows that we cannot operate on the assumption that we live in hermetically sealed political units, ignoring what is happening elsewhere in the world. We have a duty to promote global justice and this clearly requires us to foster human rights everywhere. Although most of the first generation of the English School were initially wedded to pluralism, key members became increasingly influenced by solidarist ideas. Since the end of the cold war, this move towards solidarism has strengthened amongst second-generation theorists, although there remains strong support in some quarters for a pluralist perspective.

Andrea Birdsall is one of a new generation of English School theorists and unquestionably she has solidarist leanings, but in this book she is primarily concerned with the task of examining the status of solidarist norms in an essentially pluralist world as well as putting English School theory on a firmer social science footing by strengthening the links with social constructivism. She starts from the premise that despite cultural pluralism there are undoubtedly some elements of the human rights doctrine that do potentially have *jus cogens* status. In other words, rights with this status are protected by norms that are embedded in international law and are universally accepted by the international community. Birdsall is thinking, in particular, of norms relating, for example, to torture and war crimes such as genocide. The aim of the book is to identify the ongoing status of these norms by examining to what extent it is acknowledged that states are under an obligation to ensure that individuals who have putatively violated these norms are then prosecuted. To help make this assessment, Birdsall draws on the well-known social constructivist model, formulated by Finnemore and Sikkink, that establishes three stages in the life cycle of a norm, starting with its emergence, moving through its consolidation, and ending with its internalisation, at which point, its application is simply taken for granted.

Without doubt, Birdsall is able to identify a growing body of evidence where there have been attempts to prosecute individuals who have violated norms that have *jus cogens* status. However, although she makes it clear that she favours the internalisation of this practice and argues that the evidence indicates that there is some movement towards the consolidation of these norms, she also demonstrates that there has been significant criticism of the attempts to prosecute norm violators and that there is substantial resistance to the internalisation of these norms. One of the strengths of this book is the clear exposition of the reasons why the International Military Tribunal at Nuremberg and the International Criminal Tribunal for the Former Yugoslavia, for example, are considered by some to have violated the rule of law. But despite the criticism, Birdsall is undoubtedly right to argue that these tribunals nevertheless paved the way for the establishment of the International Criminal Court, which perhaps provides the most unequivocal evidence of movement through the norm life cycle. Now even the implacable opposition to the court by the United States has given way to a more pragmatic acceptance of its existence.

For committed solidarists these developments are straws in the wind heralding the potential for more dramatic cosmopolitan change in the future. But Birdsall's sage conclusion is more circumspect. From her perspective, the International Criminal Court only comes into play as a last resort, but its existence should help to complete this particular norm life cycle. At that juncture, national courts will habitually hold norm violators to account and, effectively, solidarism will thereby have squared the pluralist circle.

Richard Little
University of Bristol

Introduction

> We must never forget that the record on which we judge these defendants is the record on which history will judge us tomorrow. To pass these defendants a poisoned chalice is to put it to our own lips as well.
>
> (Robert H. Jackson, *Chief Prosecutor at the Nuremberg Trials*)

On 8 August 1945, Nuremberg became synonymous with international criminal justice: twenty-two former Nazi leaders were tried for their roles in committing war crimes, crimes against humanity and crimes against peace during the Second World War. Nuremberg, site of the infamous Nazi party rallies to bolster support for Hitler and his policy of utter disregard of the most basic human rights, became the place for setting precedents of a different kind. For the first time, individuals were held accountable for their actions; excuses of following orders, state sovereignty and command responsibility were brushed aside. The precedents set at Nuremberg opened the way for subsequent developments in the politics of judicial intervention: intervention that aims to ensure that the most serious human rights abuses do not go unpunished and that impunity is replaced with accountability.

Both the discipline and the practice of international relations have long been based on the principles of state sovereignty and non-intervention in the domestic affairs of another state. Realist theory, which emphasizes the importance of states' self-interest and the maintenance of international order, has been the main influence on foreign policy makers. Historically, the treatment of citizens by their respective governments has predominantly been considered a domestic matter and traditionally only threats to international peace and security have been understood to justify interference by one state in the affairs of another. These norms of sovereignty and non-intervention are enshrined in the Charter of the United Nations (UN): Article 2(1) states that the UN 'is based on the principle of the sovereign equality of all its Members' and Article 2(4) that 'all Members shall refrain in their international relations from the threat or use of force against the territorial integrity or political independence of any state'.

Nevertheless, there is growing evidence in the post-Cold War world of an increased emphasis on human rights protection and universal principles of justice, which goes against the traditional realist perspective of international relations. In particular, interventions with judicial means, either by individual states or groups of states or through institutions such as the International Criminal Court (ICC) and the *ad hoc* war crimes tribunals, are recent developments that strongly suggest the increasing incorporation of new norms into international relations. This desire to secure the enforcement of justice principles sits in tension with the desire to uphold and protect state sovereignty and the principle of non-intervention.

This book evaluates the extent to which such judicial interventions are indeed expressions of the international community's ambition to promote justice within international order. It assesses the potential of these normative developments as means for resolving the problematic relationship between justice and order in the long term. For this purpose, this book analyses different case studies of unilateral and multilateral action which aimed at enforcing universally agreed human rights norms. The selected cases constitute attempts to combine justice for individuals (such as prosecution for the most serious human rights violations) with fundamental principles of international order (such as state sovereignty and the principle of non-intervention).

The overarching theoretical and analytical framework draws on the English School of International Relations and its understanding of the concept of international society that exists 'when a group of states, conscious of certain common values, form a society in the sense that they conceive themselves to be bound by a common set of rules in their relations with one another, and share in the working of common institutions' (Bull 1995: 13). The existence of international society is seen as the basis for international order, but a key merit of the English School is that it also acknowledges the importance of justice in international relations. It recognizes that a conflict exists between the order provided by states and various aspirations for justice. Within the English School, however, there is disagreement over which of these two values should be given primacy: pluralists argue that order is always prior to justice and that there will also be a permanent tension between the two, whereas solidarists look to the possibility of overcoming the conflict by developing practices that recognize the mutual interdependence of justice and order.

The theoretical framework also incorporates a constructivist approach, focusing on norms and how they enable and constrain state action. Constructivism is based on the assumption that 'realities' are socially constructed by actors through shared understandings and meanings. States shape and are shaped by the international society they exist in (Buzan 2004: 8). This approach provides a more nuanced way of analysing how new norms are developed and order is constructed. The cases chosen for the present study analyse changes and developments in the overall normative context of international society in line with the so-called 'norm life cycle' as developed by Finnemore and Sikkink (1998). Combining the English School with constructivism and the norm life cycle is a good way of looking at the dilemmas posed and how a normative order is emerging. The combination of the different approaches provides a useful starting point to illustrate the progression of norms.

The norm life cycle is a three stage process of norm emergence, norm acceptance ('norm cascade'), and norm internalization; these stages offer a framework to examine the development of human rights norms and their progress towards increased institutionalization into international order. The third stage of the cycle ties in with the solidarist understanding of international society to build a more 'just' order in which justice norms are fully internalized and 'acquire a taken-for-granted quality' (Finnemore and Sikkink 1998: 895), which means that they are seen as an integral part of the international order. The present cases illustrate the dynamic process of norm development which includes acceptance as well as resistance to changes in norms and their incorporation into the rules of international society. The book argues, however, that an *overall* progression has taken place in international society towards an increased recognition of human rights norms that are institutionalized in the international order, thereby moving the international system towards reconciling order and justice to create a more *just* order.

Cases of judicial intervention

Judicial interventions have a comparable dynamic to humanitarian interventions; they expose the conflict between order and justice on a concrete level because state sovereignty (international order) is compromised to protect human rights (individual justice). Judicial interventions are occasions of one or more states applying international law through either national or international courts. The primary focus of this book is on examining the political implications of normative developments over time that have contributed to the development of human rights law enforcement mechanisms. Judicial intervention is seen not as an alternative to humanitarian interventions but much rather as another way of promoting and incorporating human rights norms into the overall normative context without the use of force. Judicial intervention aims to institutionalize norms into the rules of international society in a way that makes them part of states' identities, thereby affecting the behaviour of states.

Judicial intervention is a solution to a complex moral and political problem that questions whether it can ever be justified to intervene in another state's internal affairs to protect universal norms of justice. It is based on the idea of legalism as 'the ethical attitude that holds moral conduct to be a matter of rule following, and moral relationships consist of duties and rights determined by rules' (Shklar 1964: 1). Legalism, in other words, means a belief that 'justice' can be achieved in courts and through judicial intervention. It manifests itself in the present case studies as an idea of *process*, i.e. rule-following in accordance with norms of criminal courts. It is based on an understanding that impunity constitutes a human rights abuse in itself because it confirms the vulnerability of victims and demonstrates an indifference to the crimes on part of international society.

This book analyses four different case studies of judicial intervention through national as well as international courts. Judicial intervention can take place as unilateral action of individual states, applying international law in their national courts to try individuals from a third country or multilaterally through the creation of international institutions. Unilateral action was taken, for instance, in the cases of Pinochet at the House of Lords and the International Arrest Warrant case of the Congo v. Belgium. Cases of multilateral action by a group of states are the establishment of the International Criminal Tribunal for the Former Yugoslavia (ICTY) and the creation of the International Criminal Court (ICC). All these cases are concrete expressions of the conflict between order and justice. In the case studies, particular attention is given to the argumentation processes and the reasons given for certain actions. The way political actors refer to existing norms and rules as justifications for their actions is an indication of the extent to which they have been accepted and incorporated into international society. Justifications are useful sources for analysing normative change because states[1] seek to explain their actions with reference to shared norms and rules that are part of the normative context in which they exist and through which they define appropriate state conduct. All the cases selected are international in nature, which means that they are concerned with the enforcement of human rights and international law that transcends state borders.

Historically, international law dealt exclusively with states, but a shift has taken place towards a recognition of individuals as subjects of international law based on the notion of 'common humanity' regardless of state borders. This change is an important challenge to the principle of state sovereignty, because it questions the idea of states as the principal bearers of rights and duties and it also questions the overall structure of an international society of states. As Bull argues: 'carried to its logical extreme, the doctrine of human rights and duties under international law is subversive of the whole principle that mankind should be organized as a society of sovereign states.' To take this position is 'simply to observe that in our times the international discussion of human rights and duties in international law is more a symptom of disorder than of order' (Bull 1995: 146–147). Even though states are still the principal bearers of rights, these rights have become increasingly dependent on fulfilling their duties towards their citizens. Challenging the existing rules of international order by increasing the recognition of human rights and justice norms through judicial intervention opens up the possibility of change towards a more solidarist international society that combines order with justice.

The case studies focus on concrete expressions of the order and justice conflict through issues of universality, immunity of state officials and the creation of international courts. The analysis is based on the understanding that certain principles of justice, such as the condemnation of genocide, crimes against humanity and war crimes are already incorporated into the international order through Conventions and other international legal agreements. The main difficulty of international law does not lie in the willingness to agree on such universal values but in the lack of political will to enforce them. The book's central conflict is therefore between two values that are both incorporated into the international order: state-centred order based principles of sovereignty and non-intervention on the one hand, versus individual justice based notions of universal human rights on the other. Both values are part of the rules of international society, but because international law has no overarching, independent authority attached to it, some form of agency is required for its application, which makes it dependent on voluntary state co-operation and political will.

International politics and international law

Primarily, international law is understood as the 'law of nations'; it is the law between states that they create and obey or disobey. Its main focus is on rights and duties of states and the relations between them. It was initially established by states to bring some order into the relations between them, while at the same time preserving their independence as sovereigns.[2] International rules and norms aim to alleviate some of the difficulties arising from the context of anarchy by binding states to co-operative relations and creating a framework for future relationships. International law thereby functions to give continuity to states' relations and to provide a mechanism through which changes based on societal values can occur. International law has changed in recent years and has expanded in terms of its subjects but also its content: it shifted away from complete state-centrism towards an increased focus on individuals and norms of justice. International law is not imposed on states, but created in a decentralized way, founded on consensus. It is created in one of two ways: it is either formulated as treaty law in international agreements that create rules that are binding on all signatories or it is created by state practice (customary law) that is recognized by the international community as providing agreed rules that have to be complied with.[3]

Though international law is not 'soft' law – it provides more than just guiding principles in a complementary fashion – it has no independent powers of enforcement and is therefore reliant on states' political will to co-operate. This makes the application of international law dependent on political considerations. Debates in international legal theory focus on the complex relationship between law and politics and what role ethics play in the overall application of human rights laws.

Debates in international law theory

International legal theorists[4] are concerned about *selectivity* in the enforcement of justice norms because, they argue, political considerations play too great a role in the application of international law. When considering the norm life cycle model, however, it becomes apparent that precedents (that are by nature selective) need to be set by norm entrepreneurs in order to facilitate change and to induce a norm cascade that can lead to further internalization of the norm into international law. Providing legal guidelines and definitions aims to reduce the political element of international law's application to make it more universal. International law theory's treatment of issues of universality, selectivity and the difficulties attached to precedent setting become further evident in the overall context of the analysis.[5]

In the discussions surrounding cases of judicial interventions, a link is made between the legitimacy of an intervention and the commitment to protect human rights norms that are established in international legal provisions. The perception that an act is legitimate assumes that the norm underlying the act is already established and codified in the rules of the international community. Further development through the process of socialization sets out new rules and laws that (re-)define what constitutes appropriate conduct in line with the rules of international society. International law is a crucial element in this development, because international law is seen as a social process that reflects common interests, negotiated between states rather than imposed by an overarching authority.

The nature of international law

International law is a system of rules and principles that are regarded as binding on states and which prevail over national laws. International law is sometimes criticized for not being 'law' in the strict sense, but rather a set of moral statements that express general political obligations for states. This is mainly due to the fact that it does not have independent coercive enforcement mechanisms attached to it, but relies on voluntary state co-operation. International law is based on reciprocity, which means that states see it as in their mutual interests to obey the established rules. Most norms of customary international law are non-controversial as they confirm powers that states already exercise, such as sovereignty over their territory. Other norms, such as human rights, are more problematic because they are based on differing cultural values and it is difficult to find agreement on their content. Some principles exist, however, that are regarded to be so fundamental and important for the international community as a whole that they supersede all other norms in international law. These norms then have *jus cogens* status and become peremptory norms that constitute obligatory law and are binding on all states. This, on the other hand, can then lead to conflicts with states' sovereign decisions on the national application of international law.

International law theorists are concerned with questions surrounding the complex relationship between international politics and international law and ethical considerations about the role of justice norms. International law is primarily concerned with providing rules and guidance that regulate behaviour between sovereign states rather than with morals and ethics. It aims to be universally applicable to every state based on objective criteria but is dependent on voluntary state co-operation for its enforcement, as there is no central overarching authority that can exert pressure on states to comply. International law needs power to enforce norms.

Possibilities for agreement on common norms exist, but their enforcement does not necessarily follow. States' politics and interests are influenced by norms and laws that enable and constrain state action. At the same time, politics determine the emergence, development and institutionalization of new norms into international law.

Ethical considerations about justice norms and their application play an important role in international politics and in this way, politics conditions international law which in turn structures politics. Legal norms can be seen as a translation of political decisions into binding rules and in this sense 'law is politics transformed' (Simpson 2004: 51). Politics, on the other hand, is concerned with making judgements about different situations including judgements as to what situation might be deemed to constitute a 'crisis', warranting intervention by other states.

International law theorists are divided whether universal values exist that are reflective of an international community or whether they are just an expression of the interests of the most powerful used to disguise the pursuit of national interests to reinforce existing power relations.

International community and universal values

More traditional, liberal theorists, such as Thomas Franck and Antonio Cassese, argue similarly to the English School that an international community of states exists that provides a shared set of rules that regulate relations between them. Franck asserts that states comply with international law on a day-to-day basis, even if it is not in their short term self-interest to do so, because states are members of an international community with a separate set of rules and laws that are prior to a state's sovereign will. He argues that state sovereignty is subordinated to obligations that derive from the membership of that community and that states 'obey rules of the community of states because they thereby manifest their membership in the community, which, in turn, validates their statehood' (Franck 1990: 8).

Franck contends that by being part of the international community, states accept that they are not completely sovereign, but that some minimum rules of coexistence exist that states follow to avoid jeopardizing their position in it (Franck 1992: 78). He asserts that states comply with international law on a day-by-day basis despite its lack of independent coercive enforcement mechanisms not because of its formal validity or its 'justness', but because of the laws' perceived legitimacy.

Cassese similarly argues that the international community incorporates universal values that override the political will of individual states. A vertically constraining system of rules exists, which is manifested in international law in notions such as *jus cogens* and universal jurisdiction.[6] Every state has the right (and even obligation) to take steps to protect and enforce such international legal provisions which place obligations on states in the international community to protect the most fundamental universal values, regardless of sovereign state borders. These provisions show that 'for the first time, the international community has decided to recognize certain values (...) that must prevail over any other form of national interest' (Cassese 1990: 168). Cassese argues that the international community has thereby made a choice in which the interests of states have taken second place to obligations towards individuals.

Cassese's approach is similar to the English School's solidarist view that agreements on the most fundamental human rights and individual justice norms exist and that these should be given priority over other, more state-centred order principles. He assumes that justice norms are already part of the international order and that their enforcement needs to be further incorporated to make them more universally applicable. He argues, in line with the norm life cycle model, that new human rights norms have emerged and are codified into rules of international society through international law, but that they still need to be enforced according to the obligations set out in those laws.

Cassese and Franck both argue that a process of international socialization can take place with regard to norms that are seen as legitimate by members of the international society. States' actions are linked and they are conditioned by the rules and norms that are part of states' membership in international society. The legitimacy of norms is important for the norm life cycle model because legitimacy enables the start of the norm cascade. The general perception that a norm is firmly rooted in international law is central for the cascade's socialization process because it gives the rule legal specificity that can then lead to changes in behaviour through a sense of obligation. A norm's legitimacy and the subsequent socialization process therefore provide the basis for the possibility of the norm being further cascaded into the rules of international society. This process occurs for instance through applying sanctions to states for obeying and disobeying emerging norms.

Distortion of law and reinforcing existing power relations

Critical legal theorists[7], such as David Kennedy and Martti Koskenniemi, are more sceptical about notions of 'universal' values of justice and human rights in the international community. They argue that international law is embedded in a specific context that reflects and reinforces existing power relations between states developed in international politics over the past decades. These relations, they argue, contain elements of imperialism and suppression of weaker states.

Koskenniemi asserts that there is a danger that, by claiming to act in the name of universal values and the international community as a whole, international law can be distorted to reflect only the interests of the most powerful even though it claims to be based on universality. He argues that 'law is a surface over which political opponents engage in hegemonic practices, trying to enlist its rules, principles and institutions on their side, making sure they would not support the adversary' (Koskenniemi 2004: 4). He asserts that 'universal values' and 'international community' can only be expressed through a state or international organization and therefore only embody *one* certain view of international law, because 'the whole' cannot be represented without at the same time representing a particular. Koskenniemi argues that even though human rights principles seek to break through sovereignty boundaries to realize universal values for the international community as a whole, this can also be seen as imposing the interests by one disguised as the interests of the whole. He maintains that laws' so-called 'turn to ethics' – i.e. the tendency for instance to justify interventions in another state's affairs in terms of universal morals and ethics – is rather problematic because the application of law is ultimately dominated by political considerations of the most powerful states rather than by universal ethics norms. He argues that this 'turn to ethics' has 'often involved a shallow and dangerous moralization which, if generalized, transforms international law into an uncritical instrument for the foreign policy choices of those whom power and privilege has put into decision-making positions' (2002: 159).

Kennedy (2004) similarly criticizes the hidden power politics in such human rights language and argues against using human rights norms as justifications for interventions. He maintains that

> humanitarians are conflicted – seeking to engage the world, but renouncing the tools of power politics and embracing a cosmopolitan tolerance of foreign cultures and political systems. These conflicts have gotten built into the tools – the United Nations, the human rights movement, the law of force – that humanitarians have devised for influencing foreign affairs.

Similarly to Koskenniemi, he asserts that the states of the centre employ the language of human rights to justify their decisions against states of the periphery. This language then constitutes a vehicle for imperialism and reinforces existing power imbalances by referring to universal values that are in fact only based on the values of the most powerful.

Kennedy sees humanitarians as misguided in their belief that humanitarian ideas and institutions are absolute virtues that can excuse any state action whereas, in reality, they are likely to be used to disguise other intentions. He argues that by relying primarily on humanitarian justifications, the issues that motivate humanitarian intervention are fudged: too much attention is placed on justifying actions in human rights terms even when the main motivating factors are entirely different.

Franck takes an entirely different approach by arguing that powerful states sometimes *have to* use justice and human rights norms to justify their actions. Such conduct would be legitimate, he asserts, if a state encountered a law that prevented it from doing what it perceived to be 'justice'. The state can then act contrary to that particular law and to justify its actions, the state needs to set out what it regards to be the most appropriate explanation that led to their moral decision to disobey that particular law (Franck 1999: 118). Franck argues that international law should then not be changed as a result of one instance of breach, but that existing legal provisions can be re-interpreted to fit the given circumstances. This approach is problematic, however, because it provides the most powerful states with an excuse to interpret international law in a way that suits them in any particular situation to make unilateral action possible. It raises the question of who decides what 'justice' means and whether a certain law can be said to prevent states from exercising 'justice'. In cases of humanitarian intervention, for instance, only the most powerful will be able to use humanitarian language and references to moral considerations as an excuse for unilateral action without fear of retribution. It is hard to conceive that powerful states would stand by and let smaller states intervene in other states under the banner of 'justice'. The most powerful are the ones that determine whether or not a certain situation is a 'crisis' and what 'justice' in that particular circumstance means. Franck's proposition leaves law open to contending interpretations based on power politics and states' interests.

Such an approach is also contrary to the norm development process and the norm life cycle which is based on the idea that norm entrepreneurs are necessary to draw attention to new norms and to start the dynamic process of the norm development (not simply re-interpret existing norms). Challenging existing state practice is necessary to find a starting point for the norm development process. The main difficulty in finding such a starting point is determining what challenges can be seen as 'legitimate' attempts to induce change that represent and are based on universal values and not just attempts by individual states to further their own interests.

Setting precedents and the political use of international law

Setting precedents is an important part of facilitating norm development and to incorporate guidelines for international law's consistent application. Cassese argues that a breach of international law based on established justice values can be used to incorporate new norms further into international law. As an example, he argues that even though the North Atlantic Treaty Organization (NATO) intervention in Kosovo was contrary to existing UN Charter provisions, it was nevertheless morally necessary. He argues that such a breach of international law could gradually lead to a more general rule of law authorizing humanitarian intervention. Such a rule could then be incorporated in the same way as Article 51 of the UN Charter that allows an exception to the prohibition of using force in cases of self-defence (Cassese 1999: 29).

Challenging existing international legal provisions and state practice with reference to existing norms is one way of setting the norm life cycle in motion. This may then lead to changes in customary international law through a norm cascade based on the norm's legitimacy. However, even though such occasions are important and necessary to facilitate change in order to incorporate human rights norms into the international order, it is difficult to determine when such a breach is indeed based on 'objective' standards and when is it simply a disguise for the pursuit of national interests.

Koskenniemi and Kennedy argue that law is inherently political and that the application of objective and general international legal provisions only takes place selectively. Kennedy argues that international legal provisions cannot resolve conflicts and ambiguities, because their vagueness opens up the possibility of self-serving interpretations. Human rights categories are interpretative and problematic and even though thresholds exist and criteria are established, borderline cases persist. This leads to the selective enforcement of international law (Kennedy 2004: 21–22).

Arguably, due to the lack of independent enforcement mechanisms, international law is always dependent on some form of agency – one or more states need to be willing to act in the face of serious human rights abuses. If they do so, it is because they focus on one particular situation, they call it a 'crisis' that warrants intervention, but it can then hardly be called an action in the name of the international community as a whole. It is much rather action by one or more states that choose to act independently in particular circumstances, but still claim to act in line with the appropriate enforcement of universal principles of international law.

Koskenniemi is concerned that 'the more international lawyers are obsessed by the effectiveness of the law to be applied on 'crises', the less we are aware of the subtle politics whereby some aspects of the world become defined as 'crisis' whereas others are not' (2002: 173). He argues that this decision is ultimately a political act, however much it is justified in terms of ethics. Establishing 'universal' standards of human rights that legitimize intervention poses problems, according to Kennedy, because 'human rights often excuses government behavior by setting standards below which mischief seems legitimate. It can be easy to sign a treaty and then do what you want' (Kennedy 2004).

The selectivity that arises from such 'crisis' language is problematic because it normalizes and justifies all other conduct that falls short of being called an 'atrocity'. The difficulty lies in devising criteria that encompass all situations on an international level. Koskenniemi argues that in the domestic context, formal rules work well; occasional injustices can be tolerated because of the 'bigger picture' resulting from the need to honour the formal validity of the law. In the international context, however, 'an injustice caused by the law immediately challenges the validity of a legal system that calls for compliance even against self-interest' (Koskenniemi 2002: 169). Establishing criteria in international law that can encompass *all* cases is difficult because such criteria are likely to be either over- or under-inclusive. The difficulty is that establishing criteria always also provides a permission: 'it would compel the well-meaning State to watch the atrocity being committed until some in itself arbitrary level has been attained – and allow the dictator to continue until that very point' (Koskenniemi 2002: 167).

A preoccupation with humanitarian language to find justifications for certain actions can lead to disguising other interests and motivations. This kind of language brings additional problems with it, because by using notions of 'morality' and 'justice' as justifications for an intervention, a specific value to a certain situation is already assigned. Judgements about the context are being made even before action is taken, which means that an objective assessment of whether or not an intervention was indeed based on general universal justice principles is not possible.

A danger exists that actions that are based on *individual* states' morality and ethics are used as precedents for the 'rightful' application of international law and are then incorporated into that law as 'objective' principles said to reflect international society as a whole. Such selectivity and situational interpretation of a 'crisis' do not lead to a consistent and universal application of international law.

This highlights the problem of the universal enforcement of justice norms that do not have an independent enforcement mechanism attached to them. States agree on some minimum standards of human rights in international society but their enforcement is still dependent on individual states' political will. This makes further codification of such norms – that are already recognized as universal values in Conventions and other legal provisions – necessary in order to make them as unambiguous as possible and thereby increase the possibility of their broad application. This is in line with the idea of the norm life cycle that norms need to be widely accepted and codified into the rules of international society before they can be fully institutionalized. The aim is for such norms to be internalized in a way that enforcing them is no longer a matter of political will, but a matter of general state practice, making outside intervention to ensure enforcement of the norm and thus reducing the problem of selectivity.

The status of some international laws as *jus cogens* rules means that agreement on some (arguably the most fundamental) human rights values exist in international law, but they still conflict at times with the sovereign right of states to decide how to interpret those laws on a national basis. Some of the case studies in this book deal with instances in which individual states have applied international laws in their domestic courts in order to create precedents to incorporate human rights norms further into the international order. Kennedy is sceptical about the motivations behind applying international law in such a way because he argues that in such cases it is likely that humanitarian outcomes are only secondary considerations to the potential impact these cases might have as precedents for international law. He believes that the primary motivation of such interventions is not to apply international law or a universal norm, but to use it to establish a precedent that can lead to changes in international law and state practice. Arguably, Kennedy is too cynical in his assessment of unilateral actions and only focuses on possible negative effects of such conduct rather than the potential positive impact such cases can have on the states in question and on international society as a whole. International law has no independent enforcement mechanisms but relies on states for its application. The difficulty lies in the fact that universal jurisdiction provisions, that place a responsibility on all states in international society, exist, but are not applied universally. It is therefore necessary for individual states to act as norm entrepreneurs and norm leaders to establish precedents to develop international law further and make these norms more universal. Even though this is far from ideal, due to the selectivity of this approach, it is nevertheless a starting point that may lead to changes in international law and the emergence of new – more appropriate and more universal – enforcement mechanisms.

The case studies for this analysis display elements of selectivity which cannot be overlooked: one or more states decided to call a particular situation a 'crisis' that warrants external intervention. Even though selectivity is problematic, a starting point needs to be found somewhere. Contravening existing state practice based on codified rules and norms is necessary in the overall framework of norm development and normative change. The focus of the analysis is only on breaches of *jus cogens* norms, such as war crimes, torture or crime against humanity, which means that agreement in international law exists that these crimes are of concern to *all* states and that all states have an obligation to act accordingly. The analysis therefore assumes only very limited agreement on the most fundamental justice norms. These norms have universal jurisdiction attached to them which means that at least a theoretical possibility exists that states can take unilateral action to enforce them.

Such instances of states taking action are important for the emergence of norms and for their development towards increased internalization into the rules of international society. The formation of international norms takes place in 'crisis situations' because such crises necessitate the negotiation of new rules and laws in response. Such situations thereby 'provide focal points for international lawyers in their efforts to determine the nature of emergent international norms and in doing so their interpretations help to constitute those norms' (Reus-Smit 2004: 288). This is an important issue which is not sufficiently explored in the debates in international law theory. The question is how ethics (justice) and law (order) can be reconciled to make normative change possible. It is this aspect that this book addresses: it uses a theoretical and analytical framework that focuses on norms and the way they develop in international relations towards increased incorporation into international laws. The case study analyses make explicit the conflict between order and justice and look at different attempts to combine international law and politics and the way these values influence each other. The case studies deal with enforcement of norms that have increasingly been incorporated in a way that makes them part of international law. The aim of their further incorporation into the rules of international society is to make them self-enforcing, which means independent from political initiatives and without external interventions. The *telos* of the norm life cycle and the aim of a solidarist international society is the internalization of norms in such a way that they are taken for granted and become an integral part of the international order: justice and order are reconciled and norms are institutionalized in such a way that political challenges to international law do not arise.

Even though critical law theorists are right in arguing that it is often the most powerful states that enforce 'universal' values, however, such instances nevertheless constitute important cases of norm entrepreneurs furthering the norm cascade. This can result in a broader acceptance of these norms by a large number of states which can then lead to instances of multilateral actions involving a great number of states, including less powerful countries. The case studies look at justifications and reasons applied by states and individual judges in the House of Lords, the International Court of Justice (ICJ), and the UN that are predominantly based on such 'universal' values. The fact that justifications and argumentations stayed within the parameters of international law and established norms shows that the exercise of politics is constrained by law but that it in turn also influences international law's further developments.

Book outline

This books starts with outlining the theoretical and analytical framework that provides the basis for the case studies. The framework centres on the English School of International Relations, combined with a constructivist view of how norms enable and constrain state action. The central focus is on the conflict between order and justice and how this conflict is dealt with in the English School's pluralist and solidarist approaches. It considers how both perspectives can be applied to decisions made in various case studies that are concrete expressions of this conflict. The framework provides the basis for an analysis to assess how both order and justice are part of argumentation and reasoning processes, how they are included in the ultimate decisions taken, and what the effects for international society as a whole are. The chapter also introduces the norm life cycle model which is used as a means for structuring the cases for the analysis. The case studies are chosen to reflect different stages of the norm life cycle that explains how norms emerge and are institutionalized in international society. The cases illustrate acceptance as well as resistance to changes along the life cycle which suggests that norm development is not a neat progression but rather a dynamic process.

The second chapter provides an overview of the historical development towards an increasing recognition of human rights in international law. It deals with the emergence of human rights norms after the Second World War and can be seen as an illustration of the norm life cycle's first stage in which norms emerge and are codified in international relations. Since international law has no overarching authority to enforce its provisions, existing enforcement mechanisms are limited to monitoring different states' compliance with the standards set out in the underlying treaties or agreements. The chapter describes examples of individual states' first attempts to go beyond these provisions to enforce human rights norms that carry universal jurisdiction. The chapter argues that even though international law lacks independent and effective enforcement mechanisms, considerable progress has taken place in the institutionalization of human rights norms. This chapter sets the contextual background for the subsequent case study analysis.

Chapters three and four analyse two cases of unilateral judicial intervention. They are cases in which individual states exercised universal jurisdiction in their national courts: the case of General Pinochet in the UK and the case of Abdulaye Yerodia Ndombasi in Belgium. Both cases are seen as expressions of the norm life cycle's second stage, the norm cascade. They are instances in which individual states intervened in another state's internal affairs to exercise jurisdiction against a former state official based on the principle of universality. Even though the cases are different in many respects, they deal with the same underlying issue: the conflict between state immunity on the one hand and individual accountability of state officials for international crimes on the other. The order and justice conflict is expressed in both cases through claims of universal jurisdiction based on the nature of the alleged crimes, which, it is argued, are incompatible with a state's right to grant immunity to its officials.

The cases are valuable illustrations of progress and resistance to normative developments as they resulted in opposing outcomes: in the case of Pinochet, the UK took an overall solidarist position and assured its right to exercise universal jurisdiction, whereas in the Yerodia case, the ICJ ruled from a pluralist stance that Belgium did not have the right to prosecute another state's official. These two cases demonstrate that even though progress had been made with regard to the incorporation of universal standards into international law in one case, the enforcement of these standards is not universal. Resistance to such developments still exists and enforcement depends on differing interpretations of the existing agreements.

Chapter five deals with the partial institutionalization of justice norms through the creation of the *ad hoc* war crimes tribunal for the Former Yugoslavia (ICTY) through a UN Security Council Resolution. This is another significant case of the norm life cycle's second stage in which the struggle between order and justice in international law and politics becomes apparent: the sovereign right of the Former Yugoslavia to exercise territorial jurisdiction was compromised in favour of an international mechanism for enforcing already established universal justice principles. The Security Council invoked Chapter VII of the UN Charter declaring the serious violations of international humanitarian law occurring in the Former Yugoslavia a 'threat to international peace and security', thus enabling it to act in response. Unlike unilateral interventions by individual states, the establishment of the ICTY constituted a multilateral intervention – through the UN as an international institution – in a sovereign state's internal affairs undertaken in the pursuit of justice.

The chapter focuses on how states responded to the Security Council's decision to create an *ad hoc* court, what their objections were and how these were overcome. It also explores the response of the ICTY to a challenge to its jurisdiction brought by its first defendant. The chapter argues that even though the ICTY was based on an overall solidarist attempt to reconcile order and justice in an international institution, the way it was set up and its limited, *ad hoc* nature makes it rather problematic. The creation of the ICTY nevertheless constituted an important development that gave renewed impetus to the establishment of the International Criminal Court (ICC) as a permanent enforcement mechanism.

The sixth chapter focuses on the process of the establishment of the ICC and highlights the main issues arising from the negotiation processes which involved a large number of states. The case is seen as an illustration of a stepping-stone towards the norm life cycle's third stage and towards norm internalization. This chapter looks at issues related to states' reluctance to compromise aspects of their sovereignty in order to establish a permanent enforcement mechanism for universal principles of justice. Most of these issues can be linked back to discussions of preceding chapters, such as questions of universal jurisdiction arising from the Pinochet analysis and the global enforcement of justice through the UN's establishment of the ICTY.

The central order and justice conflict is discernible in the ICC's negotiation processes and it is argued that a number of innovations that include pluralist as well as solidarist elements were achieved in the Court's Statute. This suggests that a change has taken place in the international order because a large number of states agreed to limiting their sovereignty by accepting the potential for the independent Court to act in order to protect agreed and established principles of justice. The chapter also deals with the active opposition of the US to the Court which, it is argued, demonstrates the continuing tension between order and justice and resistance to developments in the norm life cycle. US actions can be seen as a pluralist response to the mainly solidarist compromises incorporated into the ICC Statute because the US focuses mainly on concerns for the principle of state sovereignty and maintaining the existing international order. The chapter considers whether US opposition has an effect on the ICC and whether it will seriously hamper continued internalization of universal justice norms.

In sum, this book argues that a shift has taken place in international relations away from a predominantly state-centric view of international law towards an increased recognition of individual justice for human beings. Developments in international law and politics have challenged the existing international order to incorporate norms of justice more permanently through the enforcement of existing international human rights laws. The norm life cycle provides a useful framework to analyse the dynamic process of norm developments that starts with the emergence of new norms and concludes with institutionalizing them into the international society of states. The case studies show acceptance of these developments as well as resistance, which suggests that further developments need to take place to make norms more universal and less dependent on individual interpretations before they can be fully internalized into the rules of international society.

The principle of sovereignty has changed to include not only rights for states, but also duties towards their citizens. These developments have shown that agreement between states in international society on common justice principles is possible, which in turn opens up the possibility of change in the international order. Even though only minimum agreements on the most fundamental human rights exist, they nevertheless constitute an important starting point. This book argues that this progress is based on a solidarist understanding that order and justice are inextricably linked and need to be reconciled. Institutionalizing at least a minimum of justice norms through the ICC as an independent, international and permanent institution can then be viewed as starting point for the creation of a more *just* order in the solidarist sense.

Notes

1　Using the notion of 'states' in a personified way is shorthand for those individuals that act on behalf of states, because as Wheeler argues, it is 'individuals who sign treaties like the UN Charter, but this action does not bind them as individuals, it binds the state they represent' (Wheeler 2000: 22–23).

2　Different theories about the nature of international law exist: most importantly positive law and natural law. Natural law includes the idea that there is a kind of perfect justice given to man by nature and that man's laws should conform to this as closely as possible. This includes a moral element in theorizing law and a belief in 'god-given' principles of higher values mankind should aspire to. On the other hand, positive law is the body of law imposed by states; the empirical focus of this approach is on existing law and on what *is* rather than what ought to be. In the positive law approach, law is seen as separate from morality.

3　For discussions on the distinction between treaty law and customary law see for instance (Malanczuk 1997) or (Cassese 2001).

4　The following section focuses on views of four different writers that bring out the main issues in ongoing debates in the field of international law theory. Antonio Cassese, Thomas Franck, David Kennedy, and Martti Koskenniemi are discussed here as important representatives of traditional as well as more critical approaches.

5　The discussion about debates in international law theory is deliberately kept fairly short because it only aims to highlight the main issues relevant for the present analysis. Further issues are included as they emerge in the respective case studies. The main aim is to illustrate that international law theory as a distinct field of enquiry raises additional issues that inform this analysis and the underlying theoretical framework.

6　The concept of universal jurisdiction is built on the notion that some human rights abuses are so serious that they affect humanity as a whole and therefore need to be punished regardless of state borders. It gives states the right to exercise jurisdiction in their national courts over a criminal act regardless of where the crime took place or the nationalities of victims or perpetrators. Issues related to universal jurisdiction will be explored further in the case studies, and particularly in chapter 3.

7　Critical legal theory sees law not as a distinctive and concrete discipline but as being interlinked with other issue areas such as politics and sociology and as being dependent on morality.

1 Order and justice in international relations – a theoretical and analytical framework

This chapter outlines the theoretical and analytical framework that provides the basis for the case study analyses. The main theoretical approach is based on the English School of International Relations combined with a constructivist view to increase the focus on norms and how they enable and constrain state action. The central focus is on the conflict between order and justice and how it is dealt with in the English School through its pluralist and solidarist approaches.[1]

The English School's starting point is that states form an international society that provides rules and guidance to regulate relations between them. Bull defines international society as

> 'a group of states, conscious of certain common values, [that] form a society in the sense that they conceive themselves to be bound by a common set of rules in their relations with one another, and share in the working of common institutions' (Bull 1995: 13).

The English School approach is a move away from the traditionally predominant theory of realism and its primary focus on concepts of power and national interests. It highlights issues of coexistence and co-operation in the relations between sovereign states and thereby provides a more suitable framework to explain the growing importance of international law and human rights norms than realism. Realism's main limitation is its inability to explain adequately developments in international relations since the end of the Cold War, particularly because it is sceptical about the possibilities of co-operation and also the impact of universal values (such as norms or international law) and their potential to contribute to change in the international system. The English School approach incorporates some basic realist assumptions but emphasizes the concept of international society, which means that states see themselves to be bound by common rules and norms and that they have responsibilities by virtue of being members of the society. Buzan argues that the English School's focus on international society adds an important social element that needs to be added to realism's logic of anarchy because 'states live in an international society which they shape and are shaped by' (Buzan 2004: 8). Furthermore, the approach does not focus on order as the only value in international relations but also takes considerations of justice into account.

The English School incorporates two different views on the conflict that can occur between order and justice: pluralism, which sees order as being prior to justice, and solidarism, which tries to overcome the conflict by recognising that the two concepts are inextricably linked. Throughout the case study analyses in this study both the solidarist as well as the pluralist approaches will be considered. The pluralist view incorporates more realist elements, particularly because it emphasizes the need to subordinate demands for justice to principles of national interests and order. The solidarist approach, in contrast, is built on more liberal ideas of universal values, common morality and international law. It will be argued in the course of the analysis that a shift has taken place towards increased solidarism with regard to the enforcement of human rights laws that tries to find ways of reconciling order values with justice norms to arrive at a long term and stable solution of the conflict.

The English School is a valuable starting point for the analysis as it focuses on the concept of international society and the values of order and justice, opening up important (ethical) questions about the relationship between the two. The approach is often criticized, however, for its lack of a discussion on research methods (see for instance Finnemore 2001), which weakens its analytical strength as a tool for examining movement and change in international society. Shared values and interests are seen as sources of international society and order, but it is not explained how they develop to become part of the basis of international society and how they change. In order to theorize normative change, this book's framework incorporates a constructivist approach and the norm life cycle model, which is a valuable tool for examining how norms emerge and how they might be integrated into the rules of the international community. The model provides a useful structure which makes it possible for the case study analyses to focus on the development of justice norms. The cases to be analysed have been chosen to reflect different stages of the life cycle to examine developments in both directions: acceptance of progress towards increased incorporation of human rights norms into the rules of international society as well as resistance to it. The *telos* of the life cycle is the full internalization of norms into international relations which corresponds with the English School solidarist aim of a more just order.

Constructivism and the norm life cycle introduce a more dynamic element into the overall framework for analysis that is then not only based on aspirations as set out in the English School's solidarist approach, but focuses more on the process of change. This leads to an overall theoretical and analytical approach that places greater emphasis on norms and shared values, exploring how they affect and are affected by state action and how they change. This is important because 'states might not have a choice between acting in pluralist or solidarist ways; rather, the question becomes one of how such norms are transmitted and internalized' (Dunne 2005: 74).

This chapter starts with a brief outline of the English School and its focus on the concepts of order and justice and the conflict between them. The chapter presents pluralism and solidarism as polar ends of a continuum, ranging from very state-centred, order based views at one end to more justice based ones that focus on notions of humanity at the other. The works of four influential authors are presented in this context to illustrate different positions along the continuum. Such gradations of types of pluralism and solidarism become apparent the case study analyses in which they are reflected in justification and argumentation processes. The chapter then moves on to outlining elements of constructivism and the norm life cycle which provides constructivism with an account of change and is the basis for the choice of case studies that reflect different stages of the cycle.

The English School and concepts of order and justice

The English School of International Relations embraces the realist notion of power and sovereign states and neo-liberal ideas of co-operation, common morality and the importance of international law. The context in which states act is an anarchical society of sovereign states. Even though states have to ensure their own survival, the English School (unlike realism) argues that anarchy is not a state of war, but that a sense of belonging to a community has civilising effects on international relations.

The English School recognizes that international politics is a dialogue between three traditions of thought about the international state system: the Hobbesian or realist tradition, the Kantian or universalist tradition and the Grotian or internationalist tradition. This distinction is based on the work by Martin Wight on the three traditions of realism, revolutionism and rationalism (Wight 1994). *Realism* sees states as power agencies that focus on national interests, security and their own survival. International relations are competitive and conflictual and are primarily instrumental for states' pursuit of power. According to realism, states only co-operate with each other and obey international law if it is in their national interest to do so. *Rationalism* sees states as legal organizations that operate in accordance with international law and rules of diplomacy. International relations are perceived as rule-governed activities that are based on the mutually recognized authority of sovereign states. *Revolutionism* downplays the importance of states altogether and places the main emphasis on human beings as the ultimate members of international society. The focus of the revolutionist approach is on moral unity and the possibilities of progress and change towards a society of mankind (rather than one of states). The connection between the three traditions is apparent in the concept of international society (Buzan 2004: 9–10): it combines the realist element of an international system with the Grotian element of a socially constructed order and the pursuit of international society makes an engagement with elements of liberal revolutionism necessary. This theoretical pluralism strengthens the English School in comparison to other theoretical approaches.

Each of these traditions offers important insights into the complexities of international relations and even though they all need to be taken into consideration to gain a balanced view, the English School is most closely associated with rationalism or the Grotian approach. The main focus is on the concept of international society in which states are bound by common rules and norms and which is seen as the basis of international order. The maintenance of international order assumes that states have a sense of common interests in the elementary goals of social life, which are the limitation of violence, the stability of possession and the honouring of promises and agreements (Bull 1995: 4–5). Rules provide guidance as to what behaviour is consistent with these goals; they may have the status of international law, moral principles, and customs or established practices.

The role of international law

International law is an integral part of international society as one of its institutions which provide rules and guidance for the context in which states collaborate.[2] According to Bull, an institution is understood as

> a set of habits and practices shaped towards the realisation of common goals. These institutions do not deprive states of their central role in carrying out the political functions of international society, or serve as a surrogate central authority in the international system. They are rather an expression of the element of collaboration among states in discharging their political functions – and at the same time a means of sustaining this collaboration. These institutions serve to symbolize the existence of an international society that is more than the sum of its members, to give substance and permanence to their collaboration in carrying out the political functions of international society, and to moderate their tendency to lose sight of common interests (1995: 71).

International law is central in the context of international society because it gives meaning to the concept of 'society', in which states are bound by rules. According to the English School, international law has three main functions in the international order: first, it identifies the idea of a society of states as the key normative principle of political organisation of mankind. Second, it confirms the basic rules of coexistence among states and other actors in this society; and third, it helps mobilize compliance with these rules. Unlike national law, international law does not include a higher authority or independent means of coercing states into compliance. It is dependent on voluntary state co-operation, but 'the importance of international law does not rest on the willingness of states to abide by its principles to the detriment of their interests, but in the fact that they so often judge it in their interests to conform to it' (Bull 1995: 134).

Principles of order

International law contributes towards maintaining international order, which is 'a pattern of activity that sustains the elementary or primary goals of the society of states, or international society' (Bull 1995: 8). The most important and fundamental principles of international order are state sovereignty and non-intervention, which are regarded to be a 'minimum condition for their [states'] orderly coexistence' (Vincent 1974: 331). These principles are also enshrined in the UN Charter: Article

2(4) declares that 'All Members shall refrain in their international relations from the threat or use of force against the territorial integrity or political independence of any state, or in any other manner inconsistent with the Purposes of the United Nations.' In addition, Article 2 (7) states that

> Nothing contained in the present Charter shall authorize the United Nations to intervene in matters which are essentially within the domestic jurisdiction of any state or shall require the Members to submit such matters to settlement under the present Charter; but this principle shall not prejudice the application of enforcement measures under Chapter VII.

The UN Charter only allows exceptions to the non-intervention principles in cases of individual or collective self-defence (Article 51) and of threats to international peace and security (Chapter VII).

However, order is not the only value in international politics; states are also increasingly concerned with considerations of justice. Unlike order, 'justice' is more difficult to define as it is a subjective concept and no single definition exists that is recognized in every culture. Bull saw justice as a 'class of moral ideas, ideas which treat human actions as right in themselves and not merely hypothetically imperative' (Bull 1995: 75). English School theorists have long been concerned with the conflict that exists between the order provided by the society of states and the various aspirations for justice.

Concepts of justice

A very general concept of justice is based on the idea that all people are treated equally and are given the rights and duties that are due to them, in accordance with rules in a fair and non-discriminatory manner. Justice in the context of law is the moral idea that law upholds the protection of rights and the punishment of wrongs. Historically, individual rights were limited by the rights of sovereign states and the boundaries set by the rules of international society, but changes are taking place where the rights and duties of individuals, regardless of state borders, are gaining increasing importance.[3]

Developments in international law, such as the war crimes tribunals in Nuremberg and Tokyo are testimony of a 'growth of cosmopolitan moral awareness' (Bull 1984: 12), which transcends state boundaries, and thus pushes in the direction of minimum standards for humanity as a whole. States remain the principal bearers of rights and duties, but their responsibilities extend to include individuals and their claims to the most fundamental of human rights. This conception of justice is based on the idea of a common humanity of human beings rather than shared interests of states into which individuals are divided. States become only 'local agents for the common good' (Bull 1984: 13).

The concept of justice central to this book is that of 'individual justice', which entails 'the moral rules conferring rights and duties upon individual human beings' (Bull 1995: 79). *Rights* for individuals are based on the assumption that agreement on some common values exists between states on a universal level, ensuring at least a minimum standard of human rights protection.[4] These agreements are limited to the condemnation of the most serious human rights abuses such as genocide, crimes against humanity, torture, and war crimes which are considered to be international crimes that concern humanity as a whole. Justice also includes *duties* for individuals; it involves concepts such as individual accountability for human rights abuses in international and internal conflict situations, which means that individuals can be held accountable for their wrongs through criminal prosecution. Even though these rights are recognized to be of importance to all states, they nevertheless conflict at times with other principles of the international order such as sovereignty and sovereign immunity.

Disagreement exists in the English School about how to deal with this tension between order and justice. The pluralist and the solidarist approaches express 'a fundamental distinction between those who see international society as bound together in solidarity by common values and purposes and those who hold that states have a plurality of different purposes and that society rests solely on the observance of common rules of coexistence' (Reus-Smit 2004: 275).

Order versus justice – along the pluralism and solidarism continuum

Different variants of pluralism and solidarism exist that are evident in the case studies and are illustrated in the following section by looking at the works of four scholars that analyse the relationship between order and justice (Bull 1995; Linklater 1998; Vincent 1974; Wheeler 2000). These approaches build and expand on each other and illustrate points on a continuum that ranges from a very strict pluralist approach on the one end of the spectrum towards a more solidarist view of international relations on the other.[5] Hedley Bull and John Vincent express mainly pluralist views of the conflict between order and justice,[6] whereas Nicholas Wheeler and Andrew Linklater argue for a solidarist understanding of the tension between the two values. Linklater cannot be classified as a scholar of the English School: his approach clearly belongs to the category of critical theory, which incorporates a wider intellectual context of normative, sociological and praxeological analysis, but by moving away from the traditional theoretical framework, he introduces additional important issues to the overall framework of analysis.

These four approaches can be seen as representing different gradations along the pluralism–solidarism continuum. The spectrum reaches from a 'hard'/strict version of a very state-centred form of pluralism that favours order over justice to more extreme forms of solidarism that see norms based on a common humanity eventually leading to a breakdown of the order between states and develop towards a Kantian cosmopolitan society of peoples and world society (see Figure 1.1). The debate between pluralism and solidarism raises questions about the nature and potential of international society, the extent of shared norms, rules and institutions. Pluralists and solidarists disagree about the normative content of international society: pluralists focus on the laws of coexistence that constitute and limit international society whereas solidarists assume that a strong aspirational

Pluralism   **Solidarism**

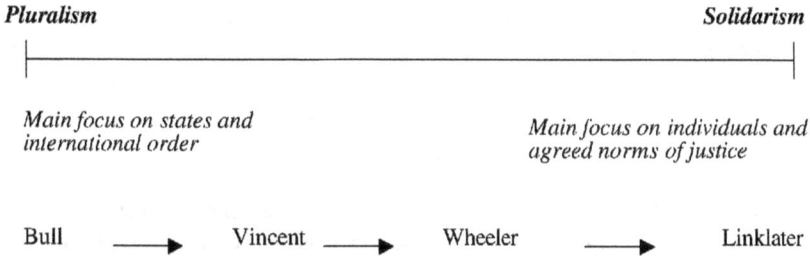

Main focus on states and   Main focus on individuals and
international order   agreed norms of justice

Bull ⟶ Vincent ⟶ Wheeler ⟶ Linklater

Figure 1.1 Pluralism–solidarism continuum.

dimension exists that includes an ethical universe beyond states that is constitutive of international society (Reus-Smit 2004: 276).

Forms of pluralism

Pluralists argue that order is always prior to justice and that there will also be a permanent tension between the two. They focus on the rules of international society which uphold international order among states that share different conceptions of justice and see international order as being built on a limited consensus to uphold the common norms of sovereignty and non-intervention. Pluralists argue that international society is based on the acceptance of a plurality of states and that its normative content is limited to states' mutual interest in continuing their existence. The principles of non-intervention and sovereignty are seen to constitute 'powerful and important norms that combine state interests, moral principles, and formal laws' (Bellamy 2005: 10). Pluralists claim that because international society cannot agree on what individual justice entails, pursuing it would undermine international order. Justice should only be pursued if order is not at stake, because order is seen as a necessary precondition for justice. Justice is therefore only possible within the context of, but never at the expense of, order. Pluralists argue that by providing a context of order, international society paves the way for the equal enjoyment of various kinds of rights and a plurality of different values.

This approach incorporates some elements of realism, such as its concerns for national interests and state sovereignty. It also includes the realist assumption that international law is positive law, i.e. a body of law imposed by states for states.[7] Yet, whereas realism emphasizes the existence of an international system in which states do not co-operate for reasons other than their own interests, pluralism focuses on the concept of international society, which assigns importance to international law and rules of co-existence. States that are members of international society have norm-governed relationships and accept at least limited responsibilities towards one another and also towards society as a whole. Pluralism assumes that even though states do not share the same views on certain values, they nevertheless agree to be morally and legally bound by a common code of co-existence through international institutions. States adhere to rules and norms of society even when these conflict with other non-vital interests. The scope for international society is limited to international order and agreements about mutual recognition and minimal rules of co-existence. Pluralism goes beyond realism in that states have some form of responsibility towards each other and society as a whole.

Different forms of pluralism – Bull and Vincent

In the *Anarchical Society*, Hedley Bull (1995) argues for a strict pluralist conception of international society which is located towards one end of the pluralism–solidarism continuum. His form of pluralism provides for an international order built on limited consensus to uphold the common norms of sovereignty and non-intervention. He argues that justice of any kind can only be provided in the context of order, because only if a pattern of social activity is realized in which the primary goals of the international society are achieved, can secondary goals, such as justice be secured (Bull 1995: 83). Bull claims that even though international society facilitates co-operation and is formally committed to much more than just minimum order (as demonstrated for instance by membership in institutions like the UN that aim to promote secondary goals such as human rights) disagreement exists between states as to what kind of human rights should be pursued and in what hierarchy. Bull argues that because international society cannot agree on what individual justice entails, pursuing it would undermine international order and 'it is here that the society of states (…) displays its conviction that international order is prior to human justice' (Bull 1995: 85).

  Bull concedes that world order, which aims to sustain elementary goals of social life among mankind as a whole, is morally prior to international order of the society of states, because

> if any value attaches to order in world politics, it is order among all mankind which we must treat as being of primary value, not order within the society of states. If international order does have value, this can only be because it is instrumental to the goal of order in human society as a whole (1995: 21).

However, at the same time, he does not see the provision of a cosmopolitan or world society as a realistic concept and maintains that two considerations always need to be kept in mind: the consequences for international order when pursuing individual justice and secondly the degree of injustice embodied in the existing order. He argues that justice should only be pursued if order is not at stake, because order is seen as a necessary precondition for justice. Yet, Bull also argues that even though order is prior to other goals, it does not mean that it is also always the *preferred* value. It is possible to bring about just change that causes temporary, local disorder and the international order that then emerges from such a change will be stronger than before. Bull concludes that 'the question of order versus justice will always be considered by the parties concerned in relation to the merits of a particular case' (1995: 93). He argues in line with realists that certain justice values are only pursued when particular states raise them, which leads to a very selective approach; one that is 'determined not by the merits of its case but by the vagaries of international politics' (Bull 1995: 86).

Building on Bull's work, John Vincent (1974) stays within the pluralist framework in his work on *Nonintervention and International Order*, but argues that because agreement exists that cases of the most extreme human rights violations cannot go unpunished, an exception to the general rule of non-intervention is possible. Like Bull, Vincent sees international society as primarily composed of sovereign states that need to observe the rule of non-intervention as a minimum condition for their coexistence. Unlike Bull, however, he acknowledges that international law has moved away from its very limited application as law only between states to include international organizations such as the UN. He argues that the UN 'unsettled the traditional doctrine of states' sovereignty' because references to human rights in its Charter 'raise the question for states of their sharing membership in the international society with individuals as well as with organisations' (Vincent 1974: 294). Vincent thereby acknowledges the role of individuals and their claims to rights independent of states. Individuals may have a claim to such rights even though they do not *expect* to find justice outside their own state's borders. He argues that because the UN Charter lacks a clear definition of human rights, however, disagreements exist between states over what human rights are, how they are to be protected, and what priority they have in the international order. He supports the principle of non-intervention because the

> minimum order among states depends upon their recognition that their interests are generally served by mutual toleration – toleration not only of the existence of each other but also of diverse behavior within them, so long as it presents no international threat (Vincent 1974: 332–333).

Vincent emphasizes that because the principle of non-intervention is important for states' coexistence as the main ordering principle, it also means that states may have to tolerate injustices, such as human rights abuses, in other states. He argues that placing order between states before justice for individuals thus 'allows states to avoid the responsibility of making decisions as to whether an act or institution within any of them is just or unjust' (Vincent 1974: 344). This, however, then also provides a 'convenient' legal excuse for states to ignore injustices committed in other states. Vincent concedes that this makes the principle an 'amoral rule' (1974: 344), but one that is still morally superior to any rule of intervention because he does not believe they can ever be fully impartial. He argues that any intervention constitutes an imposition of alien values by the one state on another since no *universal* morality exists on which such intervention can be founded.

Crucially, however, Vincent also argues that an exception to the rule of non-intervention can nevertheless be made in cases of serious human rights violations that 'outrages the conscience of mankind' (1974: 346), as is for instance the case with genocide. He argues that 'by urging the legitimacy of certain exceptions to the rule, this doctrine asserts that there are internationally sanctioned minimum standards of human conduct and that the state failing to meet them has no recourse to the principle of nonintervention' (Vincent 1974: 346). He argues that the less worthy consequences of intervention, such as partiality, need to be tolerated in such cases because of the positive outcomes intervention can achieve. The dilemma for international law, he argues, is to find a middle way to resolve this problem. For Vincent, however, until such a middle way can be found, 'nonintervention (...) provides the more dignified principle for international law to sanction' (1974: 349).

Vincent builds on Bull's approach by looking at different cases of past state practice in which justice had been given priority over order. Like Bull, he believes that because there is no overall agreement in international society about the meaning of human rights, it is not possible to accommodate a general framework that can provide for a consistent emphasis of justice over order. However, he concedes that agreement on some human rights exists which warrants an exception to the inviolability of the non-intervention principle. This is a move away from the very strict pluralist view, moving along the pluralism–solidarism continuum to incorporate an acknowledgement of the existence of limited agreement on some universal justice norms. For Vincent's view on a pluralist international society, the disagreement between states therefore does not lie so much in the 'what', but in the 'how' to protect these agreed human rights and in how to devise objective criteria to make their protection impartial and less dependent on national interests and power politics.

Forms of solidarism

In contrast to the pluralist approaches, solidarism is based more on the Grotian tradition as described by Bull (1966)[8]. Solidarism looks to the possibility of overcoming the conflict between order and justice by recognising the mutual interdependence of the two values. Its main focus is on individuals as principal holders of rights and duties in international relations and on the realisation of individual justice. It emphasizes the fact that states are comprised of human beings as the ultimate members of international society. Unlike realists, solidarists argue that states recognize not only their responsibility to protect the individual justice of their own citizens, but also their responsibility to guard individual justice everywhere. Agreement among states and collective action for the cause of individual justice are seen as possible and can be reconciled with principles of order. Solidarism assumes that states

> have reached an agreement about a range of moral principles such as individual human rights (...) which they believe they should promote together. (...) there is some consensus about the substantive moral purposes which the whole society of states has a duty to uphold (Linklater 1998: 166–167).

The ultimate aim of solidarism is to achieve a more just international order that can accommodate individual justice in a way in which it becomes an integral part of international order. The potential scope for international society is therefore much wider and includes the possibility of including shared norms and values in addition to the minimum rules of coexistence. State sovereignty is seen as embracing more than merely the principle of non-intervention and as including relationships between states and their citizens (which also include human rights). Developments of human rights and state sovereignty do not contradict each other and a certain degree of collective enforcement is possible.

Different forms of solidarism – Wheeler and Linklater

Nicholas Wheeler in his book *Saving Strangers* (2000) develops a (constructivist) solidarist argument from the approaches of Bull and Vincent. He argues that international society is rule-governed and that rules that enable and constrain state actions do not exist independently of the practices of human agents. He sees states as structures which provide a framework for action for individuals who hold positions of responsibility within those states. Wheeler argues that the order principle of sovereignty has no objective meaning, but that it 'exists only by virtue of the intersubjective meanings that conjure it into existence' (Wheeler 2000: 22). He thereby assumes a constructivist position, arguing that sovereign boundaries are moral constructions that are therefore changeable – there is nothing natural or given about sovereignty as an outer limit of moral responsibility.

Wheeler argues that the mere fact that states have to justify their actions to the society of states already limits their possible courses of action. Through an analysis of cases of humanitarian intervention before and after the Cold War, Wheeler establishes that international society has become more open to solidarist themes in the 1990s, with interventions in the 1970s mainly being driven by pluralist and realist justifications. He sees the reason for this development in the changing norms that legitimate new state actions on the domestic as well as the international level. The UN Security Council, for instance, increasingly treats humanitarian crises as threats to international peace and security, paving the way for the enforcement of global humanitarian norms. Wheeler goes further and argues in favour of establishing a right to humanitarian interventions without UN authorisation, to ensure that justice is always given priority over order in cases of the most severe human rights abuses. He argues that because states are already part of international legal institutions that commit them to upholding basic standards of human rights it is evident that states can agree on those normative standards, but they fail to agree on the means that can be legally employed to enforce them.

Like Bull and Vincent, Wheeler believes that most of the time in practice, considerations of international order are given priority over considerations of individual justice in international society. He argues that the universal enforcement of justice is still restricted, because state leaders are reluctant to risk more than just a minimum of costs to protect human rights unless the state's national interests are at stake. But in contrast to pluralist writers, he rejects the view that realising a doctrine of humanitarian intervention would be subversive of international order. He argues that 'there is often a mutual compatibility between protecting the national interest, promoting international order, and enforcing human rights' (Wheeler 2000: 309). He therefore sees order and justice as inextricably linked and argues that 'an unjust world will be a disorderly one' (Wheeler 2000: 301). He asserts that a link exists between internal conflicts and international aggression which means that ignoring concerns for individual justice in conflict situations can lead to a breakdown of the international order. Wheeler argues that recent history demonstrates that even though state leaders have accepted that it is sometimes necessary for justice to be given priority over order, they have not yet taken the moral risks to create international law that encompasses such a doctrine for universal humanity. He argues, however, that the acceptance by Western governments that humanitarian intervention is both morally permitted and also morally required in cases of 'supreme humanitarian emergency' is a key moral transformation in the current international society which has occurred since the end of the Cold War.

Wheeler takes account of emerging norms and sees the solidarist project as 'premature' (2000: 310), because realist considerations still play an important role in states' considerations. However, he argues that examples of humanitarian intervention after the Cold War have shown that the society of states is capable of agreement on minimum standards of individual justice and of accommodating them at times even at the expense of international order. He argues that human rights are becoming increasingly important on a domestic level and also in international institutions such as the UN Security Council, and these changes have an impact on international state action. According to Wheeler, the challenge lies in establishing a general framework for the pursuit of justice in international society that will eventually lead to a more just order less dependent on state borders.

Andrew Linklater (1998) follows a similar argument in his critical theory approach that moves away from the English School and reification of the Westphalian state system towards a strong form of solidarism in terms of the overall pluralism–solidarism continuum. His approach includes a notion of a solidarist society of peoples that makes the recognition of universal responsibility of justice for mankind possible. His work on *The Transformation of Political Community* is based on the concept of political communities, which he defines as 'systems of inclusion and exclusion' (Linklater 1998: 2). He argues that communities establish their identities by accentuating differences between insiders and outsiders but they nevertheless need to define their interest in light of a more general good if they want to survive. He argues that 'citizens have to reconcile their identity as citizens with their conception of themselves as subjects of universal duties and rights' (Linklater 1998: 2). Linklater aims to reaffirm a cosmopolitan critique of the state system and questions the adequacy of Westphalian principles because of geopolitical rivalries and wars between sovereign states. He argues that states are capable of fundamental changes that are mainly driven by the effects of globalisation and fragmentation, which erode the moral significance of existing national boundaries. Opportunities exist for more universalistic values and therefore a move towards a world society.

Linklater sees unit-driven transformations as possible and also believes in an 'inside-out' approach to international political change, which means that national actors can utilize their moral capital to join outsiders and thereby extend the moral and political boundaries of their community (Linklater 1998: 216). He argues that the ultimate aim of society is to create more co-operation between states and replace domination and force with dialogue and consent. Modern ideas about citizenship are seen as important because they give states the possibility to overcome their internal moral deficits by promoting the 'triple transformation of political community' (Linklater 1998: 6–7). Such a transformation involves the creation of social relations that are more universalistic, less unequal and more sensitive to cultural differences.

Linklater argues that the ultimate goal is a solidarist international society of peoples (rather than states) that can encompass a better balance between universality and difference in the post-Westphalian era by breaking the connection between sovereignty and citizenship, and by promoting wider, diverse communities (Linklater 1998: 60). He assumes that political communities have the fundamental moral duty to assess the impact of their actions on outsiders and avoid causing them unnecessary harm. For Linklater, political communities need to widen their horizons to ensure that no individual is systematically excluded from moral considerations. All loyalties need to be assessed as to whether they treat others as different and unequal. Linklater aims to combine a general morality for a common good with cultural differences in an equal world and argues for a move towards a world society that is characterized by a non-territorialized form of politics. His project is very idealistic and he himself asserts that his approach might be at times utopian (Linklater 1998: 219–220) because it is mainly based on Kantian aspirations of moving towards a complete emphasis of justice over order towards a world society of peoples.

Arguably, Bull and Vincent's analyses do not take enough account of the impact that changing morals and norms have on state practice; a limitation Wheeler tries to overcome in his more constructivist approach that focuses on norms and their effects on legitimate state practice. Wheeler classifies the solidarist project as premature, which means that the potential for a more solidarist international society is given, but more changes and developments need to take place before it can be fully realized. Linklater goes even further by suggesting that Westphalian principles need to be abolished in a changing world that is influenced by globalization and fragmentation. His view of structural changes which would abolish inequalities and create a community that encompasses common values (while at the same time respecting cultural differences) is very ambitious and could be argued to be utopian. However, his emphasis on the eroding importance of state borders and the effects of globalization and fragmentation add further important dimensions to Wheeler's normative analysis of changes in international society.

The main difficulty that international society faces is not a lack of solidarity with regard to reaching agreements on the most fundamental human rights norms, but the problem of enforcement and political will. State borders still matter in today's world and they at times constitute barriers to the universal enforcement of justice norms. However, recent cases of humanitarian intervention and the establishment of international criminal tribunals can be seen as first steps in the direction of integrating a generally accepted norm to protect human rights universally – regardless of state borders. States have already agreed on some fundamental standards of justice, but the challenge lies in the consistent and non-selective enforcement of these standards. As Buzan argues:

> at the pluralist end of the spectrum, where international society is thin, collective enforcement of rules will be difficult and rare. Towards the solidarist end, where international society is thicker, a degree of collective enforcement in some areas might well become generally accepted and common (Buzan 2004: 149).

The different approaches towards pluralism and solidarism along the continuum become evident in the case study analyses which illustrate different ways in which the conflict between order and justice has been approached by the various decision makers involved in cases of judicial intervention.

Pluralism, solidarism and international judicial interventions

International judicial intervention is a concrete expression of the conflict between order and justice. Similar to cases of military humanitarian intervention, it involves external intervention by one or more states into the internal affairs of another sovereign state to enforce human rights norms and protect principles of justice. The intervention takes place with judicial means rather than the use of force in national or international courts. The pluralism/solidarism debate highlights a number of issues with regard to intervention based on humanitarian motives in which 'solidarists argue that a new norm of intervention in times of supreme emergency has been created, whilst pluralists continue to argue that individual acts of intervention are illegitimate because they breach the fundamental rule of international society: the principle of non-intervention' (Bellamy 2003: 321–322).

Interventions that are motivated by human rights concerns – by military or judicial means – raise important questions about the link between the legitimacy of an intervention and the commitment to protect universal human rights norms. Legitimacy involves legality (i.e. existing legal provisions) but also morality, political will and constitutionality.[9] Judicial interventions are justified with reference to international legal provisions such as treaties or Conventions that deal with human rights issues. Yet, because international law has no independent enforcement mechanism, it must rely on the political will of individual states for its application, raising questions about conflicting values and norms which determine state action.

Pluralists and solidarists agree on the concept of international society, but 'differ markedly over precisely how international society is to be further understood, with important implications for how they see international law' (Reus-Smit 2004: 275). Pluralists see international law purely as rules of co-existence, whereas solidarists see an ethical dimension that is constitutive of international society and its laws. Pluralists focus on international law as positive law, i.e. an empirical focus on existing law, whereas solidarists emphasize natural law which includes moral theorizing about a 'higher' law of perfect justice. It can be argued that developments in international relations suggest a move from a predominantly pluralist understanding of the conflict between order and justice towards an increasingly solidarist view. As Hurrell, for instance, argues, there has been growing support for the idea that international society

> could, and should, seek to promote greater justice as in the broadening agenda of human rights, (...) a minimally acceptable notion of order is increasingly held to involve the creation of international rules that deeply affect the domestic structures and organizations of states that invest individuals and groups within states with rights and duties, and that seek to embody some notion of a global common good (Hurrell 2003: 31–32).

Developments since the end of the Cold War suggest a move towards an increased recognition of human rights and of their position in international relations through a number of treaties and Conventions, international courts and national prosecutions of international crimes. To analyse *how* these changes from complete state-centrism in international law occurred, a theory of change needs to be incorporated with the English School and its central concepts. This can be achieved by integrating elements of constructivism and the norm life cycle model.

Theorising the norm life cycle

Constructivism and norms

Constructivism is a method of approach rather than a distinct theory of international relations and is based on three core ontological propositions (Reus-Smit 2001: 216–218). First, normative and ideational structures are seen to be as important as material structures. A system of shared ideas, beliefs and values exists that defines appropriate forms of conduct, which has structural characteristics and thereby exerts influence on political action. Second, understanding how these structures condition actors' identities is important, because identities inform interests which in turn influence actions. This contributes to understanding how actors develop interests that explain significant international political phenomena. Unlike realism, which takes the interests of actors for granted, constructivism argues that interests are related to actors' identities and have constitutive as well as behavioural effects. Third, agents and structures are seen as interacting and being mutually constituted, which means that 'state interests emerge from and are endogenous to interaction with structures' (Checkel 1998: 326). In contrast to realist and liberal approaches that understand structure purely as a constraint on states, constructivists argue that agents can influence structure.

Actors behave consistently with identities, values and norms to which they have been socialized and which have been internalized. They act according to the 'logic of appropriateness' which means that actors deliberate what action would be consistent with their values and interests. Constructivists view 'realities' as socially constructed by actors through shared understandings and meanings that are produced and reproduced through continuing action and interaction. The social world does not exist independently from its actors. Actors are embedded in a normative structure influenced by the rules that constitute international society and

> to endorse a norm not only expresses a belief, but also creates impetus for behavior consistent with the belief. While ideas are usually individualistic, norms have an explicit intersubjective quality because they are collective expectations (Risse and Sikkink 1999: 7).

Concepts like 'international society' and 'state sovereignty' are not exogenously given, but are based on the meanings and interpretations actors assign to them. These concepts are not seen as having fixed meanings but as being socially constructed principles that are changeable and embedded in a system of other norms and values. Sovereignty, for instance, includes a mutual recognition of one another's right to exercise political authority within a given territory. Constructivists argue that 'the sovereign state is an ongoing accomplishment of practice, not a once-and-for-all-creation of norms that somehow exist apart from practice' (Wendt 1992: 413).

International law and politics are both seen by constructivists as inherently so-cial processes that provide a framework for rules and norms defined and redefined through practices. Law embodies an understanding of the structure of international society, its processes and developments. It does not determine relations between states, but can be an important indication for the nature of change and development in society and the relations between states: 'law has an important expressive function – it formally restates social values and norms' (Lutz and Sikkink 2000: 657). International human rights law can therefore be seen as an expression of international norms. Legal and social norms are influential not because they regulate behaviour but because they constitute identities and preferences.

In contrast to realist approaches that argue that norms have no causal force, constructivists assert that 'norms are collective understandings that make behavioral claims on actors. Their effects reach deeper: they constitute actor identities and interests and do not simply regulate behavior' (Checkel 1998: 327–328). Understanding the processes through which norms and rules are being constituted and how they are interpreted by different actors is necessary in order to evaluate the process that leads to the incorporation of justice norms into the international order. 'New' understandings of concepts such as sovereignty, and a re-evaluation of the role of human rights norms, can therefore lead to changes in state behaviour and the underlying rules and institutions of international society as well as its order principles.

The norm life cycle and the case studies

The starting point for the present analysis is the assumption that states form an international society that is constituted by rules of co-existence, such as the principle of non-intervention. These rules are challenged by emerging norms of justice that are also increasingly incorporated into international society. The intersubjective dimension of norms is important, 'because norms by definition embody a quality of 'oughtness' and shared moral assessment, norms prompt justifications for action and leave an extensive trail of communication among actors that we can study' (Finnemore and Sikkink 1998: 892). The primary focus of the analysis is an examination of the underlying development of international society towards increased solidarism and a new normative capacity for enforcing minimum standards of humanity by attempting to combine justice with order to overcome the conflict between the two.

Justifications given for actions in the different case studies are important because states seek to explain their actions with reference to shared norms and rules that are part of the normative context in which they exist and that define what appropriate conduct entails. Judicial interventions are based on justifications with reference to international law and analysing these justification processes can therefore provide an insight into the normative context and shared social purpose of international society. As Finnemore argues, 'through an examination of justifications, we can begin to piece together what those internationally held standards are and how they change over time' (2003: 15).

The present analysis focuses on identifying pluralist as well as solidarist justifications of attempts to create universal enforcement mechanisms independent from states and their national interests.[10] In line with a constructivist approach, states are seen as existing in a normative structure that enables and constrains their choices of behaviour. The analysis aims to show how existing human rights laws affect states in their attempts to enforce justice norms in the international order. Norms and rules that have been created over a long period of time increasingly influence the decision making process and provide legitimising reasons for certain actions.

> The interesting question is whether and how human-rights norms are becoming not only regulative injunctions designed to overcome the collective action problems associated with interdependent choice, but also constitutive, a direct reflection of the actors' identity and self-understanding (Adler 1997: 332).

The case studies allow an assessment to be made as to whether a progression has taken place that has led to a change in international order, making human rights norms an integral part of it. The cases chosen demonstrate different aspects of the underlying order and justice conflict that is expressed in various ways: concerns for state sovereignty, non-intervention, the right to state immunity etc. are in conflict with notions of justice for victims of the most serious human rights abuses and attempts by one or more states to uphold universally agreed human rights norms even without state consent. Finnemore and Sikkink's (1998) norm life cycle model provides an effective tool for the analysis. It seeks to explain how new norms are generated and disseminated and how they may become part of the rules of international society and thereby enable and constrain state action. The cases are chosen to reflect different stages of the norm life cycle, they illustrate acceptance and resistance to change in accordance with the model which suggests that norm development includes progress as well as set-backs. The life cycle is a different way of looking at these issues and adds to the aspirational dimension set out in the English School's solidarist approach by providing a dynamic element for the overall analysis.

The norm life cycle model illustrates how international norms emerge and develop and how they are incorporated into the rules of international society. The 'life cycle' consists of three stages: norm emergence, norm cascade, and norm internalization (see Figure 1.2). Different actors, motives and influences are involved in different stages of the process. The life cycle starts with the emergence of a new norm, followed by its diffusion and cascade towards greater acceptance and is completed with the internalization of a new norm as a fully incorporated rule in international society. Complete norm internalization can be seen as being similar to the solidarists' ultimate aim of a more 'just' order because 'norms acquire a taken-for-granted quality and are no longer a matter of broad public debate' (Finnemore and Sikkink 1998: 895). The order and justice conflict is thus overcome through enforcement and compliance with individual justice norms which are then permanently incorporated into the international order and become an integral part of international society.

In accordance with the different stages of the life cycle approach, the different case studies in this book seek to demonstrate that an overall progression has taken place from initial attempts to enforce justice norms universally (either on a unilateral or a multilateral basis) to the establishment of the ICC as an independent and permanent institution, aimed at the universal enforcement of human rights provisions. This progression has also been resisted which is reflected in the cases chosen.

The first stage of the norm life cycle, *norm emergence*, is dominated by the attempts of 'norm entrepreneurs' to call attention to 'new' issues and to convince

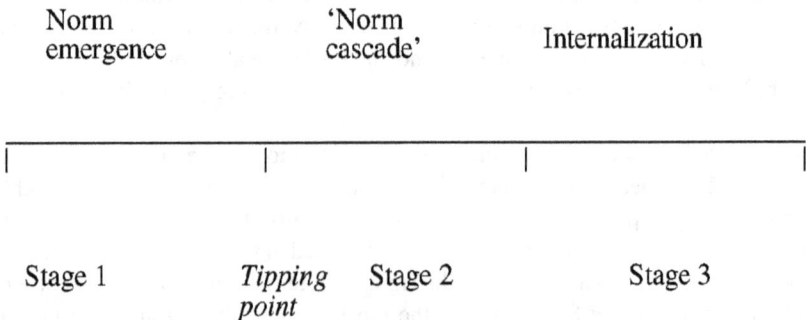

Norm emergence	'Norm cascade'	Internalization

Stage 1	*Tipping point*	Stage 2	Stage 3

Figure 1.2 Norm life cycle (Finnemore and Sikkink 1998: 896).

a 'critical mass' of states (as norm leaders) to embrace new norms. Norms are 'actively built by agents having strong notions about appropriate or desirable behavior in their community' (Finnemore and Sikkink 1998: 896). Emergent norms are institutionalized, usually in international law, to clarify their content, determine what constitutes a violation and to specify procedures for sanctioning norm breaking. This process of legalisation aims to induce compliance with norms based on the view that codified rules and norms affect behaviour. These new norms do not enter into a normative vacuum, but compete with other norms, ideas and interests.

The next chapter sets out the emergence and development of human rights norms and their increased recognition in international law since the end of the Second World War. The chapter describes how such norms became increasingly recognized and incorporated into the rules of international society through international law and provides the context for the subsequent case studies.

In order for a norm to reach the life cycle's second stage, a 'tipping' point or threshold needs to be reached, which occurs when 'a critical mass of relevant state actors adopt the norm' (Finnemore and Sikkink 1998: 895). The norm then enters into the second stage of the '*norm cascade*', at which point a different dynamic starts: more and more states adopt the new norm and a process of international socialization begins, in which norm breakers are induced to become norm followers. The norm cascade is a collection of norm affirming events, which are 'discursive events – that is they are verbal or written statements asserting the norm' (Lutz and Sikkink 2000: 655). Such events can take the form of treaties and declarations, statements by government officials or domestic laws that are based on international law. Most of the case studies constitute norm affirming events by focusing on legal judgments with regard to judicial interventions.

Socialization is the dominant mechanism of the norm cascade, it involves applying diplomatic sanctions on states for obeying or disobeying new norms either multilaterally or unilaterally through states, international organisations or pressure groups. This process is aimed at changing states' behaviour towards adopting the new norms and thereby reflects changes in the understanding of what is deemed to be appropriate behaviour in line with the rules of international society.

The life cycle's second stage is illustrated in three of the case studies: the Pinochet case analysed in chapter three and the case of Belgium v. The Congo analysed in chapter four constitute unilateral attempts by individual states to act as 'norm entrepreneurs' to enforce new norms that were codified in international law in line with the cycle's first stage. Chapter five analyses a multilateral attempt to enforce such human rights norms through the creation of the International Criminal Tribunal for the Former Yugoslavia (ICTY).

In the third stage of the life cycle, the *norm internalization*, 'norms may become so widely accepted that they are internalized by actors and achieve a 'taken-for-granted' quality that makes conformance with the norm almost automatic' (Finnemore and Sikkink 1998: 904). Norm cascade and norm internalization are very lengthy and difficult processes, involving a number of concessions and compromises with regard to traditional understandings of the principles of international order. The new norms become standards of appropriateness, requiring a re-evaluation of established values and raising questions such as what sovereignty entails and whether the principle of non-intervention is always inviolable.

The completion of the whole life cycle is not inevitable, it is dependent on the intrinsic characteristics of the norm and the inherent belief system that needs to transcend cultural or political contexts. The relationship to existing norms also influences the likelihood of the new norm's influence, particularly in the context of international law, because 'the persuasiveness of a normative claim in law is explicitly tied to the 'fit' of that claim within existing normative frameworks; legal arguments are persuasive when they are grounded in precedent' (Finnemore and Sikkink 1998: 914–915).

In chapter six, the establishment of the ICC is used as a case to illustrate this third and final stage of the cycle. It ties in with already existing and universally agreed upon international norms that are already part of the international order through international legal provisions, but have no effective enforcement mechanisms attached to them. The ICC can then be seen as an attempt to incorporate norms and their enforcement more fully into provisions of the international order

Table 1.1 The stages of the norm life cycle and the case studies (adapted from Finnemore and Sikkink 1998: 898)

	Stage 1 *Norm emergence*	*Stage 2* *Norm cascade*	*Stage 3* *Internalization*
Actors	Norm entrepreneurs with organizational platforms	States; international organizations; networks	Law; professions; bureaucracy
Motives	Altruism; empathy; ideational commitment	Legitimacy; reputation; esteem	Conformity
Dominant mechanisms	Persuasion	Socialization; institutionalization; demonstration	Habit; institutionalization
Main characteristics of stage	Emergence of new issues and norms; codification into international rules and laws to clarify norms	International socialization shapes state identities linked to their membership in international society	Norms are widely accepted and achieve taken-for-granted quality; universal enforcement
Case studies	Emergence of new human rights norms in international law after the Second World War (chapter three).	Selective enforcement to institutionalize norms and laws and resistance to such efforts: the cases of Pinochet and Yerodia (chapters four and five); and the establishment of the ICTY as an *ad hoc* court (chapter six).	Attempt to (partially) institutionalize human rights law enforcement through the ICC as an independent and permanent court and resistance to it mainly through US opposition (chapter seven).

through an independent supranational institution. The creation of the ICC ties in with the solidarist understanding of international society towards building a more just order in which norms are fully internalized and are seen as an integral part of the international order. The chapter also explores resistance to the norm internalization in form of US opposition to the Court.

Table 1.1 illustrates the links between the stages in the norm life cycle model and the cases analysed in the present study. The different stages of the life cycle model should not be seen as discrete categories with clear cut boundaries, but as more general divisions used to illustrate the development of new norms. Each case study is assigned to one stage of the model but some of their characteristics also overlap with the adjacent stages. Norm development in accordance with the norm life cycle is closely linked to changes in international law as the progress of a norm to the next stages of the model is dependent on its codification into international legal provisions and the perception of that norm as being legitimate. Legitimacy is important in order for norms to be accepted by a large number of states and to be cascaded along the life cycle towards increased institutionalization.

Notes

1 This distinction between pluralism and solidarism was first made by Hedley Bull in his article on 'The Grotian conception in international society' (Bull 1966).
2 According to Bull (1995), the five institutions of international society are balance of power, international law, diplomacy, great powers, and war.
3 Bull recognizes this, for instance, by arguing that 'it is a profound change in our perception of this matter that in the second half of the twentieth century the question of justice concerns what is due not only to states and nations but to all individual persons in an imagined community of mankind' (1984: 12).
4 Criticism exists that concern with individuals and analyses of human rights is a weakness of recent works in the English School tradition. See for instance Buzan (2004: 17) who argues that this leads to an assumption that human rights principles must be universal and affect humankind as a whole: 'one of those dangers is that both the possibility and the fact of regional developments of international society get ignored.' Such criticisms certainly have their place, however, in the context of the present analysis the focus is on very limited/minimal agreement on some of the worst human rights abuses that are recognized in international law as being of universal concern and as constituting *jus cogens* norms.
5 This continuum is similar to Buzan's (2004) distinction between 'thin' (pluralism) and 'thick' (solidarism) international society according to the degree of shared norms, institutions etc.
6 Both Bull and Vincent developed more solidarist themes in their later works. Wheeler and Dunne argue that in the course of his life and work, Hedley Bull was 'increasingly drawn to the idea that without justice there could be no lasting order' (1996: 100). John Vincent's work on 'Human Rights and International Relations' can even be seen as a complete contradiction to his earlier work (Wheeler 1992: 478), but in the context of this chapter, his early work on 'Nonintervention and International Order' is used to illustrate one particular version of pluralism.
7 Positive law is distinguished from natural law, which is the idea that there is a kind of perfect justice given to man by nature and that man's law should conform to this as closely as possible.
8 The Grotian tradition's central assumption is described as 'solidarity, or potential solidarity, of the states comprising international society, with respect to the enforcement

of law. This assumption is not explicitly adopted and defended by Grotius, but (…) the rules which he propounds for international conduct are such as to presuppose that it is made' (Bull 1966: 52).

9 For an in-depth discussion of this point, see (Clark 2005).

10 In the case studies, the analysis focuses on the reasons given by states and their representatives, such as judges in the House of Lords as well as delegations in meetings during negotiations to create international criminal courts, for justifying intervention in another state's affairs by judicial means. These argumentations reflect broader debates occurring in international law and politics, played out in these concrete instances.

2 The emergence of human rights and the limits of their enforcement

This chapter provides the context for the subsequent case study analyses. It outlines the emergence of human rights norms in international relations after the Second World War and some of the problems attached to the lack of effective independent enforcement mechanisms. In line with the norm life cycle's first stage, new norms emerged after the war that were incorporated into the rules and laws of international society. Since the end of the Second World War, a major shift has taken place in international law that is no longer only concerned with states and the relations between them but also recognizes individuals as having rights independently of states. This recognition of individual human rights challenges the very foundations of international law, based on order principles of state sovereignty and non-intervention, to include norms of individual justice. States are still the principal bearers of rights but their duties extend to include concerns for their citizens and human rights more generally. In addition, individuals can be held responsible for their actions.

Human rights laws that emerged after the Second World War can be divided into two categories: broad guidelines that set out very general rights, and more specific crimes that are seen to be fundamental to all states in international society and therefore warrant special provisions for their enforcement. This chapter argues that the main difficulty facing international law is that it operates without a central overarching authority to ensure the enforcement of its provisions and is dependent on some form of agency and voluntary state co-operation. Even though states agree on codifying human rights into international law, no effective independent enforcement mechanisms are attached to them. Existing enforcement through UN institutions is limited to monitoring and reporting on states' compliance. Two well-documented attempts to go beyond these limited powers briefly discussed in this chapter are the International Military Tribunal at Nuremberg and the trial of Adolf Eichmann in Jerusalem. Both are examples of judicial intervention by one or more states aimed at enforcing existing human rights provisions. Despite a number of problems and issues raised in these cases, this chapter argues that they constitute valuable precedents and starting points from which subsequent developments in human rights law implementation, in line with the norm life cycle, could take place.

The emergence of international human rights and the Nuremberg precedent

International relations have historically been dominated by the Westphalian principles of state sovereignty and non-intervention in the internal affairs of another state. Traditionally, states were seen as the principal actors in international relations and the treatment of their citizens was solely considered to be within their national jurisdiction. In line with realist approaches, international law was seen to be primarily concerned with regulating relations between states and protecting the own interests of those states. This changed after the Second World War when it was recognized that Nazi aggression and the atrocities committed resulted from a 'philosophy based on utter disregard for the dignity of human beings' (Cassese 2001: 351). It was decided that basic standards for human rights needed to be formulated and promoted in the international community to ensure a recognition that individuals have rights independently from states. Initially, a set of general principles on human rights that provided broad guidelines for the UN and its members was negotiated, followed by their gradual elaboration and implementation through more concrete legal provisions. This was the start of the first stage in the norm life cycle: the emergence of 'new' issues of importance that were codified into international law to clarify their content and to include new standards of appropriate behaviour.

The UN Charter, established at the end of the Second World War, was the first legal document to incorporate notions of universal human rights. It introduced the idea that not only states, but also individuals are subjects of international law with rights and duties. The Preamble of the Charter reaffirms 'faith in fundamental human rights, in the dignity and worth of the human person, in the equal rights of men and women and of nations large and small.' Article 1 also states that 'all human beings are equal in dignity and rights.' Further notions of this 'new' and important issue of human rights norms are set out in Articles 55 and 56[1], which include a pledge by all members to promote and respect international human rights. This was the first time that human rights had been explicitly mentioned in an international document, signed by a large number of states. Even though the human rights provisions in the UN Charter were rather vague, it was the first treaty that recognized human rights as a matter of global – and not just domestic – concern (Robertson 2002: 27). Human beings were acknowledged as subjects of international law that have rights based on their humanity and not only on their membership of a particular state.

At the same time, however, the very same document also reaffirmed the notion of state sovereignty and the principle of non-intervention, and thus further incorporated the conflict between order and justice. Article 2(1), for instances, states that the UN 'is based on the principle of the sovereign equality of all its Members' and Articles 2(4) and 2(7) set out the principle of non-intervention.[2] Even though states endorsed the general idea of human rights, their realisation still depended on traditional state diplomacy: 'much of world politics in subsequent years was to deal with the contradiction between affirmation of universal human rights and the reaffirmation of state sovereignty over domestic social issues' (Forsythe 2006: 38).

A first serious attempt to enforce human rights by developing standards of universal application based on the rule of law was made in the Nuremberg tribunal. This is a concrete expression of the underlying order and justice conflict because Germany's sovereign right to exercise jurisdiction over its own nationals was compromised by the decision of a number of states to create an international tribunal to deal with the most serious human rights abuses committed during the Second World War.

Setting a precedent – the International Military Tribunal at Nuremberg

The Nuremberg tribunal was established after the Second World War as an attempt to create 'new rules of international conduct and agreed boundaries in the violation of human rights' (Overy 2003: 23). It was a first attempt to enforce human rights provisions through an international judicial intervention and can be seen as the 'starting point for the new era of international human rights law' (Bindman 2002: 146).

During the Second World War the Allied forces agreed that they had to deal with the human rights abuses committed by the Nazi regime. Although Churchill and Roosevelt initially favoured summary execution of Nazi leaders without trial, the victorious states eventually agreed to set up the International Military Tribunal (IMT) at Nuremberg to bring Nazi criminals to justice in an international court (Overy 2003: 3–5). The Allied forces set out to create an international legal framework to match those taken for granted on the domestic level in most sovereign states. This external judicial intervention required some surrender of power and sovereignty by Germany. The main aims of the tribunal were to establish documentary evidence of the crimes committed by the regime in order to determine questions of responsibility and to prevent the creation of myths and fantasies about the Second World War and the Nazi regime.

On 8 August 1945 the London Agreement was signed with the Charter for the IMT as an annex containing the law and the procedures of the trial. In the major trial before the IMT, twenty-two defendants were tried in a trial that lasted almost one year and resulted in nineteen guilty verdicts and three acquittals.[3] Even though the IMT is often criticized for a number of reasons, it set a precedent for new rules of international conduct regarding human rights law, because 'for the first time States broke the monopoly of national jurisdiction over international crimes, a monopoly that until then had been the rule' (Cassese 2001: 267).

A number of important innovations were made by the IMT that had (and still have) considerable effects on the development of international human rights law and its enforcement. The decision to establish a tribunal to deal with human rights atrocities through an international legal mechanism rather than to exercise revenge through summary executions constituted a first step towards realising the potential to achieve justice through law. As Shklar argues,

> the Trial fulfilled an immediate function which is both the most ancient and the most compelling purpose of all criminal justice. It replaced private,

uncontrolled vengeance with a measured process of fixing guilt in each case, and taking the power to punish out of the hands of those directly involved (1964: 158).

States acknowledged the importance of rectifying injustice by applying generally agreed international norms and rules concerning human rights through a formal system that adhered to principles of legal proceedings with respect to the rights of victims as well as the accused (Minow 1998: 25). The Nuremberg tribunal can be seen as a starting point of a norm life cycle which could ultimately end the culture of impunity for atrocious human rights abuses and replace it with one of accountability. The motivation behind enforcing justice principles through an international court is based on the view that impunity in itself constitutes a human rights violation because it confirms the defencelessness of vulnerable victims and does not challenge the legitimacy of the acts committed. International criminal justice also includes the idea that enforcing human rights through rules and institutions established by the international community can lead to greater recognition and application of these norms on a universal basis. Other important precedents set by the IMT included the creation of new crimes in international law and the recognition of individual accountability for international crimes.

New categories of crimes

Article 6 of the IMT Charter set out the crimes the defendants were charged with. These fell into three categories: crimes against peace, war crimes, and crimes against humanity (Harris 1998: 739–740). One of the rule of law's most fundamental principle was violated through the creation of new categories of crimes that were applied in this case: the principle of *nullum crimen sine lege, nulla poena sine lege* means that crimes cannot by defined retroactively. This principle is fundamental to the rule of law because it provides clarity and makes law predictable. Even though the crimes under Article 6 of the IMT Charter were defined as such for the first time and therefore constituted retroactive law in the strict sense, the court decided that 'many acts covered by the Indictment were in fact known to be criminal at the time they were committed, and would have been subject to criminal proceedings had the law not been perverted by the dictatorship' (Overy 2003: 22–23). The IMT thereby established a precedent by emphasising the importance of enforcing certain justice norms over one of the most fundamental principles of international law.

The category of 'crimes against humanity' further challenged established principles of the international order because it included crimes committed by the Nazi regime on German soil that were not covered by the laws of war. By establishing crimes against humanity as an *international* crime, the systematic atrocities that took place within the German state were placed in international law and could be included in the trial proceedings. This is significant because it 'represents the first breach of the 'fences' of sovereignty, indicating that certain crimes are so egregious that the international community has a right to punish them wherever they take place' (Rodman 2006: 28).

Individual accountability

The way all the crimes were defined was innovative and set an example for future human rights laws in an additional way because the defendants were charged as individuals, regardless of their position in the Nazi government, whether they acted under national law or under orders given by their superiors.[4] The IMT thereby based its judgements on the concept of individual accountability which means that individuals can be held accountable for the crimes they committed in the context of international conflicts. Arguments of state sovereignty were rejected as acceptable defence for violations of human rights, because as the IMT's Chief Justice Stone famously commented, 'crimes against international law are committed by men, not abstract entities, and only by punishing individuals who commit such crimes can the provisions of international law be enforced' (quoted in Harris 1998: 742).

This recognition of individual responsibility with regard to international crimes was key to the development of international enforcement of human rights law through international courts. It is a significant aspect of the IMT because prior to this tribunal, international law was primarily concerned with states and not individual persons. This shift away from states' responsibility towards individual responsibility marks a turning point in the understanding of sovereignty. It constitutes a dominant development in international human rights law which 'was moving toward direct applicability to individuals – endowing them with rights and protections and in return demanding adherence to international norms' (Maogoto 2004: 6). The principle of individual accountability recognizes that international law gives individuals rights but in return also sets out obligations. Individuals are no longer protected by the doctrine of state sovereignty but can be held responsible for their individual actions under international law. The IMT set a precedent in that international human rights law can be applied to individuals and not just states.

Shortfalls of the IMT

The IMT is often criticized for applying victors' justice and its lack of impartiality because only German crimes committed during the war were tried in the court. It was also not a truly 'international' court because even though it was jointly established and operated, the trials were in many respects domestic trials of the Allied Forces. The IMT was therefore an expression of one-sided justice: that of a victorious party over a defeated one. This makes the delivery of equal and universal justice questionable when only the enemy is brought to trial in its own occupied territory. For instance, British forces have never been held accountable over the carpet bombing of Dresden which some argue could be considered to have amounted to war crimes. There were also some serious legal challenges attached to the trials, most importantly (as outlined above) the application of *ex post facto*[5] law and the violation of the *nullum crimen* principle.

Despite these shortfalls, however, Nuremberg established a very important precedent for the subsequent development of international human rights law enforcement. It changed and clarified international law in many ways and it was a first attempt by more than one state to prosecute individuals for international crimes concerning human rights regardless of state borders. Individuals were held accountable for their acts and new categories of crimes were established that still serve as a basis for today's international human rights laws. The Nuremberg tribunal was the first example of the enforcement of international human rights provisions through an international judicial institution. Arguably, one of the most significant aspect of Nuremberg, however, is that it happened at all. As Bosch argues,

> Nuremberg is a fact of history; international law will never be the same. Legal precedents have been declared, and new procedures for international criminal courts have been developed. The Tribunal has affirmed personal responsibility; the court has asserted judicial protection for human rights (1970: 238).

Justice was *seen* to be done: the accused were accorded the right of a defence counsel, the trials were translated into their own language and the accused were given the right to make final unchallenged summations. The IMT set a precedent for the international enforcement of human rights norms and therefore constituted the first stage of the norm life cycle. It gave rise to the idea that human rights transcend state borders and need to be protected by the international community as a whole, thereby placing a limit on state sovereignty. Judicial intervention through the IMT confirmed the emergence of these new norms and their increasing significance in the relations between states. Further developments of human rights norms and their enforcement were slowed down, however, during a Cold War that was dominated by power politics and only secondary concern for individual justice.

International human rights laws and their limited enforcement

The onset of the Cold War halted progress in furthering universal norms of human rights, because the era was dominated by mistrust, fear and rivalry between the US and the Soviet Union as the two great powers, and their respective allies. Even though Nuremberg had given rise to the idea that human rights can limit state sovereignty, during the Cold War, sovereignty considerations were reinforced. The UN was used to cultivate national agendas rather than to further human rights norms. The rules in the UN Charter that included the responsibility for all states to preserve international peace and security where abused by both sides to further national interests. International justice suffered considerably during this time, because generally, states' main concern lay in strengthening their sovereignty and observing the principle of non-intervention rather than enforcing human rights universally.

Even though possibilities for actual co-operation to enforce human rights norms on a universal basis were limited, some progress was still made in the negotiation and establishment of human rights norms in international legal provisions. States negotiated a number of treaties and conventions to further incorporate human rights into international law, but they failed to include effective independent enforcement powers. As Maogoto argues, 'the Cold War era was a mixed bag for international humanitarian law. Advances were made in the codification and broadening of international humanitarian law, but East-West rivalries prevented real enforcement at the international level' (Maogoto 2004: 136).

Agreements in international treaties and Conventions

The Universal Declaration of Human Rights and the two Covenants

In 1948, the UN General Assembly adopted the Universal Declaration of Human Rights (UDHR), which specifies the general guidelines on human rights set out in the UN Charter. It details the basic civil and political rights to which all human beings are entitled, such as the rights to life, liberty and security. It is the first legal document that outlines specific rights for individuals in international law and can be seen as part of the norm life cycle's first stage in which the content of human rights norms is clarified and incorporated into international law.

The UDHR sets standards for the international protection of human rights by providing rules for states' internal governments, which is as a 'decisive step in codifying the emerging view that the way in which states treat their own citizens is not only a legitimate international concern but subject to international standards' (Donnelly 1999: 73). However, the Declaration does not constitute binding law for the states that signed it, but is merely a 'statement of aspirations' (Forsythe 2006: 39) which outlines only very general duties to promote human rights standards. There is no legal duty to comply with the UDHR's standards and no independent enforcement mechanism is attached to it. It is a declaration only, rather than a treaty or Convention, primarily aimed at raising human rights consciousness around the world.

The UDHR was established through the General Assembly. There were no votes against it and only eight abstentions, a result which is not surprising given that negotiations were dominated by Western states that had pushed towards its creation. Non-Western states were either under-represented or their governments reflected Western values.[6] 'To say that it was very much a 'western' creation is by no means *ipso facto* to demean it; it is, however, to recognize a simple truth essential to the understanding of so much that has happened since' (Best 1990: 8). The UDHR was not a multilateral treaty that had to be signed and ratified by states, but simply a General Assembly Resolution that was not *per se* legally binding.

To overcome this limitation and to give human rights binding force, states eventually negotiated treaties to provide binding law for the protection of human rights. These efforts to translate the UDHR into enforceable treaties proved time-consuming and controversial due to the Cold War environment in which none of the great powers showed great enthusiasm and support to continue the UN's human rights developments. It took until 1966 to agree on the International Covenant on

Civil and Political Rights and the International Covenant on Economic, Social and Cultural Rights. These two Covenants take the general provisions of the UDHR a step further by translating them into legally binding commitments; they specify rights for individuals in international relations, such as the right to freedom of movement and the right to an adequate standard of life.[7] Even though the Covenants constitute binding international law and include provisions for setting up bodies to monitor compliance by states, they still lack more effective enforcement mechanisms that coerce states into compliance. States were willing in principle to agree to follow certain human rights standards and incorporate new norms into the rules governing international society. Yet, they were still reluctant to do so at the expense of permanently limiting their sovereignty by establishing effective independent enforcement mechanisms that could (at least in theory) be used against their own interests.

Conventions and jus cogens rules

Most of the human rights norms incorporated through the UDHR and the Covenants are very broad and constitute rather general guidelines such as the right to life or the freedom of speech. To take account of some more specific, narrowly defined provisions, a number of Conventions were elaborated or extended. Conventions deal with particular human rights issues such as the Conventions against Torture and Other Cruel, Inhuman or Degrading Treatment or Punishment (1984) and the Convention on the Rights of the Child (1989). These issues are seen to belong to a different category of rights and as being important to *all* states, which justifies establishing special provisions in international law to protect them. Such Conventions go a step further than only drawing attention to human rights issues, they establish offences with *jus cogens* character which means that they 'may be punished by any state because the offenders are common enemies of all mankind and all nations have an equal interest in their apprehension and prosecution' (Chigara 2000: 118). *Jus cogens* norms are special because they are binding on all states and allow no exceptions or contradiction by other treaty provisions or customary law. They constitute a new way of perceiving relations between states and individuals, because 'for the first time, the international community has decided to recognize certain *values* (…) that must *prevail* over any other form of national interest' (Cassese 1990: 168).

Jus cogens norms are seen as being fundamental to the interests of all states. They are given special status in international law by imposing obligations on every state to assist in the trial and punishment of those offences. Such a commitment is found in international legal provisions such as the Torture Convention or the definition of crimes against humanity, where a link to all states in international society exists through the notion of common humanity. This is not a new development, 'but it marks an extension of the principle, in a modified form, into a new subject area' (Sands 2003: 87) and suggests that a special category of crimes exists that is universally agreed upon by states. Such norms can conflict with order principles of non-intervention if a state fails to protect them and other states are subsequently required to take external action. *Jus cogens* offences create the possibility of universal jurisdiction by individual states.[8]

Universal jurisdiction

A number of Conventions incorporate the principle of universal jurisdiction, which gives states the right (and even duty) to exercise jurisdiction over a criminal act irrespective of where the crime was committed or the nationalities of victims or perpetrators. This principle is based on the idea that some human rights violations are so serious that they concern humanity as a whole and therefore need to be punished everywhere, regardless of state borders (Goldsmith and Krasner 2003: 48). The principle aims to strengthen international human rights law enforcement by giving states broad competence to enforce these human rights norms universally.

Piracy and slavery have traditionally been recognized as international crimes that attract universal jurisdiction, primarily because they tend to occur across borders, but the application of universal jurisdiction in cases of human rights abuses is not as clear. Universal jurisdiction is not self-enforcing but dependent on individual states' political will to take action. One of the main difficulties for the enforcement of these principles on an international basis lies in the fact that international human rights laws create rights for individuals, but the obligations to honour these provisions are for states. Universal jurisdiction gives states the right to act unilaterally and infringe another state's sovereignty if they believe a human right has been violated, but even though guidelines on these provisions exist, what constitutes a violation remains a matter of interpretation. Decisions of why to intervene in one case but not another are influenced by political considerations and not only humanitarian motives, which means that a consistent application of the laws cannot be ensured.[9]

Universal jurisdiction is problematic for two reasons: first because it assumes that universal values shared by all states exist and second because of the selectivity in its application. Conventions set out guidelines for the content of crimes that attract universal jurisdiction, but these remain open to interpretation and also require some form of agency to be enforced. As discussed above, it is also debateable whether universal values are truly universal or based on the interests of the most powerful and whether a vertically constraining system of rights exists that places obligations on states. The selective enforcement of these standards can also lead to a distortion of international law. However, universal jurisdiction provisions are significant because they include a recognition that some human rights are seen as being fundamental to all states and have the potential to take precedence over other principles incorporated in international society. It opens up the possibility of enforcing a very limited and specific set of human rights that are of concern to humanity as a whole. Such enforcement makes the creation of precedents possible that can lead to changes in the normative context towards a more universal incorporation of justice norms into the rules of international society.

Despite these practical limitations it is important to recognize that states were in favour of creating laws to incorporate justice norms into international relations.

Such laws included at least the theoretical possibility that they could be enforced against a state's will and thereby compromise state sovereignty. The fact that these treaties exist can already influence actual state behaviour in the long term: 'human rights standards are indeed a liberal fact of international relations, and the possibility of their actually generating some beneficial influence on behalf of human dignity can not be discounted out of hand' (Forsythe 2006: 48). The increased recognition of human rights norms in international law also suggests that order principles have changed over recent years in line with a constructivist approach to international relations. Order principles increasingly include notions of a common humanity which make sovereignty and the principle of non-intervention dependent on how states treat their own citizens. This illustrates the conflict between order and justice because sovereignty grants states authority within their territorial borders without a higher authority, but human rights with *jus cogens* status place limits on how states treat their own people and therefore compromise sovereignty.

On balance, the Cold War witnessed a steady expansion of the institutionalization of human rights in international relations through more and more international laws. This began to erode the traditional immunity of sovereign states from international scrutiny, but international law is not effective unless specific provisions for enforcement and compliance are made by states on national levels. States not only need to sign treaties they also need to ratify them into their national laws because no central authority exists that has the power to enforce these standards. Some form of agency is required to bring them to the domestic level: 'formal acceptance by a state party is often not the end, but the beginning of a prolonged struggle about the implementation of the norms (Schmitz and Sikkink 2002: 529).

Even though international law's enforcement is primarily dependent on states' voluntary co-operation, the UN has some powers that are limited to monitoring states' compliance and reporting on failures to do so. These supranational monitoring mechanisms are not very powerful, but they can nevertheless be seen as attempts to strike a compromise between state sovereignty and the requirement for states to comply with international standards of human rights.

UN reporting mechanisms

A number of UN institutions were established to enforce existing human rights provisions. The Human Rights Commission was created in 1946 as a permanent subsidiary body of the Economic and Social Council (ECOSOC). It consisted of fifty-three state representatives and was until 2006 the main UN body charged with protecting and promoting human rights. The Commission concentrated on identifying and setting standards as well as monitoring the application of these standards by states (White 2002: 223). To avoid only dealing with certain states, it introduced 'thematic procedures' that allowed the Commission to consider particular kinds of human rights violations. It had the power to appoint special rapporteurs and working groups to investigate alleged violations of human rights and report on human rights abuses in particular states. The Commission was dependent on states' co-operation and did not have any enforcement powers of its own; it could only request more information and make recommendations. When the Commission was first set up, states took its proceedings very seriously, but its reputation declined steadily over time. The Commission suffered from accusations of creating double standards, particularly with regard to the permanent members of the Security Council. The permanent members were always elected as representatives to the Commission and were seen by other states to only protect their own interests and those of their allies (Forsythe 2006: 75). The Commission lost legitimacy in the eyes of many over the years because it could not ensure the consistent application of universal standards.

The Commission was replaced in 2006 by the Human Rights Council that was established by the General Assembly as one of its subsidiary organs which makes it directly accountable to all member states of the UN. The creation of the Council was opposed by four states, including the US that claimed that it wanted a stronger new institution. The Council was created to 'strengthen the promotion and protection of human rights around the world'. It is very similar to its predecessor in that it monitors, advises and publicly reports on human rights situations in specific countries or territories (country mandate) or on particular human rights issues in the world (thematic mandate). It aims (*inter alia*) to aid the development of international human rights law by making recommendations to the General Assembly, promote the full implementation of human rights obligations undertaken by states, respond to emergencies and serve as a forum for dialogue on different human rights issues.

The Council consists of forty-seven members that are elected by the General Assembly for three years. The distribution of seats is in accordance with geographical representation which means that the African and Asian Groups hold the largest number of seats, the Eastern and Western European ones the least. The rules for membership of the Council stipulate that members 'shall uphold the highest standards in the promotion and protection of human rights' and that membership will be subject to periodic review. The election of the initial members of the Human Rights Council was very controversial as they include a number of states with poor human rights records such as China, Cuba, Saudi Arabia, Pakistan and Russia.

The Council was created to be a stronger body than the Human Rights Commission but with forty-seven members, it is still relatively big and it is questionable how much can be achieved. Unlike the distribution of membership of the Commission, new members of the Council had to compete for their seats and successful candidates needed to win the support of a majority of all UN member states in a secret ballot. The fact that membership included scrutiny of states' human rights records was designed to discourage the worst human rights offenders. However, considering the states that were successful in being elected to the Council, it is questionable how well this has worked in practice. Nevertheless, for the first time ever, states gave a voluntary commitment to promote and uphold human rights or otherwise face suspension from the Council. The Council is based on ideas of universality, impartiality, objectivity and non-selectivity and also stresses the importance of ending double-standards. It contains a periodic review mechanism that includes examining the human rights records of *all*

192 UN member states. The Human Rights Council is still a very new institution and it needs to be determined in the longer term whether it improves on the Human Rights Commission it replaced.

The UN also incorporates treaty-specific bodies such as the Human Rights Committee (HRC) and the Committee on Economic, Social, and Cultural Rights to monitor states' implementation of and compliance with the two Covenants. These Committees are treaty-specific bodies which means that they are only concerned with provisions set out in the respective Covenants. They consist of panels of independent experts that review and comment on reports by states on measures they have taken in national laws to implement their obligations under the Covenants. The Committees also monitor states as well as individuals with regard to possible violations of the Covenants' provisions. The Committees' findings are made public and produced in annual reports to the General Assembly. In addition, states are obliged to submit reports on their national human rights situation every five years. Yet, states also have the opportunity to enter reservations to their acceptance of the Covenants, which means that the universal implementation of their standards is weakened (Malanczuk 1997: 215). The two Committees suffer from the same weaknesses as the Human Rights Commission because they also have to rely on voluntary state co-operation and can only comment on reports or request additional information.

In 1993, the UN established the Office of the High Commissioner for Human Rights, with the aim of strengthening the co-ordination of the UN's human rights activities. The High Commissioner is the principal UN official responsible for the UN's human rights activities. He or she is appointed for a period of four years and performs their duties under the direction of the Secretary-General, independent and not representative of a state. The High Commissioner has a fairly vague and ambitious mandate of 'promoting and protecting all human rights: civil, political, economic, social and cultural.' Their duties involve compiling annual reports on international human rights at the UN and establishing human rights field missions to obtain information on alleged human rights abuses in individual countries. Even though these missions require the particular state's consent, the aim is that highlighting and publicising certain situations might lead to an end of these offences being committed and 'shame' governments into compliance.

Mary Robinson was the second High Commissioner from 1997 to 2002. She was praised by human rights activists for being very outspoken about human rights violations taking place in China, Russia and Israel. Her open and uncompromising criticism, however, angered a number of governments around the world. The US in particular became increasingly dissatisfied with Mary Robinson following criticisms she made after 9/11 about the war in Afghanistan and China's use of the 'war on terror' as a pretext to suppress ethnic minority groups. Then Secretary-General Kofi Annan was put under pressure not to renew her contract – which he subsequently followed. This shows the limits of the 'real' independent powers of the High Commissioner and also states' reluctance to have a strong human rights enforcement arm within the UN (Forsythe 2006: 69). The High Commissioner at the time of writing, Louise Arbour, is the former prosecutor of the ICTY and is regarded to be more diplomatic than Mary Robinson.

Limitations of the UN reporting mechanisms

The UN's reporting system is problematic because it requires states to co-operate with the monitoring bodies and engage in critical self-evaluation of their national laws and practices. States maintain control over human rights law implementation and it is likely that states' reports will be 'self-serving and omissions and inaccuracies may be difficult to identify' (Chinkin 1998: 118). The potential influence of the UN is limited due to its own structural constraints, because as an intergovernmental organisation it only has the powers states give to it. At the same time, states are also the principal violators of human rights. The UN also includes a strong political element through the Security Council in which some states are given more influence than others through the power of veto. This power allows the permanent members of the Security Council to protect their national interests whenever they are in conflict with proposed UN action. The monitoring bodies 'operate in an area where States, although they may have assumed international obligations, are not prepared to submit to international judicial scrutiny; and this area covers matters that are politically extremely sensitive' (Cassese 2001: 365). Under these circumstances, the UN mechanisms are arguably at least reasonably effective because they focus on problematic countries or issues, draw attention to human rights concerns, exert pressure on states, contribute to the creation of an international ethos and serve as catalyst to the gradual elaboration of new international conventions. Whether this has any independent effects, however, can only be assessed in the longer term.

Since these mechanisms lack independent powers and are dependent on voluntary co-operation, decisions of which country or issue to investigate are highly political. There is a lack of substantive criteria for determining when countries should be investigated, which leads to accusations that particular states are targeted for predominantly political reasons (Farer and Gaer 1993: 288). This illustrates arguments made by critical law theorists that concerns for human rights are dependent on individual states' interpretations of existing provisions and also on the political will of these states to act. As discussed in the Introduction, Kennedy, for instance sees the use of human rights language as a 'vehicle for imperialism' which is only used as part of furthering powerful states' national agendas. This selectivity in human rights law enforcement can then lead to powerful states and their allies enjoying a degree of *de facto* immunity from sustained scrutiny by UN institutions (Alston 1998: 351) and prevents the universal application of established justice norms.

However, monitoring the implementation of human rights standards and exposing violations is arguably a first step towards implementing justice norms into the rules of international society. The historically entirely inviolable principle of state sovereignty is compromised through an increasing recognition of individuals and their rights in international relations. Implementing and monitoring these standards widely into different international legal provisions creates expectations of how states should behave towards their citizens. This in turn establishes a culture of increased human rights respect and thereby constitutes a starting point for the norm life cycle to reach its next stages.

Unilateral enforcement during the Cold War – the Eichmann trial in Jerusalem

One attempt to go beyond mere reporting and acting on the principle of universal jurisdiction during the Cold War was the trial of Adolf Eichmann. This judicial intervention was based on one state's claim to universal jurisdiction to enforce *jus cogens* norms and to act in the interest of universal human rights that are codified in international law. The trial of Adolf Eichmann is an example of judicial intervention based on universal human rights, but unlike the IMT which was established by a group of states, Israel acted unilaterally by making a claim of universal jurisdiction to try Eichmann.

Adolf Eichmann was an important figure in the Nazi party, responsible as the proclaimed 'Jewish expert' for the logistics and co-ordination of the deportation of Jews to the death camps. He fled Germany after the end of the Second World War and lived in Argentina for ten years under an assumed name before being kidnapped by the Israeli secret service and transferred to Israel to stand trial in May 1960. Eichmann was charged with fifteen separate counts under the Israel Nazi and Nazi Collaborator (Punishment) Act of 1950, which included charges of crimes against the Jewish people, crimes against humanity and war crimes. Eichmann based his defence mainly on the claim that he was obeying orders. After a four month trial, he was eventually found guilty on all charges and of being instrumental in implementing the 'Final Solution'. Eichmann was sentenced to death, his appeal against the judgment was rejected and he was hanged on 31 May 1962.

The trial raises a number of issues particularly in relation to state sovereignty: a German national was tried in Israel's domestic court based on laws that did not even exist at the time the offences were committed and for crimes not committed on Israel's territory. Eichmann's defence asserted that because the crimes were not committed on Israeli soil, Israel could not claim jurisdiction under the principle of territoriality. Since the state of Israel did not even exist at the time the crimes were committed, jurisdiction based on the principle of victims' nationality could also not be applied. However, the prosecuting court argued that Israel did have jurisdiction over this case because of the principle of universal jurisdiction and also due to Israel's role as protector of the Jewish people. The principle of universal jurisdiction can be applied in cases of prosecuting crimes that affect humanity as a whole and in the Eichmann trial, the court ruled that: 'the abhorrent crimes defined in this Law are not crimes under Israel law alone. These crimes, which struck at the whole of mankind and shocked the conscience of nations, are grave offences against the law of nations itself. (*delicta juris gentium*)' (Harris 1998: 281). Israel invoked the principle of universal jurisdiction with reference to Article 6 of the Genocide Convention and the definition of crimes against humanity which both place obligations on states to not let these kinds of crimes go unpunished.

Similar to criticisms made against the IMT, the Eichmann trial proceedings were criticized because of the retroactivity of the law applied in the proceedings. However, as Arendt argues, in this particular case, the principle of *nullum crimen, nulla poena sine lege* was not substantially violated because it only applies to acts *known* to the legislator. She rightly points out that if a crime such as genocide, suddenly appears, 'justice itself demands a judgement according to a new law' (Arendt 1994: 254). The court recognized that in cases in which this principle conflicts with fundamental concerns about justice, justice should prevail.

Eichmann's defence claimed that he, as an individual, could not be held responsible for 'acts of state', because 'any act performed by a person in his position as agent of the state, whether he be the head of state or merely a functionary acting on government orders, should be considered solely as an act of the state for which the state alone is responsible' (Papadatos 1964: 72). This argument was rejected by the court because it was argued that ultimately laws need to serve justice and 'lawless laws'[10] must concede to justice. Rejecting the claim of 'act of state' sets an important precedent because it presupposes a limitation of the principle of state sovereignty. The recognition of individual responsibility independent from the state furthermore confirmed that individuals do not only have rights under international law, but can also be held accountable for their actions by states in the international community.

One major controversy of the trial centred on the charge of 'crimes against Jewish people'. Arendt argues that Eichmann should have been tried instead with crimes against *humanity*, because the crimes committed by the Nazis were crimes affecting the whole of humanity and not just the Jewish people. She argues that the 'very monstrousness of the events is 'minimized' before a tribunal that represents one nation only' (Arendt 1994: 270). It would have been possible to set a more powerful precedent by prosecuting these offences as crimes against humanity instead. The fact that in this particular case the victims were Jewish should only matter for the jurisdiction of the court, but not the definition of the offence (Stone 1961: 8). By prosecuting these crimes in the name of one nation only, Israel did not truly exercise universal jurisdiction with a primary focus on the interests of humanity as a whole but rather on the rights of its own people.

Basing a court's jurisdiction solely on the principle of universal jurisdiction still carries the possibility of politically motivated prosecutions or of other states perceiving the trial to be unfair and illegitimate. This is problematic for the norm development that is based on the concept of legitimacy because if states perceive the way a particular norm is being enforced as illegitimate, the norm life cycle's socialization process can be obstructed, preventing the norm to progress further. Even though the danger exists that universal jurisdiction might be used for political ends, this should not be used an argument against the principle in general, but much rather an argument in favour of *international* courts' exercise of universal jurisdiction (Robertson 2002: 258) free from domestic pressures. Trying Eichmann in an international court would have overcome possible concerns about impartiality and fairness because the main emphasis would have been on international society as a whole rather than just Israel. Enforcing human rights through international courts leads to greater uniformity and consistency in the application of international law. Trying crimes on an international level also signals the willingness of the international community as a whole to break with the past and to condemn (and prosecute) human rights abuses (Cassese 2001: 208–209).

The fact that Eichmann was singled out as one criminal among many that deserved to be brought to justice was based on Israel's individual interpretation of international legal provisions and its political agenda. Such unilateral actions to apply international legal standards demonstrates problems attached to the *universal* application of 'universal' jurisdiction provisions that lack independent enforcement and are reliant on some form of agency. However, it is necessary to find a starting point somewhere in order to set precedents to facilitate further norm developments and to integrate justice norms more fully into international society. The Eichmann trial was important and as Arendt argues it 'had to take place in the interests of justice and nothing else' (Arendt 1994: 286).

Conclusion

This chapter set the context for the subsequent case study analyses by looking at the emergence of human rights norms since the end of the Second World War. The recognition of human rights in international legal provisions represents the first stage of the norm life cycle model in which new issues of importance emerge and are slowly incorporated into the rules and laws of international society. The developments in international relations show that agreement on justice norms between states is possible although they lack independent enforcement mechanisms to make them more effective. The main enforcement mechanisms that exist on an international basis only entail monitoring states' compliance with general guidelines and lack 'teeth' to coerce states into implementing international legal provisions. Limited agreement exists on a special category of human rights that are seen as fundamentally important to international society as a whole. These rights include special provisions of universal jurisdiction, placing a responsibility on all states to act to protect them. A major shift has taken place in international law that is no longer only concerned with the relations between states but also recognizes rights of individuals. International law increasingly includes the notion that individuals have rights and ought to be able to enforce these rights against their governments. This shift from complete state-centrism towards a recognition of a common humanity can be seen as a major turning point in international law since the end of the Second World War.

The emergence of human rights in international relations illustrates the central order and justice conflict because it places limits on states' treatment of their own citizens, thereby compromising the inviolability of the sovereignty principle. Concerns over state sovereignty and the right to self-determination on the one hand conflict with claims to international human rights on the other. In line with a constructivist approach, sovereignty is seen not as a static given, but as changing with time and context. Sovereignty has changed to include notions of human rights resting on the belief that all human beings have rights by virtue of their humanity which transcend state borders. Sovereignty has also changed with regard to states' international legitimacy. Traditionally states were seen to be legitimate if they exercised authority over their territory and accepted legal obligations they had contracted, but in today's world, human rights provide a standard of moral legitimacy which has been incorporated into international society. These developments are based on the understanding that

> if sovereignty is a shared set of understandings and expectations about state authority that is reinforced by practices, then changes in these practices and understandings should in turn change sovereignty. The expansion of human rights law and policy in the postwar period is an example of a conscious collective attempt to modify this set of shared norms and practices (Keck and Sikkink 1998: 37).

The main limitation of international law is that it has no overarching, independent authority attached to it that can coerce states into compliance. It is reliant on state co-operation, which makes the enforcement of human rights norms not universal but dependent on states' political will. Two examples of states' individual attempts to enforce these universal norms through judicial intervention were discussed in this chapter in the examples of the Nuremberg and the Eichmann trials. The order and justice conflict became evident in these cases whereby a state's sovereign right to exercise jurisdiction was compromised to enforce universal norms of justice. Both cases can be seen as first attempts by norm entrepreneurs to take action to enforce norms that are incorporated into the rules of international society in order to implement them further and to make their application more universal. These two cases set important precedents that affect decisions made by states in subsequent cases of judicial intervention after the end of the Cold War.

Such interventions are discussed in the case study analyses presented in the following chapters. The cases of Pinochet and Yerodia are unilateral attempts by states to implement existing justice norms whereas interventions based on the creation of international criminal courts (such as the ICTY and ICC) constitute multilateral efforts involving a number of states. The emergence and development of human rights laws in line with the norm life cycle's first stage and as outlined in this chapter provide the background and normative context for the case studies which are primarily concerned with the enforcement of these existing provisions.

Notes

1 Article 55: 'With a view to the creation of conditions of stability and well-being which are necessary for peaceful and friendly relations among nations based on respect for the principle of equal rights and self-determination of peoples, the United Nations shall promote: a. higher standards of living, full employment, and conditions of economic and social progress and development; b. solutions of international economic, social, health

and related problems; and international cultural and educational cooperation; and c. universal respect for, and observance of, human rights and fundamental freedoms for all without distinction as to race, sex, language, or religion.'

Article 56: 'All Members pledge themselves to take joint and separate action in co-operation with the Organization for the achievement of the purposes set forth in Article 55.'

2 Article 2(4): 'All Members shall refrain in their international relations from the threat or use of force against the territorial integrity or political independence of any state, or in any other manner inconsistent with the Purposes of the United Nations.'

Article 2(7): 'Nothing contained in the present Charter shall authorize the United Nations to intervene in matters which are essentially within the domestic jurisdiction of any state or shall require the Members to submit such matters to settlement under the present Charter; but this principle shall not prejudice the application of enforcement measures under Chapter VII.'

3 A number of subsequent trials in the years that followed (from 1945 to 1949) dealt with other, lesser war criminals.

4 Article 8 of the IMT Charter concedes that the fact that the accused acted under orders may be considered as a mitigating circumstance regarding the punishment, but it cannot free the accused from responsibility.

5 *Ex post facto* law: passing a law after an act has been committed which retrospectively changes the legal consequences of such acts. *Nullum crimen* principle: an act cannot be considered a crime and punished accordingly unless there is a provision of criminal law in force at the time of its commission.

6 Best describes the situation as follows: 'The drafting committee contained not one African, and the General Assembly only weak delegations from Ethiopia and Liberia; most of the members who were not 'western' had received 'western' educations or professional formations; the most eloquent Islamic member was a British-educated member of a sect regarded by most Moslems as heretical; and so on' (1990: 8).

7 The UDHR and the two Covenants constitute the International Bill of Rights.

8 Jurisdiction in international law can be exercised based on the following principles: (1) territoriality principle (giving the state in which the crime has occurred jurisdiction); (2) nationality principle (jurisdiction is based on the nationality of the alleged perpetrator); (3) protective principle (the injured state can exercise jurisdiction when its national interests are threatened); (4) passive personality principle (jurisdiction is based on the nationality of the victim of the crime); (5) universality principle (breach of law with *jus cogens* status) (See Martin 2002: 273).

9 The problems attached to universal jurisdiction will be discussed in more detail in the context of the case studies analysis and particularly chapter 5.

10 For a discussion of the relationship between morality and law, see Radbruch's Formula, which states that 'when the contradiction between positive law and justice reaches an intolerable level that the law is supposed to give way as a 'false law' [unrichtiges Recht] to justice. (…) appropriately enacted and socially effective norms lose their legal character or their legal validity when they are extremely unjust. (…) Extreme injustice is no law' (Translation cited in Alexy 1999: 16–17).

3 The Pinochet decisions in the House of Lords

On 16 October 1998, British police arrested the former Chilean head of state General Augusto Pinochet in London in response to an extradition request issued by a Spanish judge. The House of Lords decisions and the public debates that followed this arrest in the months that followed brought out a number of issues related to unilateral attempts by individual states to enforce justice norms that are incorporated in international law and carry universal jurisdiction provisions. It exposes the central conflict between order and justice that are both values incorporated in the rules of international society at a concrete level: Chile's sovereign right to grant immunity to its former state official conflicted with the UK's attempt to extradite him to Spain to face prosecution for international human rights abuses.[1] The case can be seen as an example of the norm life cycle's second stage, the norm cascade, which follows the initial institutionalization of new norms into international law. International human rights norms have emerged, given legal specificity in the cycle's first stage and thereby provide the normative context which shapes states' identities and behaviour. In line with the norm cascade the UK and Spain engaged in norm affirming action by applying these codified justice norms in their justifications for prosecuting Pinochet in their national courts. The House of Lords decisions have great political significance, because for the first time a UK court exercised jurisdiction over a matter that did not directly involve UK nationals or interests, but *international* human rights concerns.

This chapter starts with a brief outline of the background to the case to set the context for an analysis of the two decisions taken by the House of Lords with regard to the extradition request by Spain. The chapter analyses both judgments and the arguments given by the Lords in light of the underlying theoretical framework and its pluralist and solidarist approaches towards the conflict between order and justice. The majority judgments in both House of Lords decisions suggest an overall solidarist understanding of resolving the conflict by upholding justice norms at the cost of infringing Chile's sovereign right to claim state immunity. It is argued that the majority judgments demonstrate an acceptance of changes that have taken place in the normative context in line with the norm life cycle. The dissenting opinions suggest, however, that resistance to such developments also exists and that norms have not progressed far enough to make their enforcement a matter of course, undisputed by all. The first decision allowed Pinochet's extradition purely based on an analysis of the nature of the crimes in question based on international law, whereas the second decision limited the scope of the case to keep within more narrow parameters of applicable national laws. The final section of this chapter compares the two decisions and raises issues related to unilateral action based on universal values.

Background to the case of Pinochet and the House of Lords

Pinochet had come to power in 1973, heading a coup which overturned the democratically elected government of Salvador Allende. It is alleged that during the seventeen years in which Pinochet ruled Chile, more than 3,000 people were murdered or disappeared. He left office in 1990 but continued to have a role in the Chilean government advising on arms purchases. Pinochet enjoyed a close personal friendship with Margaret Thatcher and visited Britain frequently, travelling on a diplomatic passport.

In September 1998, while Pinochet was visiting London to receive medical treatment, the Spanish government issued an arrest warrant, asking the British government to extradite him to Spain in order to face charges on suspected crimes against Spanish citizens and crimes against humanity during his rule of Chile. Spain primarily sought extradition because some of the victims were Spanish nationals but also on the basis of the principle of universality for the crimes of torture and hostage taking. Pinochet had been made senator-for-life by Chile in 1998 and therefore enjoyed complete immunity from prosecution in that country.

Two arrest warrants were issued by a UK Metropolitan Magistrate in accordance with the Extradition Act 1989 following this request from Spain. The first warrant was issued in haste, and only included allegations of murder of Spanish citizens, a crime for which Pinochet could be tried in Spain under Spanish law but not under UK law. The warrant was quashed by the Divisional Court because of the 'double criminality rule' which means that the offence for which extradition is sought needs to be recognized as a crime in both states involved.

The second warrant was more carefully drafted and was based on evidence that

> between 1 January 1988 and December 1992, being a public official, [Pinochet] intentionally inflicted severe pain or suffering on others in the performance or purported performance of official duties within the jurisdiction of the Government of Spain (Pinochet I 1998).

Unlike the first warrant, the second warrant included crimes of torture and hostage taking that could be tried in the UK and could therefore constitute the basis for extradition. The UK accepted torture as a crime that carried universal jurisdiction by incorporating the Torture Convention into the Criminal Justice Act of 1988. From the date the Act came into effect, torture became a crime under UK law wherever committed and therefore constituted an extraditable offence.

On 23 October 1998, Pinochet was arrested under the second warrant. The arrest was challenged by Pinochet's defence on two grounds: firstly they argued that Pinochet enjoyed immunity as a former head of state and secondly that Britain (and for that matter Spain) had no legal right to exercise jurisdiction. The Divisional Court quashed the second warrant as well on the grounds that Pinochet was entitled to state immunity with respect to the alleged offences, arguing that these offences were committed as part of official acts performed in exercise of his functions as head of state. However, even though the second warrant was quashed, the Divisional Court granted leave to appeal to the House of Lords, the highest Court of Appeal in the UK, because

> a point of law of general public importance is involved in the Court's decision, namely the proper interpretation and scope of the immunity enjoyed by a former Head of State from arrest and extradition proceedings in the United Kingdom in respect of acts committed when he was Head of State (Pinochet I 1998).

Table 3.1 The Pinochet case: Timeline of events

1973–1990	General Augusto José Ramón Pinochet Ugarte ousted the socialist President Salvador Allende in a coup in 1973, starting a seventeen year military dictatorship.
1990–1998	Pinochet stepped down as head of state but remained army commander-in-chief.
1998	Pinochet was made senator-for-life, guaranteeing life-long immunity from prosecution in Chile.
16 October 1998	Spanish judge Balthazar Garzón issued an international warrant for the arrest of Pinochet from the Central Court of Criminal Proceedings in Madrid to UK Metropolitan Magistrate Nicholas Evans. The warrant was quashed due to the double criminality rule.
22 October 1998	Second warrant issued to overcome some of the first warrant's shortfalls to satisfy the requirement of including 'extradition crimes'.
23 October 1998	Pinochet arrested in London and placed under house arrest.
28 October 1998	Divisional Court quashed warrant but decides to allow an appeal to the House of Lords to rule on the extradition request.
25 November 1998	*Pinochet I*: House of Lords gave first decision, voting 3–2 in favour of the extradition request. In favour: Lords Hoffmann, Nicholls and Steyn; Against: Lords Lloyd and Slynn.
17 December 1998	*Pinochet II*: House of Lords rendered decision that Pinochet I could not be upheld because of suspected bias of Lord Hoffmann.
24 March 1999	*Pinochet III*: House of Lords' second verdict resulted in a 6–1 vote in favour of the extradition request. In favour: Lords Browne-Wilkinson, Hope, Hutton, Millet, Saville and Worth Matravers; Against: Lord Goff.

It was decided that while head of state, Pinochet was entitled to immunity for *all* acts committed, but once he had left office, immunity was limited to acts which were done in exercise of official functions of head of state. This decision opened the question of whether the acts Pinochet was accused of were carried out by him in an official capacity. In other words, the question was whether he committed the alleged human rights abuses in a private capacity or as part of his acts as head of state. Even though this question seems almost incomprehensible to most sensible people, it demonstrates the difficulties attached to the consistent application of international law.

On 25 November 1998, the House of Lords gave its first verdict with three votes to two in favour of reversing the Divisional Court's decision and allowing Pinochet's extradition to Spain to face prosecution for the alleged human rights abuses. This decision was set aside because of suspected bias of one of the judges: Lord Hoffmann had failed to declare his links to Amnesty International, which had been involved in the prosecution as intervener.[2] A new hearing before a panel of seven Law Lords was scheduled. Its decision was rendered on 24 March 1999 with an even clearer verdict of six to one in favour of extradition, but with the scope of the case considerably changed. In the first decision, the most important issue surrounded the question of what constituted official acts exercised in the function of head of state, whereas the second decision focused on the double criminality rule and the identification of extradition crimes.

Questions of state doctrine and the nature of official acts – *Pinochet I*

The first hearing at the House of Lords took place in front of five Law Lords. It was concerned with the question of Pinochet's right to claim immunity under UK law and the correct interpretation of the State Immunity Act 1978.[3] The hearing resulted in a three to two vote in favour of allowing Pinochet's extradition to Spain. Lord Nicholls, Lord Steyn, and Lord Hoffmann were in favour of extraditing Pinochet, whereas Lord Slynn and Lord Lloyd argued in favour of Chile's sovereign right to grant immunity. The majority of Lords ruled that Pinochet could be held personally responsible for his actions because no distinction could be made 'between the man who strikes, and a man who orders another to strike' (Pinochet I 1998).

All Lords agreed that because Pinochet was head of state at the time in question he enjoyed immunity *ratione personae*[4] while he was acting in this capacity. They agreed that once he had left office, Pinochet enjoyed immunity from criminal jurisdiction in the UK with respect to official acts that were part of his head of state functions (immunity *ratione materiae*), but not private acts. The main questions therefore surrounded the issue of what constituted an 'official act in exercise of a head of state's functions', whether the alleged crimes fell into the scope of these acts and whether or not Pinochet was therefore entitled to immunity. The Lords agreed that it was sometimes necessary for state officials to commit crimes as part of their governmental conduct. They disagreed, however, over the question of whether a line should be drawn with regard to the *nature* of the alleged offences in order to qualify for immunity. In other words, they disagreed on whether other states could morally evaluate what conduct can be seen to be part of a state's official functions and therefore attract immunity *ratione materiae.*

The Lords' argumentations bring out the tension between order and justice on a concrete level: Chile's right to claim state immunity for its former head of state *versus* the recognition of certain categories of crimes that are considered by international society to be so serious that they are not the sole responsibility of one state but affect all states and therefore justify universal jurisdiction. These crimes constitute *jus cogens* norms and are already established as such in international law in the Torture and Taking Hostages Convention, but they do not have independent enforcement mechanisms attached to them. The Lords had to decide whether the UK had the right to exercise universal jurisdiction unilaterally with regard to international crimes which had been committed in Chile against Spanish citizens.

The proceedings were significant 'because they challenged judges and politicians in the United Kingdom to exercise the universal jurisdiction available to them' (Byers 2000: 422), i.e. enforcing justice norms that are established as international law. The two sides of the Lords' arguments bring out both the pluralist and solidarist positions on the conflict between order and justice in line with the underlying theoretical framework. They also illustrate different responses to developments in line with the norm life cycle in the form of recognition of progress on the one hand and rejection of it on the other. The arguments of the Law Lords focused on the question whether international law had changed since the Second World War to include notions of individual accountability and limits to complete sovereign immunity. At issue were therefore two competing visions of international law: the traditional approach that gives primacy to the interests of states and a more modern approach that focuses on individuals and their rights and duties under international law.

The need to draw a 'meaningful line' – the majority opinion

The majority of Lords in the first decision ruled in favour of extraditing Pinochet to Spain. Lords Hoffmann[5], Nicholls, and Steyn argued that it was vital to draw a line between different official acts in order to not 'make a mockery of international law' (Pinochet I 1998). The Lords argued in favour of the possibility of states in international society to evaluate and make normative decisions based on the 'justness' of other states' official conduct. They concluded that certain acts could never be regarded as being part of official governmental functions and therefore required other states to intervene. They argued that international agreements like the Torture and Taking Hostages Conventions already established special categories of crimes which were seen as 'high crimes' by customary international law and therefore justified external interference. Upholding these principles of justice was seen by the majority of Lords as being more important than a state's sovereign right to grant state immunity.

Lord Steyn criticized the initial Divisional Court's decision that no line could be drawn in order to establish a limitation on immunities and argued that 'it follows that when Hitler ordered the 'final solution' his act must be regarded as an official act deriving from the exercise of his functions as Head of State.' Some acts of head of state do fall 'beyond even the most enlarged meaning of official acts' and 'there is indeed a meaningful line to be drawn' (Pinochet I 1998). Lord Steyn argued that developments in international law demonstrated that a line had already been established through a number of international legal agreements: genocide, torture, hostage taking, and crimes against humanity were all recognized as international crimes that need to be punished. He argued that 'given this state of international law, it seems to me difficult to maintain that the commission of such high crimes may amount to acts performed in the exercise of the functions of a Head of State' (Pinochet I 1998). He asserted that the charges brought by Spain against Pinochet fell beyond the scope of official head of state functions and that Pinochet was therefore not entitled to state immunity.

Lord Nicholls similarly recognized certain categories of crimes as attracting universal jurisdiction for which former state leaders could not claim immunity and therefore needed to be punished – even if the state of the alleged offender did not intend to take action to that effect itself. He argued that

> international law has made plain that certain types of conduct, including torture and hostage-taking, are not acceptable conduct on the part of anyone. This applies as much to heads of states, or even more so; as it does to every-one else; the contrary conclusion would make a mockery of international law (Pinochet I 1998).

He argued that not drawing a line to qualify official conduct would take the principles of order too far and reduce international law to absurdity. Lord Nicholls asserted that Pinochet could not claim immunity under the State Immunity Act, because immunity can only be conferred

> in respect to acts performed in the exercise of functions which international law recognizes as functions of a head of state, of the terms of his domestic constitution. (…) And it hardly needs saying that torture of his own subjects, or of aliens, would not be regarded by international law as a function of a head of state (Pinochet I 1998).

He referred to the precedent set in the judgment of the IMT in Nuremberg that state representatives cannot claim immunity based on their official position. He argued that because this precedent is generally accepted and established in customary international law, heads of states and other officials had no uncertainty about potential personal liability when participating in international crimes. Lord Nicholls claimed that it was not consistent with the definition of torture as set out in the Torture Convention that former officials (however senior) could be immune from prosecution outside their own jurisdiction. Furthermore, universal jurisdiction provisions in the Torture and the Hostage Taking Conventions made clear that trying crimes in national courts was a possibility.

Lords Nicholls and Steyn recognized that international society had already reached agreement on certain universal justice principles such as prohibition of torture which are established in laws such as the Torture Convention. The Lords argued in favour of drawing a line to qualify state immunity in the interest of international law to uphold these principles. They argued that state officials could not be given complete free range in their actions without the possibility of facing prosecution for crimes they might commit. They asserted that if a state official killed his gardener in a fit of rage, he would undoubtedly not be granted immunity – so why should he when he committed torture and other crimes that are so grave that they could morally never be justified to be necessary for the proper conduct of state affairs? The Lords therefore concluded that a fine line needed to be drawn to enforce justice norms that are already incorporated in the international order.

The majority decision by the three Law Lords is an attempt to reconcile order and justice in line with solidarist approaches that are both incorporated in the rules of international society. Principles of international order – such as sovereignty and non-intervention – are still seen as necessary for states in international society to regulate states' conduct and their relations with each other, but they should not be taken to an extreme whereby states and their officials can act with complete disregard for other existing norms concerned with justice. This decision qualifies the order principle of state sovereignty by including a duty to protect universal human rights that affect all states and are established as such in the rules of international society. The Torture Convention, for instance, includes conduct that can never be justified as 'official' acts and attract immunity. The Pinochet case signals 'a shift from a State-centred order of things' (Fox 1999: 207) which means that it confirms developments in international law which recognized that individuals have rights independently from states.

The protection of certain categories of human rights has become an issue for international society as a whole and not just an individual state because 'matters which once indisputably belonged to the domestic jurisdiction of states, such as the way a state treats persons under its jurisdiction, nowadays may be the object of international scrutiny' (Bianchi 1999: 272–273). This is a fairly strong solidarist position taken by the Lords that argue that some norms of justice are recognized as being of universal concern and that they can trump considerations for order principles.

The Lords' reliance on existing norms in international law in their argumentation is fundamentally important, because it 'signalled that the most basic human rights are enforceable against anyone regardless of conflicting rules of international law that might otherwise apply' (Byers 2000: 430). This interpretation of international law is in line with the developments of human rights norms in accordance with the norm life cycle that have taken place in subsequent years. As outlined earlier, agreements on certain human rights norms exist and are incorporated in international law in the cycle's first stage but they still require individual states' political will to enforce them. The norms are clarified in international law and set expectations of appropriate state behaviour in international society. States see these new norms as legitimate and see enforcing them as consistent with their identity as members of international society in harmony with the 'new' rules rooted in international law. The majority judgment to allow the extradition of Pinochet to Spain was very surprising and made headlines around the world. The decision was hailed as evidence for the transformation of the international legal order.

Supporting sovereign immunity – the dissenting opinions

Lord Slynn and Lord Lloyd disagreed with the majority opinion and argued in favour of Chile's right to grant immunity, maintaining that the international community did not have the right to draw a line between official acts 'whose criminality and moral obliquity is more or less great'[6] (Pinochet I 1998). Both Lords agreed that Pinochet committed the alleged offences as part of his *official* governmental functions and that he therefore enjoyed immunity. They argued that it was part of the prerogative of sovereign states to determine whether an act constituted part of official functions or private conduct and that it was neither possible nor justifiable to intervene externally to morally evaluate other states' conduct. The two Lords argued that the only meaningful distinction for the purpose of deciding whether Pinochet could claim immunity could be made between 'private' and 'official' acts but not between acts that were morally right or wrong. They thereby affirmed the primacy of the principle of sovereignty that gives states the right to act free from external intervention.

Lord Slynn argued that it was recognized in international law that official functions of state leaders varied from country to country and that international law therefore did not prescribe what these functions included and what they excluded. He asserted that

> the critical test would seem to be whether the conduct was engaged in under colour of or in ostensible exercise of the Head of State's public authority. If it was, it must be treated as official conduct and so not a matter subject to the jurisdiction of other States whether or not it was wrongful or illegal under the law of his own State (Pinochet I 1998).

Lord Lloyd argued similarly against drawing a line to qualify immunity on the grounds that 'it would be unjustifiable in theory, and unworkable in practice, to impose any restriction on head of state immunity by reference to the number and gravity of the alleged crimes. (...) This would not make sense (Pinochet I 1998).'

The two Lords argued from pluralist perspectives maintaining that states have different views on what constitutes official conduct as part of government functions. The sovereign right to grant immunity *ratione materiae* could not be compromised by other states with reference to universal norms of justice, regardless of the nature of the alleged offences. Lord Slynn exhibited a more moderate pluralist position than Lord Lloyd, because he conceded at least the possibility that immunity for official acts could be affected by an emerging notion of individual justice in international law. He argued that there is 'no doubt that states have been moving towards the recognition of some crimes as those which should not be covered by States or Head of State or other official or diplomatic immunity when charges are brought before international tribunals' (Pinochet I 1998). Such a challenge to state immunity, he asserted, could only take place through international legal agreements that included provisions for national jurisdiction and an express waiver of immunity. He further argued that the recognition of international crimes that attracted universal jurisdiction in national courts were more like 'aspirations' and rather 'embryonic', because developments in international law were very slow and much debate and uncertainty still existed.

Lord Slynn opposed the notion that a universal rule existed that *all* international crimes were outside immunity *ratione materiae*, because he saw the right of states to grant immunity as still being important. He argued that this right could only be lost if states signed treaties or Conventions which included express waivers that provided clarity on whether a crime attracted immunity or not. He thereby acknowledged universal jurisdiction as a possibility in international law, but argued that states needed to proceed cautiously because no clear guidelines existed as to when it could be applied. Furthermore, Lord Slynn argued that universal jurisdiction could only be applied in international and not national courts. He thereby recognized that norms of universal justice have emerged in international relations and law in line with the norm life cycle's first stage, but unlike the Lords in the majority opinion, he did not see them as having progressed far enough to be part of the rules of international society. This view demonstrates resistance to norm affirmative action in line with the norm cascade because Lord Slynn argued that further clarifications of the contents of the 'new' norms are needed before they can be enforced as part of the general rules of international society.

Lord Lloyd expressed a stronger pluralist view than Lord Slynn and displayed more resistance to the developments of the norm life cycle by arguing that the UK could not apply universal jurisdiction in this case. He agreed with Lord Slynn that prosecutions could only take place in international courts, but he also maintained that the nature of the crimes a head of state is accused of could never be used to restrict the state sovereignty principle. Lord Lloyd argued that since the crimes Pinochet was accused of were committed as part of his governmental functions, only the state in question had the right to decide on the possibility of prosecution. This view is opposed to the majority opinion's recognition of developments with regard to justice norms that have taken place in the norm life cycle that make a moral evaluation of official acts possible. Lord Lloyd did not agree that these justice norms had developed in a way that they could be regarded to be part of international society as a whole and universally applicable. He demonstrated a strong pluralist view by placing primary emphasis on maintaining principles of order that can not be externally assessed as to whether or not they violated universal justice principles.

National laws and the double criminality rule – *Pinochet III*

The original House of Lords decision was set aside due to suspected bias of Lord Hoffmann, and a new hearing before a panel of seven Law Lords was scheduled. The second vote on the extradition request's appeal was six to one in favour of extradition, but the scope of the case changed considerably. Unlike the first decision that mainly focused on the nature of the crimes Pinochet was accused of, the second decision concentrated on the 'double criminality rule', which means that the conduct in question needed to amount to a crime in the UK as well as in Spain at the time it was committed.[7] The emphasis shifted from looking at state practice and customary law to focussing on treaty law, i.e. the law incorporated in the treaties concluded between states in written form. The main focus was on the 1984 Convention against Torture and Other Cruel, Inhuman and Degrading Treatment and Punishment. It was decided by the majority of Lords that Pinochet could claim immunity for acts which had occurred after 8 December 1988, the date the Torture Convention came into force in all three states concerned (Chile, UK, Spain). The loss of immunity was therefore limited to acts committed after a certain date when torture became a crime with universal jurisdiction provisions in all three states. The majority of Lords agreed that torture could not be part of official functions because by definition it can only be committed by an official.[8]

This new focus narrowed down the scope of the allegations considerably: by relying on the dates the Convention became effective in UK law, the Lords ruled that Pinochet was immune from prosecution in respect to all crimes alleged to have been committed before that date. Only acts allegedly committed after the date torture and hostage-taking became international crimes under UK law could be retained in the request. The majority of the Lords thereby decided to rely on national rather than international legal provisions to reach a decision.

Two of the Lords dissented from the majority opinion in either direction: Lord Goff was the only one who opposed the overall judgment and dismissed the appeal for extradition, while Lord Millett disagreed with the changed scope of the case and argued in favour of retaining all charges brought against Pinochet.

'A prime example of an official torturer' – the majority opinion

The majority of Lords argued that the Torture Convention did not establish a new crime in international law, because torture was recognized as a crime long before the Convention came into effect. The Convention only strengthened existing prohibitions through a number of supporting measures, including provisions for prosecution. The Lords agreed that universal jurisdiction was given in cases of torture and that by signing the agreement, the UK, Spain and Chile had all accepted this provision. Most of the Lords argued that torture could not be regarded to be part of official functions under international law, because international law expressly prohibits torture and defines it as an international crime. As Lord Browne-Wilkinson argued: 'How can it be for international law purposes an official function to do something which international law itself prohibits and criminalizes?' (Pinochet III 1999).

The majority of Lords agreed that states could not grant immunity *ratione materiae* for acts of torture even though the Convention did not include an express waiver of immunity. States that signed the Convention recognized that torture attracted universal jurisdiction which excludes immunities for individual persons.

The Lords argued that it was part of 'common notions of justice' (Pinochet III 1999) that individuals that act as agents of the state could be held individually responsible for their actions and could be prosecuted for them. They agreed that a plea for immunity was entirely inconsistent with the definition of torture, because according to Article 1 of the Torture Convention, the offence could only be committed by persons acting in official capacity thus making a head of state 'a prime example of an official torturer' (Pinochet III 1999). The Lords agreed that the 'official' nature of the act - that forms the basis for the claim of immunity *ratione materiae* - was at the same time an essential aspect of the definition of the offence of torture. They argued that other states were required to act precisely because the offending state could not be relied upon to do so itself. They conceded that Chile had the *primary* right to exercise jurisdiction over Pinochet, but not the *exclusive* right.

In their arguments, the Lords acknowledged a number of developments in international law (in line with the norm life cycle), identifying

> a clear recognition by the international community that certain crimes are so grave and so inhuman that they constitute crimes against international law and that the international community is under a duty to bring to justice a person who commits such crimes (Pinochet III 1999).

Lord Phillips further argued that the international community had recognized justice principles that needed to be pursued sometimes even at the expense of the existing order and its principle of non-intervention. He argued that 'some types of criminal conduct cannot be treated as a matter for the exclusive competence of the state in which they occur' (Pinochet III 1999). The Lords acknowledged that the international community has moved towards international agreements on certain principles of justice and that state sovereignty could be compromised if these agreed principles of justice were violated.

The Lords acknowledged that it was no longer accepted in international law that the way in which a state treated its own citizens was a purely internal matter. They argued in line with a solidarist view that minimum agreement on upholding certain human rights as matters for the international community was possible and agreed that Chile's sovereignty could be compromised to protect such existing principles of justice. However, by limiting the scope of the case to only include acts covered by UK domestic laws they took an overall more limited solidarist approach in which universal justice can only be enforced in line with existing *national* rather than international law provisions. The Lords acknowledged that torture was a crime with *jus cogens* status before the relevant UK laws came into effect, but they did not agree that these norms of individual justice could take precedence over order principles in any case. Justice principles can only be enforced at the expense of order in line with already existing limitations incorporated in domestic legal provisions.

The Lords' argumentation reflects an acknowledgement of developments that have taken place in line with the norm life cycle by referring to norms that have been incorporated into law. They engaged in norm affirming action that leads to a norm cascade and a socialization process in which appropriate behaviour is redefined in line with these norms, thereby leading to their further integration. The Torture Convention sets out a clear definition of the crime of torture which requires a reassessment of what can be regarded as 'official conduct' that attracts immunity *ratione materiae*. The change in what is regarded to constitute appropriate behaviour, i.e. the acknowledgment that state immunity cannot be claimed for such crimes, is then in line with the newly incorporated norm and developments in the norm life cycle.

Concerns for international order – the two dissenting opinions

Two of the Lords dissented from the majority decision, in opposite directions: Lord Goff was the only one who dissented in his overall judgment to dismiss the appeal for extradition, whereas Lord Millett disagreed with the majority opinion on the changed scope of the charges brought against Pinochet. Lord Millett took a strong solidarist view, advocating that Pinochet should stand trial for *all* alleged offences, wherever and whenever committed.

Ensuing 'international chaos' – Lord Goff

Lord Goff voted against the extradition request, arguing that the Torture Convention did not include an express waiver of immunity. He asserted that the simple fact that the crime in question was torture did not exclude immunity *ratione materiae* immediately, because only the state in question had the right to waive immunity. Lord Goff argued that state immunity was necessary to protect states from external intervention into their internal affairs and to ensure that they could act independently and make sovereign decisions. He rejected the suggestion that a waiver of immunity was implied in the Torture Convention, because it would have been 'unwise' for state parties to give up this protection. Lord Goff argued that failing to incorporate such a universal enforcement mechanism was a 'small price to pay' (Pinochet III 1999) in order to reach agreement on the Torture Convention. Lord Goff argued that he could not see any benefits for the international community as a whole to establish universal enforcement mechanisms and favoured leaving a possible escape clause for states that sign up to such international legal agreements to protect them in the event of their national interests being in conflict with these universal norms.

Lord Goff exerted a strong pluralist view that also includes realist elements by emphasizing that national interests can override the rules of international society. Lord Goff affirmed a sovereign's sole right to exercise jurisdiction on its own territory and to decide on the question of what constitutes 'official' conduct as part of governmental functions. He was concerned that reaching decisions on a case-by-case basis on whether waivers of immunity were implied in different international agreements would lead to 'international chaos' (Pinochet III 1999) and a breakdown of order.[9] Lord Goff emphasized the importance of maintaining the existing order and its principles of sovereignty and non-intervention and argued that principles of justice independent from states do not have value in themselves. In his view, no normative qualification is attached to international order, because agreement on justice principles is limited and pursuing justice would lead to chaos.

Lord Goff's argumentation illustrates some of the difficulties attached to the complex relationship between law and politics as discussed earlier: law is concerned with devising clearly defined guidelines whereas politics is about making case-by-case decisions. Enforcing norms unilaterally in individual situations exposes the problem of selectivity of universal values. Lord Goff did not see the norm life cycle as having developed far enough to make the application of these particular justice norms truly universal. He argued for a need for more guidelines to be devised and incorporated into international law to prevent chaos and a breakdown of international order. He acknowledged the existence of agreements between states with regard to defining norms that prohibit torture, but argued that they were not institutionalized to a degree that would allow them to be enforced at the expense of other, more fundamental, order principles such as sovereignty. Lord Goff argued that further developments had to take place to ensure the consistent application of the emergent norms.

'An attack on the international legal Order' – Lord Millett

Lord Millett, on the other end of the spectrum, gave the most determined support in favour of the extradition request. He argued from a strong solidarist perspective in favour of including all offences Pinochet was accused of – regardless of where and when they had been committed. He recognized Chile's right to grant immunity *ratione personae*, but argued that developments in international law had led to a move away from an unchallenged right to claim immunity *ratione materiae*. He asserted that the IMT at Nuremberg and the Eichmann trial had rejected the possibility of immunity for criminal acts for state officials. He argued that international crimes attracted universal jurisdiction if they violated *jus cogens* norms and if they were 'so serious and on such a scale that they could justly be regarded as an attack on the international legal order' (Pinochet III 1999).

Lord Millett argued that torture was recognized as an international crime that attracted universal jurisdiction well before 1984 when the Torture Convention was signed. It therefore did not create a 'new' crime but rather redefined, affirmed and extended it.

> Whereas the international community had condemned the widespread and systematic use of torture as an instrument of state policy, the Convention extended the offence to cover isolated and individual instances of torture provided that they were committed by a public official. I do not consider that offences of this kind were previously regarded as international crimes attracting universal jurisdiction. The charges against Senator Pinochet, however, are plainly of the requisite character. (...) Whereas previously states were entitled to take

jurisdiction in respect of the offence wherever it was committed, they were now placed under an obligation to do so. Any state party in whose territory a person alleged to have committed the offence was found was bound to offer to extradite him or to initiate proceedings to prosecute him (Pinochet III 1999).

He further maintained that the definition of torture was entirely inconsistent with a plea of immunity *ratione materiae*, because the offence could only be committed by an official person and that 'no rational system of criminal justice can allow an immunity which is co-extensive with the offence'[10] (Pinochet III 1999). He argued that the UK was therefore obliged either to extradite Pinochet to another requesting state or to prosecute him itself.

Lord Millett took a strong solidarist position, arguing for the necessity to pursue justice even if that involved compromising other principles of the existing order. He argued that if states failed to do so, order would break down, which is a solidarist statement in line with the English School's understanding that 'an unjust world is a disorderly one' (Wheeler 2000: 301). Lord Millett made a connection between order and justice and argued for a need to reconcile the two values, because some crimes were so severe that they could be regarded as an 'attack on the international legal order' (Pinochet III 1999). Lord Millett based his decision on the view that torture was already an offence with *jus cogens* status before the Torture Convention was negotiated and that states had recognized that this particular crime could not go unpunished.

Lord Millett acknowledged progress of the norm life cycle's first stage that included the increasing incorporation of human rights norms and the principle of universal jurisdiction into the rules of international society. He argued that Chile lost its right as sovereign in this case by not prosecuting a crime with *jus cogens* status and that other states in the international community therefore had a responsibility to act. He saw emerging and newly established principles of justice as being more important than the principles of non-intervention and sovereignty. In existing international law, some crimes are considered to be so serious that they concern humanity as a whole and need to be punished, which places an obligation on states in the international community to act if the state in question cannot be relied upon to do so itself. This obligation includes the possibility of external intervention by other states to pursue justice norms. Lord Millett's position is similar to Cassese's view as outlined in the Introduction that a vertically constraining system of rules exists which manifests itself in international law in notions of *jus cogens* and universal jurisdiction. This position includes a recognition of universal values that prevail over other forms of national interests and place an obligation on all states to protect them.

Unlike the majority opinion, Lord Millett based his arguments on the *nature* of the crimes Pinochet was accused of and justified his decision solely with reference to international rather than domestic law. He thereby exhibits a progressive view of international law, acknowledging developments in the norm life cycle of special human rights categories' position in the relations between states. These categories of human rights are seen as legitimate and grounded in precedent (as can be seen from references he made to Eichmann and the IMT) and are therefore seen as part of the existing rules of international society.

Comparison of the two House of Lords decisions

The two decisions of the House of Lords raise a number of issues important for the overall analysis. The first decision went a lot further than the second one, because it was argued that certain international crimes can *never* be qualified as official acts as part of government functions. The second decision (*Pinochet III*) was confined to acts of torture after the date the Torture Convention became effective law. The discussions and outcomes of both House of Lords decisions are significant for the development of human rights norms in international law for a number of reasons (Bianchi 1999: 248–249).

In *Pinochet I*, for the first time, an UK court relied solely on international agreements to reach a verdict and argued that a (moral) line could be drawn in international law to distinguish between wrongful acts by state organs and acts that could be regarded as international crimes. The House of Lords asserted that immunity *ratione materiae* in criminal proceedings was not always given but needed to be qualified with considerations of the nature of the crimes. This is significant because it normatively qualifies the existing international order and recognizes the existence of generally agreed justice principles already incorporated into that order.

Pinochet I focused mainly on the nature of the crimes Pinochet was accused of and established that torture, hostage taking and other crimes against international law could not benefit from protection through state immunity. The majority of Lords in that case argued that international crimes could never be recognized by international law to constitute official acts of states and hence attract immunity. They were in favour of 'drawing a line' and thereby argued for the possibility to morally evaluate existing principles of order in terms of states' sovereign right to declare certain acts to be official acts of states.

All in all, the first majority decision was based on a solidarist understanding of the order and justice dilemma; it was based on international law and the understanding that agreement on justice principles existed and that the moral value of order was important. Order and justice principles were both seen as being part of the rules of international society and also as being interlinked. Justice needed to be protected even if that included compromising other principles of order. The two dissenting judges, Lord Slynn and Lord Lloyd, were also in favour of bringing Pinochet to justice, but they argued that this could only be done either in Chile or through an international criminal court. They therefore also recognized the existence of generally shared ideas of justice, but they argued from a more pluralist viewpoint that these could only be upheld by respecting the more traditional order principles of non-intervention and sovereignty, and not by unilateral action.

This is a moderate pluralist position in terms of the pluralism–solidarism continuum, because the two Lords recognized the importance of justice norms and that some agreements exist. Yet, they also argued that international order principles could not be compromised on the basis of states' individual interpretations of justice norms. This position also highlights the problems attached to selectivity and politicized application of international law. Since international law has no overarching authority attached to it and relies on states for its enforcement, decisions to intervene in one case but not another are always based on political considerations and are therefore arguably selective. Enforcement of these norms is then not based on universality but much rather on individual states' interests and actions. The two dissenting Lords did not agree that these particular norms have developed far enough in line with the norm life cycle to allow them to be applied consistently.

The majority of Lords in both decisions, *Pinochet I* and *III*, recognized changes that have taken place in international society with regard to human rights norms being established and codified in international law. Even though the first decision was more innovative because it focused purely on the nature of the alleged crimes, the second decision was arguably based more firmly on existing provisions that were integrated into national laws.

The second decision (*Pinochet III*) was much more cautious than the first, and did not include an expansive interpretation of international legal obligations. The Lords based their decision primarily on the Torture Convention, and because this limited 'the denial of immunity to those instances where universal jurisdiction had specifically been accepted by way of treaty and statute, [this decision] was inherently more conservative than that of the first panel' (Byers 2000: 434).

Pinochet III focused on the interpretation of domestic laws and their relevant operating dates, rather than international laws and the nature of crimes, which led to a considerable change in the scope of the case. The majority of Lords emphasized the importance of existing international legal agreements that included principles of justice, but based their decision on international laws' application through domestic laws. This is a solidarist element in their reasoning that acknowledges the possibility of agreement on some justice principles that have already been reconciled with, and are incorporated into, the international order. The Lords clearly fought with the order and justice dilemma, because even though they recognized that torture was a serious international crime long before the Torture Convention, they only argued in favour of prosecuting Pinochet for acts allegedly committed *after* the Convention became binding in domestic law. They thereby emphasized the importance of the rule of law, which includes the principle of *nullum crimen sine lege, nulla poena sine lege*, i.e. the prohibition of retroactive application of law. They argued that justice principles could only be upheld within the framework of existing international agreements and their application in domestic laws.

Arguably, this is a cautious resolution of the order and justice dilemma but order and justice principles were reconciled, albeit in a more limited way. Justice principles were upheld in the context of international order – even if the interpretation was not wide enough to further challenge the moral and normative value of the existing order. The principle of sovereign immunity was challenged and it was confirmed that not just states but also individuals can be held accountable for their actions in accordance with international standards. Sovereign immunity is a principle that sets out that individuals who are members of a government cannot be held personally responsible for the conduct of their office. This is based on the notion that *states* are the subjects and objects of international law and not the individuals that hold particular offices in those states. This principle is necessary to ensure that state officials can exercise their state functions without fear of prosecution. The House of Lords decisions undermine this principle: individuals can be held accountable for their actions in accordance with international standards (even for 'official' acts). The Lords decided that heads of state still have the right to exercise their authority but only in accordance with international law which forbids torture. This places a limit on sovereign immunity for which state officials can be held accountable once they have left office. This is an important change because the previously unchallengeable principle of state sovereignty is now qualified to distinguish between official and unofficial acts for which individuals can be held accountable.

Overall, both majority decisions to allow the extradition of Pinochet were based on solidarist understandings of the conflict between order and justice. The Lords recognized that agreements on some fundamental justice norms exist that are institutionalized in international law and the international order and thereby place obligations on states to protect them. This application of universal values is limited, because 'genuinely universal crimes are defined quite restrictively and with great care and precision' (Weller 1999: 617). The Lords in *Pinochet I* based their decision purely on international law, which shows that they saw universal values as clearly established as such internationally. The second decision resisted this broad application of international law and focused on domestic laws instead, which further establish and incorporate norms into international society.

Unilateral action and the problem of selectivity

Unilateral actions by individual states raise a number of issues, but most importantly the problem of selectivity in terms of applying universal international laws in only one specific instance. As outlined earlier, critical law theorists such as Koskenniemi and Kennedy argue that such selective enforcement of universal rights can lead to a distortion of international law. Koskenniemi raises the concern that unilateral action is based on one state's particular view of international law rather than 'genuine' universality. Kennedy criticizes human rights for being vague and not providing enough clarity to be used as standards that can be used to justify external intervention. He sees the danger that human rights language can be used as a vehicle for imperialism, raising the question of whether challenges to international law are indeed 'legitimate' attempts to transform the international system based on universal values or whether they are based on other (national) interests.

The question remains why Pinochet was singled out as a former head of state involved in serious human rights abuses. A large number of people were killed after the coup that brought Pinochet to power and numerous human rights atrocities are known to have taken place under his dictatorship. By gaining status as senator-for-life he secured his constitutional protection against national jurisdiction in Chile. However, his is not the only case of a former head of state who has stood accused of serious international crimes, which raises the question of why the Spanish government decided to take action in this particular case. Yet, as Hawthorn for instance, argues 'one has to seize the political moment, and cannot in advance determine where and when it will present itself' (1999: 254). Prosecutions by successor regimes are rare and the decision to take unilateral action in one situation and not another is likely to be political. Such situations are selective, but it can be argued that they are nevertheless important because they provide focal points to determine the nature of emerging norms and how to interpret them (Reus-Smit 2004: 288). It is necessary to set precedents in order for norms to enter the norm cascade and thus to create a normative context in which they are increasingly internalized and can be developed further. International law has no independent enforcement mechanisms attached to it, which means that some form of agency is needed to enforce its principles. Even though such action is then not based on universality, it provides a starting point that needs to be found somewhere.

The Pinochet decisions were only based on norms with *jus cogens* character which means that agreement already existed between states that these norms affect international society as a whole and need to be protected universally. The difficulty therefore does not seem to lie in agreeing on certain principles, but in finding ways of applying them consistently. Through norm affirming action in the form of unilateral intervention as in the Pinochet case, these norms and their enforcement are incorporated further and cascaded into the rules of international society with the aim of making them more universal. Such a reconciliation of ethics considerations with international law can then facilitate normative change.

Unilateral enforcement is problematic because of its selectivity and can only be seen as one step in the norm life cycle towards further internalization of more universal human rights law enforcement in international society. Consistent and repeated enforcement of these norms together with the threat of punishment leads to a deterrent effect and therefore, 'what really matters is to set clear normative standards and to enforce them consistently whenever prosecution is possible under the circumstances' (Bianchi 1999: 274). The fact that prosecutions are perceived to be legitimate and firmly rooted in international law is important for further norm developments towards greater compliance with these norms.

Unilateral action is not sustainable in the longer term because it is based on an individual state's political will to intervene in a particular situation to enforce existing international legal provisions. It is likely that the 'new politics' of international law will remain selective and partial until a more neutral form of enforcing international laws can be found, because as Roht-Arriaza for instance argues: 'the very nature of transnational prosecutions makes them opportunistic, supplemental, ad-hoc. They will never be the only mechanism for achieving justice. But they are one piece of the emerging architecture, an architecture with a number of pillars.' (2005: 198).

It is likely that powerful states will continue to protect their citizens' close allies from prosecution by other states, but it can be argued that 'nonetheless, the political mood is changing, and with it, the political means of bringing putative violators to book' (Hawthorn 1999: 256).

Conclusion

The extradition request and subsequent decisions at the House of Lords in relation to Pinochet suggest that states are beginning to take their responsibilities with regard to special categories of human rights more seriously and to give established norms new powers of enforcement through unilateral action. This is in line with the norm life cycle's second stage as these actions are based on norms that are established in the rules of international society. Some of the Lords resisted the application of these norms, which suggests that they are not implemented far enough to be universally perceived as being part of international society. The norms are still emerging from the first stage of the norm development and more progress needs to take place before they are enforced consistently as part of what is deemed to be appropriate behaviour for the members of international society. The arguments made in the Pinochet judgments have demonstrated a number of developments that have taken place in international law. These developments have been ongoing since 1945, but 'until Pinochet, few may have realized the implications of all these developments taken together, which amount to a very advanced international legal order' (Weller 1999: 616).

The House of Lords confirmed, in line with an overall solidarist approach, that justice and order values are both part of international order and need to be reconciled to contribute to the institutionalization of new norms into international society. The case suggests that international society is slowly moving towards increased solidarity and new norms of a more just order in which both values can be realised. The first House of Lords decision was often criticized for getting too involved in political decision-making rather than concentrating on applying international law. In the second decision, the Lords avoided this accusation by asking the then Home Secretary Jack Straw to reconsider his decision on the extradition request. Rather than seeing this as an indication that the Lords wanted Straw to return Pinochet to Chile, 'the House of Lords was simply confirming that, while the courts could rule on the process, in the end the decision whether or not to extradite was political. They were thus returning the matter to its rightful place' (Woodhouse 2000: 11). Straw confirmed that Pinochet could not claim immunity and that extradition proceedings could resume, but when Pinochet was eventually declared to be unfit to stand trial and sent back to Chile, doubts were raised about whether he would ever in fact face prosecution for the alleged offences. This decision was very controversial particularly because it was claimed that Pinochet had left the UK in a wheelchair as a frail and weak man but upon arrival in Chile was able to walk unaided. Sending him back to Chile raised doubts whether he would ever face prosecution for the alleged offences.

Initial reactions in Chile to Pinochet's arrest in the UK were mixed, but the majority of Chileans were positive about the fact that action was finally being taken against their former head of state. A report by Human Rights Watch written one year after the final House of Lords decision confirmed that changes had taken place in Chile which had opened up the possibility of prosecution. These changes also forced the country more generally to deal more openly with matters that had previously been swept under the carpet. This suggests that unilateral action by one state can have an impact on the application of universal norms on other states. Chile was compelled to change its initial decision to grant Pinochet immunity for life and started to take action to bring him to justice. The Supreme Court also allowed prosecutions in 'disappearance' cases against a number of generals and officers to proceed despite amnesty laws established in 1978. In May 2004, Chile decided to strip Pinochet of his immunity from prosecution, opening up the possibility to try him for his part in human rights abuses committed in what was known as Operation Condor – a co-ordinated campaign by Latin American military governments of the 1970s and 1980s to crack down on their suspected opponents. This case was dismissed, but in September 2006, Pinochet was stripped of *all* immunity from prosecution of rights violations. The aim was to open the way for Pinochet to be charged with kidnapping and torture in the infamous Villa Grimaldi prison in the 1970s. He was placed under house arrest, but died before he faced any charges in December 2006, leaving a lot of his victims feeling that they have been denied 'justice'.

In spite of these limitations and the fairly restrictive nature of the second House of Lords ruling, the Law Lords' decisions can be said to constitute a 'quite remark-able challenge to the norms of the Westphalian system' (Brown 2002: 218) and particularly the concept of sovereign immunity. The case confirmed the emergence and incorporation of new norms into the rules of international society, but resistance to these changes was demonstrated some months later: the case of the Congo's Foreign Minister Abdulaye Yerodia Ndombasi before the International Court of Justice (ICJ) in 2002 confirmed that resistance to the norm life cycle's developments still existed. This case equally dealt with one state's unilateral challenge to the immunity for a state official accused of serious human rights abuses, but had a different outcome: the Congo's right to grant immunity was confirmed in the ICJ. This case is the subject of the next chapter that also draws comparisons with the Pinochet decisions and discusses issues relating to the problem of universal jurisdiction. Both cases – Pinochet and Yerodia – expose the difficulties attached to enforcing these provisions on a universal and consistent basis.

Notes

1 This case cannot be seen as an important *legal* precedent for a number of reasons, mainly because the House of Lords is not bound by its own decisions and most of what has been said can be ruled out as *obiter dicta*. *Obiter dictum* (Latin: a remark in passing), does not form part of the *ratio decidendi* of the case and therefore does not create a binding precedent, but may be cited as persuasive authority in later cases. The Pinochet decisions nevertheless constitute precedents with great political significance.

2 *Pinochet II* and issues arising from the question of suspected bias are not relevant for the present analysis and will therefore not be discussed further. For an in-depth analysis of these issues see for instance Woodhouse (2000).

3 Rules of state immunity concern the protection which a state is given from being sued in the courts of other states. These rules developed at a time when it was thought to be

an infringement of a state's sovereignty to bring proceedings against it or its officials in a foreign country.

4 Two different types of state immunity exist: immunity *ratione personae*, which is personal immunity attached to the status of an individual person. A serving head of state, for instance, is immune from prosecution by another state under this provision. Immunity *ratione materiae*, on the other hand, is subject-matter immunity, which is attached to official acts of states.

5 Lord Hoffmann decided to concur with Lord Nicholls' arguments and voted in favour of allowing the appeal. He did not outline a separate opinion.

6 This argument is in line with the 'Act of State Doctrine', which stipulates that no judgment can be passed on the validity of acts of foreign governments performed within their national territory.

7 In *Pinochet I* all Lords agreed that the date the extradition request was *received* mattered most which meant that the double criminality rule did not have any impact on the scope of the case.

8 Article 1 (1) of the Torture Convention defines torture as 'any act by which severe pain or suffering, whether physical or mental, is intentionally inflicted on a person for such purposes as obtaining from him or a third person information or a confession, punishing him for an act he or a third person has committed or is suspected of having committed, or intimidating or coercing him or a third person, or for any reason based on discrimination of any kind, when such pain or suffering is *inflicted by or at the instigation of or with the consent or acquiescence of a public official or other person acting in an official capacity.* It does not include pain or suffering arising only from, inherent in or incidental to lawful sanctions' (emphasis added).

9 This position is contrary to the solidarist view that argues that international order breaks down if it is *unjust.*

10 This is a similar argument to the one made by Lords Slynn and Nicholls in the first decision, who argued that attempts to maintain international order can be taken too far and make a 'mockery' of international law.

4 The International Arrest Warrant case – the Congo v. Belgium

The International Arrest Warrant case of the Congo v. Belgium at the International Court of Justice (ICJ) is another unilateral attempt by one state to enforce universal justice norms but with an opposing outcome to the Pinochet case. The ICJ confirmed the availability of state immunity for the Congo's Foreign Minister Abdulaye Yerodia Ndombasi and ordered Belgium to cancel the arrest warrant it had issued to try him for international human rights abuses. This chapter analyses the judgment given by the ICJ and the judges' separate opinions in light of the analysis' central order and justice debate, expressed in the Congo's claims to state immunity and Belgium's attempt to exercise universal jurisdiction over international crimes.

Unlike the Pinochet case, the Yerodia case deals with immunity granted to an acting Minister of Foreign Affairs rather than a former head of state and it deals with an arrest warrant being issued *in absentia*. Both cases, however, deal with the same underlying issues: the conflict between state immunity and individual accountability of state officials for international crimes, and the question of unilateral exercise of universal jurisdiction established in international law. The main difference between the two cases lies in their outcomes: whereas in the Pinochet decisions the judges ruled in favour of a state's claim to exercise universal jurisdiction, the judges at the ICJ decided that the Congo could grant immunity to its former state official and ordered Belgium to cancel its arrest warrant. Both cases can be seen as illustrations of the norm life cycle's second stage which deals with attempts to enforce human rights norms that are already established in international law. Norms that have emerged in the cycle's first stage are being enforced on the basis that they are accepted to be part of the rules of international society. These norms are not fully institutionalized and resistance to their enforcement may still occur, as is evident from the case study in hand.

This chapter starts by outlining the main (relevant) issues of the ICJ's judgment and those aspects of the separate opinions of the individual judges in which the conflict between order and justice becomes apparent. The implications of the ICJ's decision, together with the judges' separate opinions, will be assessed in the context of the underlying theoretical framework and in comparison to the Pinochet case. The two cases demonstrate different interpretations of the development of the norm life cycle: in the Pinochet case, new norms were considered by the majority of judges to be part of the normative framework that constrains state action. In the Yerodia case, in contrast, these norms were not seen by the judges to have progressed far enough to be applied in a way that made compromising other, more traditional order principles possible. Unilateral action was based on claims of universal jurisdiction in both cases. As argued in preceding chapters, universal jurisdiction is problematic because decisions about whether or not to intervene are based on political considerations and lead to selective application of international law. These issues are discussed in the final section of this chapter and it is argued that the ICJ's decision to disallow the exercise of universal jurisdiction in this particular instance suggests that further developments in line with the norm life cycle need to take place before these norms are fully institutionalized and their application made universal.

The case and the judgment

On 11 April 2000, a Belgian judge issued an international arrest warrant *in absentia* against the Congo's Minister for Foreign Affairs Abdulaye Yerodia Ndombasi, charging him 'as perpetrator or co-perpetrator, with offences constituting grave breaches of the Geneva Conventions of 1949 and of the Additional Protocols thereto, and with crimes against humanity' (Arrest Warrant Case 2002: 8). Yerodia was accused of making various speeches inciting racial hatred during August 1998 in his capacity as principal private secretary to the then President Laurent Kabila. These speeches allegedly encouraged the Congolese population to kill members of the government opposition and resulted in several hundred deaths, arbitrary arrests and unfair trials of Tutsi residents in Kinshasa.

The crimes Yerodia stood accused of were punishable under the Belgian 'Law of 16 June 1993 concerning the Punishment of Grave Breaches of the International Geneva Conventions and the Additional Protocols as amended by Law of 19 February 1999 concerning the Punishment of Serious Violations of International Humanitarian Law'. This Law lists a number of acts that constitute grave breaches of the Geneva Conventions, including crimes against humanity and war crimes. Under Article 7 they are declared crimes under international law that can be prosecuted regardless of where they are committed. With this Law, Belgium incorporated universal jurisdiction for certain international crimes into its national laws, opening the possibility to prosecute such crimes regardless of where and by whom they were committed. Belgium thereby took the provisions set out in the Geneva Conventions seriously by making them enforceable principles in its domestic legal system. These provisions place a duty on states to prosecute perpetrators of particular crimes in the interest of humanity as a whole.

Belgium claimed that it could exercise universal jurisdiction in the case against Yerodia entirely due to the nature of the alleged crimes. The alleged crimes had not been committed on Belgian territory and had not involved Belgian nationals (neither victims nor the alleged perpetrator) and Yerodia himself was not on Belgian territory when the warrant was issued and circulated. Article 5 (3) of the Belgian Law provides that the Act 'shall apply equally to all persons without distinction based on official capacity' (Reydams 2003: 107) and could therefore be applied to a Foreign Minister. The alleged crimes took place *before* Yerodia became Foreign Minister, but he was acting in that capacity at the time the arrest warrant was issued and circulated.

On 17 October 2000, the Congo filed an application with the ICJ, challenging the legality of the arrest warrant under international law. It argued that Belgium had violated the principles of non-intervention and sovereign equality of states by exercising jurisdiction on the Congo's territory through issuing the arrest warrant. The Congo submitted that '[t]he *universal jurisdiction* that the Belgian State attributes to itself under Article 7 of the Law in question' constituted a

> [v]iolation of the principle that a State may not exercise its authority on the territory of another State and of the principle of sovereign equality among all Members of the United Nations, as laid down in Article 2, paragraph 1, of the Charter of the United Nations (Arrest Warrant Case 2002: 9).

The Congo further claimed that its Foreign Minister had a right to diplomatic immunity while in office.

Belgium argued that, at the time of the judgment in 2002, Yerodia was no longer Foreign Minister, had not held a ministerial position since a new government took office[1] and could therefore not claim state immunity. Belgium maintained that it had not violated the principle of diplomatic immunity because it never intended to arrest Yerodia while he was in office; the arrest warrant included an exception for official visits.[2] The 'Red Notice', which requires other states to act in line with the arrest warrant, was only issued after he had left office. Belgium argued that the purpose of the international *circulation* of the disputed arrest warrant was 'to establish a legal basis for the arrest of Mr. Yerodia …abroad and his subsequent extradition to Belgium' (Arrest Warrant Case 2002: 27).

On 14 February 2002, the ICJ delivered its judgment on the *Case Concerning the Arrest Warrant of 11 April 2000 (the Congo v. Belgium)* in which it ruled in

Table 4.1 The Arrest warrant case: Timeline of events

August 1998	Abdulaye Yerodia Ndombasi made various speeches in his capacity of principal private secretary to the then President Laurent Kabila, inciting racial hatred against members of the government opposition
14 March 1999 – November 2000	Yerodia held office of Minister for Foreign Affairs
11 April 2000	Belgium issued arrest warrant against Yerodia
17 October 2000	Congo filed an application with the ICJ challenging the legality of the arrest warrant
November 2000 – April 2001	Yerodia held office of Minister for Education
15 April 2001	New government took office. Yerodia ceased to have a governmental position.
14 February 2002	ICJ Judgment: vote of 10–6 ordered Belgium to cancel arrest warrant

favour of the Congo by confirming the availability of state immunity against charges of international crimes for its Minister of Foreign Affairs. With a vote of ten to six[3] it ordered Belgium to cancel the arrest warrant and inform all authorities to which it had been circulated to that effect. The Court restricted its judgment to the question of immunities and refrained from passing judgement on whether Belgium had acted *ultra vires*[4] by exercising universal jurisdiction. This limitation in the judgment prompted most of the ICJ judges to outline separate opinions to clarify their views on this issue.

The judgment of the ICJ and the separate opinions illustrate the way the judges struggled with the conflict between state immunity (as a principle of order) on the one hand and individual accountability of state officials for international crimes (as a principle of justice) on the other. Both are incorporated in the rules of international society and Belgium's claim of universal jurisdiction demonstrated the incompatibility of state sovereignty and the enforcement of universal values. In the context of this analysis, two issues of the ICJ judgment are most significant: firstly the question whether Belgium acted *ultra vires* by exercising universal jurisdiction; and secondly whether Belgium had violated principles of state immunity or whether immunities cease to be available when a Foreign Minister is suspected of serious abuses of international human rights.

Claims to universal jurisdiction

As outlined in chapter two, universal jurisdiction gives states the right (and even duty) to exercise jurisdiction over a criminal act regardless of where the crime was committed or the nationalities of the victim or perpetrator. This is based on the idea that some human rights violations are so serious that they concern humanity as a whole and therefore need to be punished anywhere, regardless of state borders. The universal jurisdiction principle aims to strengthen international human rights law enforcement by giving states broad competence to enforce these human rights universally in their national courts.

This makes the claim of universal jurisdiction controversial because on the one hand, it is incorporated into international law through treaties and Conventions, but on the other its exercise is not regulated in a way that makes it truly universal and consistent. Universal jurisdiction relies on voluntary state co-operation and there is a possibility that the decision to act in one case but not another may be politicized and selective. Individual states decide on a case-by-case basis whether to honour their responsibilities with regard to international crimes with *jus cogens* character and to take action.

In the Yerodia case, the ICJ decided not to formally rule on the question of whether Belgium had acted *ultra vires* by claiming universal jurisdiction because both parties to the dispute had requested to limit the judgement to the question of immunities. The ICJ clarified that 'this does not mean, however, that the Court may not deal with certain aspects of that question in the reasoning of its Judgment, should it deem this necessary or desirable' (Arrest Warrant Case 2002: 17).

A number of legal writers criticized the ICJ's failure to take a clear stand on whether or not universal jurisdiction was admissible and argued as Cassese, for instance, that 'the Court has thus missed a golden opportunity to cast light on a difficult and topical legal issue' (2002: 856). The ICJ avoided taking a lead role in establishing a precedent either way, which may have resulted from the fact that 'the judges were very much divided on this controversial issue' (Wouters 2003: 263). However, ten of the ICJ's judges outlined their separate opinions to clarify their views on the matter of universal jurisdiction and even though the ICJ did not formally rule on it, this 'made a significant contribution to elucidating existing law' (Cassese 2002: 856).

The question of state immunity

The second question of significance in relation to the ICJ judgment is that of state immunity, i.e. the notion that a sovereign state should not be subject to the jurisdiction of another state. In its judgment the ICJ decided that state immunity was necessary to ensure that a Foreign Minster can exercise his official functions on behalf of the state without fear of external intervention. The Court did not distinguish between acts committed before assuming office and during the period of office nor did it qualify what constituted 'official' and 'private' acts of a Foreign Minister. These distinctions would have been important for the final judgment because the crimes Yerodia was accused of took place *before* he became Minister for Foreign Affairs.

The ICJ confirmed the availability of immunity *ratione personae* arguing that such immunity for an acting Foreign Minister was necessary in order not to deter him from travelling internationally when required for purposes of the performance of official functions. This is in line with the Pinochet decision where immunity was confirmed while Pinochet was in office. The ICJ did not make a distinction between immunity *ratione materiae* and *ratione personae* and did not qualify what constituted 'official acts'; issues that were essential in the case against Pinochet. The ICJ judgment held that it was

> unable to deduce from [national state] practice that there exists under customary international law any form of exception to the rule according immunity from criminal jurisdiction and inviolability to incumbent Ministers of Foreign Affairs, where they are suspected of having committed war crimes or crimes against humanity (Arrest Warrant Case 2002: 21).

The judgment was mainly based on the understanding that immunities for acting Foreign Ministers are necessary to ensure they can properly exercise official functions on behalf of their state. The ICJ stressed that immunity did not mean impunity, it only meant that prosecution was barred for a certain period or for certain offences; immunity could not exonerate a person from criminal responsibility. The Court outlined four possible scenarios under which an incumbent state official could still face prosecution: first, in a court of his own country; second, if his country decided to waive immunity; third, when he left office; and fourth, through an international criminal court. This can be seen as recognition by the ICJ in line with a pluralist view that agreement on universal values of justice is possible, but that they cannot be enforced at the expense of state sovereignty and the non-intervention principle. The ICJ emphasized the order principle and the concept of state immunity over holding Yerodia accountable for alleged war crimes and crimes against humanity.

Ten of the judges submitted their separate opinions in order to qualify the overall judgment and to outline their positions on the issue of universal jurisdiction.

The separate opinions

'Upholding the rule of law' – the majority opinions

Judges Guillaume, Koroma, Ranjeva, Rezek and *ad hoc* Judge Bula-Bula outlined their separate opinions in support of the overall ICJ judgment and argued that Belgium did not have the right to exercise universal jurisdiction against Yerodia.

Judges Guillaume and Rezek argued that universal jurisdiction *in absentia* was 'unknown in conventional law' (Guillaume 2002: 5) and that jurisdiction was usually based on either the territoriality or the nationality principle. They argued that the UN Charter's recognition of the sovereign equality of states, as well as developments in international law and politics, strengthened the territorial principle. They therefore asserted that universal jurisdiction needed to be restricted to include a link between the alleged crime and the prosecuting state.

Judge Guillaume stated that because a crime was recognized as such under international law did not automatically mean that other states had jurisdiction to try it. He referred to Lord Slynn's argument in *Pinochet I* that 'there is no universality of crimes against international law' (Pinochet I 1998). Judge Guillaume argued further that even though international criminal law had developed considerably, and it was possible to confer jurisdiction, this should only be to *international* courts, not to national ones. To confer jurisdiction to national courts, he argued, would

> risk creating total judicial chaos. It would also be to encourage the arbitrary for the benefit of the powerful, purportedly acting as agents for an ill-defined 'international community'. (...) such a development would represent not an advance in the law but a step backward (Guillaume 2002: 8).

Judge Bula-Bula similarly argued that the Court upheld 'the rule of law against the law of the jungle' (Summary of Opinions 2002). These views are in line with a pluralist approach that enforcing justice norms that are in conflict with other order principles can lead to chaos and a breakdown of international order. The arguments are also similar to critical law theorists' view that international law may be used by the most powerful states to further their own interests. The ICJ judges questioned whether universal values exist that reflect the interests of all states and argued that enforcing international law based on claims of *universality* can lead to a distortion of law.

With regard to the question of immunity, Judge Koroma agreed with the overall judgment that Yerodia was immune from Belgium's jurisdiction to ensure he could act effectively in his capacity as Foreign Minister. Judge Koroma acknowledged that the Belgian Law established universal jurisdiction when certain grave breaches of international humanitarian law were committed, but argued that 'international law imposes a limit on Belgium's jurisdiction where the Foreign Minister in office of a foreign state is concerned' (2002: 2). He argued that universal jurisdiction was possible in general, but not in this particular case:

> Belgium is entitled to invoke criminal jurisdiction against anyone, save a Foreign Minister in office. It is unfortunate that the wrong case would appear to have been chosen in attempting to carry out what Belgium considers its international obligation (Koroma 2002: 2–3).

Judge Koroma concluded that universal jurisdiction was available for certain crimes and that 'the Judgment cannot be seen either as a rejection of the principle of universal jurisdiction (...) or as an invalidation of that principle' (Koroma 2002: 3). His opinion thus differed from the overall ICJ judgment in that he acknowledged the existence of universal jurisdiction in general, but did not agree that it could be exercised in this particular case because it dealt with the case of an *acting* state official. He thereby recognized that agreement on certain justice norms exists and that they are incorporated into international law, but he also argued that fundamental principles of state immunity for acting state officials should take precedence over such 'newly' emerged norms.

Unlike arguments made in the Pinochet case, the majority of judges did not deliberate the potential implications of the nature of the crimes Yerodia was accused of. They did not make a distinction between what constituted 'private' and 'official' acts. The judges argued that the arrest warrant was not based on customary international law and was therefore not valid in the first place, making such a distinction irrelevant in this context. The judges emphasized the functional argument by focusing on a Foreign Minister's responsibilities and the notion that immunity was vital to ensure he could act without others states' external interference. In so doing, however, they buried an important moral argument which distinguishes between different acts.

The failure of the ICJ's majority judges to not clearly distinguish between private and official acts and to not clarify whether immunity can be granted for international crimes has been criticized by a number of legal writers. Cassese, for instance, argues that 'by ambiguously excluding that state agents could be brought to trial after leaving office, the Court has arguably left in the event the demands of international justice unheeded' (2002: 874). Arguably, a qualification of what 'official' acts entail is important, because it clarifies that the 'official' capacity of an alleged perpetrator cannot be accepted as a valid defence. As asserted by the House of Lords in *Pinochet III*, a number of serious international crimes, such as torture and crimes against humanity can by definition only been committed by state officials. The 'official' nature of the act is a constituting element of the definition of the crime, which makes them (by definition) incompatible with state immunities.

The ICJ judges focused mainly on the principles of state sovereignty and non-intervention arguing that there was no basis for universal jurisdiction and that states should not be allowed to intervene in another state's affairs, regardless of the nature of the alleged crimes. They argued that otherwise chaos and abuse of this principle by the powerful could ensue, resulting in politicized decisions about possible prosecutions. The judges thereby gave an overall pluralist view, stressing international law's primary function of dealing with relations between states to maintain international order rather than universal justice principles, such as individual accountability for international crimes. Judge Koroma exhibited a more moderate pluralist view by acknowledging that justice norms are incorporated into the rules of international society, but are not institutionalized in a way that they can supersede the principle of state immunity.

The majority judgment and related separate opinions show that the norms that constituted the basis for the Pinochet decisions are not incorporated far enough to make their enforcement universal in all cases. They are still dependent on interpretations by individual states and in this case, the decision was taken that they were not an essential part of the rules and the normative context of international society. The majority of the judges argued that agreement on universal norms was possible and that these have been incorporated into international law in line with the norm life cycle's first stage. They argued, however, that further clarifications are necessary before these norms can be cascaded into international society, thereby changing 'appropriate' behaviour in line with shifts in the overall normative environment. The majority of judges were opposed to applying such international rules in national courts because of a lack of clear and uniform guidelines that ensure their enforcement is universal.

'Balancing divergent interests of international law' – the dissenting opinions

Six of the judges[5] disagreed with the overall judgment that Belgium should cancel the arrest warrant. They based their arguments mainly on the fact that Yerodia was no longer in office and could therefore not claim immunity as part of his official position as Foreign Minister. They asserted that immunity was an exception to a rule and therefore needed to be defined narrowly. The dissenting judges acknowledged the existence of the conflict between order and justice and argued that the case

> was about balancing two divergent interests in modern international (criminal) law: the need of international accountability for such crimes as torture, terrorism, war crimes and crimes against humanity and the principle of sovereign equality of States, which presupposes a system of immunities (Van den Wyngaert 2002: 4).

Judges Higgins, Kooijmans and Buergenthal in a joint separate opinion argued that two different sets of interests existed in the international community: on the one hand the interests of the community of mankind to prevent and stop impunity for perpetrators of grave human rights abuses; and on the other, the interests of the community of states to act freely on the interstate level without unwarranted interference. They argued that a balancing of these differing interests was necessary because they were both valued by the international community. In this case, Belgium and the Congo both gave particular emphasis to the opposing sets of interests. The judges argued that the balance was constantly changing, but that

> a trend is discernible that in the world which increasingly rejects impunity for the most repugnant offences, the attribution of responsibility and accountability is becoming firmer, the possibility for the assertion of jurisdiction wider and the availability of immunity as a shield more limited (Higgins, Kooijmans and Buergenthal 2002: 18).

The judges stressed the important function immunity has in international relations to maintain order in international society. They argued (in line with an overall solidarist approach) that the challenge for the international community was to reconcile and accommodate both values – justice and order – that are interlinked and not to let one triumph over the other.

In terms of the pluralism–solidarism continuum, Judges Van den Wyngaert and Al-Khasawneh displayed a stronger solidarist position by arguing that norms of justice are seen to be so important that they can always supersede order. Judge Al-Khasawneh for instance maintained that

> the effective combating of grave crimes has arguably assumed a *jus cogens* character reflecting recognition by the international community of the vital community interests and values it seeks to protect and enhance. Therefore when this hierarchically higher norm comes into conflict with the rules of immunity, it should prevail (2002: 3).

The dissenting judges argued that universal jurisdiction was possible, because the duty to prosecute was established in international agreements such as the 1949 Geneva Conventions and in a series of multilateral treaties with special jurisdiction provisions that 'reflect the determination by the international community that those engaged in (…) [international crimes] should not go unpunished' (Higgins, Kooijmans and Buergenthal 2002: 13). Judge Van den Wyngaert argued that the present case was a test case which needed a principle decision to determine what actions states can take to respond to allegations of such human rights violations. The dissenting judges argued that the crimes Yerodia was accused of, which included war crimes and crimes against humanity, affected the international community as a whole and seemed to 'fall within this category in respect of which an exercise of universal jurisdiction is not precluded under international law' (Higgins, Kooijmans and Buergenthal 2002: 16).

The judges argued that immunity could not exculpate an offender from criminal responsibility, even though immunity could be granted as long as the suspected state official was in office. This, Judge Van den Wyngaert, concluded means that the ICJ judgment might lead to different kinds of abuse: of states claiming immunity for their officials and that 'perhaps the International Court of Justice, in its efforts to close one box of Pandora for fear of chaos and abuse, has opened another one: that of granting immunity and thus *de facto* impunity to an increasing number of government officials' (Van den Wyngaert 2002: 42).

The dissenting judges agreed that even though the ICJ judgment set out different scenarios of how Yerodia could still be prosecuted, granting immunity led to *de facto* impunity, because the essence of the problem lay in the unwillingness of national courts to prosecute their own state officials. They argued that the ICJ should have made clear in its final judgment that the Congo had not fulfilled its obligations to investigate Yerodia for the alleged crimes. They argued in line with both Pinochet decisions that immunity was only available for official acts, whereas international crimes could *never* be regarded as part of official functions. They agreed that Belgium's arrest warrant was illegal while Yerodia had been in office, but opposed the overall ICJ judgment that it remained illegal once he had left office. The dissenting judges argued that a clear distinction of what constitutes 'private' and 'official' acts needed to be made. They asserted that immunities for Foreign Ministers cease to exist for acts other than those exercised as part of official state functions, because 'immunity should never apply to crimes under international law, neither before international courts nor national courts' (Van den Wyngaert 2002: 20).[6]

The dissenting judges confirmed the availability of state immunity while a Foreign Minister was in office and thereby emphasized the importance of the order principle to ensure that a Minister can perform their official functions without external intervention. This immunity they argued, however, ceased to exist in cases of allegations of serious international crimes once that Minister had left office. The dissenting judges argued, in a similar way to both Pinochet decisions, that international crimes could never be considered to be official acts. The right to immunity *ratione materiae* needed to be qualified once a state official leaves their post. They maintained that state immunity could not be used as a shield behind which alleged perpetrators could hide. Judge Van Den Wyngaert validly pointed out that abuse of a different kind (initiated by states) could become a possibility after the ICJ's judgment: states might invoke the state immunity principle to avoid prosecution of their own state officials even when they were accused of international crimes.

In their argumentation, the dissenting judges favoured an overall solidarist view of the tension between order and justice and the need to find a balance between universal jurisdiction and state immunity as two different recognized sets of values. They argued in favour of enforcing universal justice norms with *jus cogens* character by compromising the inviolability of state sovereignty and non-intervention. In line with the norm life cycle, the judges identified a developing trend in international society towards a more solidarist position by incorporating the possibilities of universal jurisdiction and individual accountability for *former* state officials. The judges recognized the emergence and development of certain human rights norms into the rules of international society by referring to them in their argumentation. This reflects a recognition of changes that have taken place in the overall normative structure that enables and constrains action and also creates expectations in line with the norm life cycle. The dissenting judges accepted that enough progress had taken place with regard to these norms that enforcing them was consistent with states' membership of international society. This is a different interpretation to the one advanced in the majority opinion: the dissenting judges argued that such norms can be enforced through unilateral action because they are based on already established and codified universal values.

Comparing the Pinochet case and the Arrest Warrant case – claims to universal jurisdiction

The International Arrest Warrant case is similar to the Pinochet case in a number of respects, most importantly, because they both deal with the conflict between immunity for state officials on the one hand and claims of universal jurisdiction by individual states for serious international crimes on the other. Both cases dealt with 'the struggle between two competing visions of international law' (Sands 2003: 103): one vision sees international law as including broadly shared norms and values that involve a commitment to bring impunity for the gravest international crimes to an end, the other understands international law's main function as facilitating relations between states which are seen as the principal actors.

Both cases confirmed the availability of absolute immunity (*ratione personae* and *ratione materiae*) for incumbent state officials, but they differed in their treatment of state immunity for *former* state officials. The ICJ judgment ruled that state officials cease to be immune from prosecution for private acts, but continue to have immunity *ratione materiae* for all official acts, without qualifying what official acts entail. In the Pinochet judgments, in contrast, it was decided that serious international crimes could never be regarded as official acts and that former state officials could therefore not claim immunity from prosecution.

A number of legal scholars (Cassese 2003; Clapham 2003; Sands 2003; Wirth 2002) have criticized the overall ICJ judgment for its failure to qualify what it saw as 'official' acts for which immunity could be sought. Wirth, for instance, argues that the ICJ judgment does not reflect the current state of customary law and that 'this decision might be conceived as a step backwards to before the House of Lords' *Pinochet* judgment' (2002: 881). Cassese argues that the ICJ's proposition that no exception to the rule of state immunity exists is 'questionable' (2002: 865), because it failed to refer to the customary rule lifting immunity *ratione materiae* for former state officials in cases of serious international crimes. He argues that the ICJ had to strike a balance between the need to safeguard the prerogative of sovereign states to unimpaired conduct of international relations with the demands for safeguarding universal values. The ICJ ruled in favour of the former, but Cassese argues that current international law allows for the protection of both requirements – through the distinction between immunity available for incumbent as opposed to former state officials (2002: 874).

The judges in both cases argued from different bases in trying to find a balance between order and justice values that are both incorporated in the international order: in the Pinochet case, the judges started from a presumption *against* immunity and limited the role of immunities available to states, whereas the judges in the ICJ started from a presumption *in favour of* immunities unless removed by express act (Sands 2003: 103). The different emphases placed on the different values demonstrate that the two courts had diverse views of international law's function and how it developed over the past decades. In the Pinochet case, the judges recognized that changes towards increased recognition of human rights norms have taken place, that these norms are incorporated into international law and that they need to be taken into account as a part of international law. The ICJ, on the other hand, was more conservative in its view of international law and favoured a state-centred approach, emphasizing more traditional principles of order over newer justice norms. The ICJ thereby did not recognize developments with regard to human rights norms and interpreted existing legal provisions differently from the judges in the House of Lords. The different outcomes of the two cases suggest that the judges relied on contending interpretations with regard to how far norms have changed and developed in the norm life cycle.

Most of the ICJ judges demonstrated in their separate opinions that they struggled to make a decision on the conflict between order and justice in this particular case. Some of the judges that voted in favour of the Congo's right to state immunity still recognized the existence of universal jurisdiction. They were mainly against its application without clearer guidelines to make it more consistent and less selective. Some international law scholars recognize that the ICJ's ruling is rather conservative: 'refusing to examine what is really at stake here, namely the balancing of two divergent interests in international criminal law: the need for international accountability for core crimes and the principle of sovereign equality between states.' (Winants 2003: 499).

The ICJ placed greater emphasis on the importance of unhindered conduct of international relations between states over the prosecution of crimes that concern international society as a whole. However, this ignores

> the fact that since 1945 the international community has increasingly evolved towards an international legal order in which the traditional limits on criminal prosecution are no longer applicable with regard to the most serious international crimes and in which individual criminal responsibility increasingly gains the upper hand over immunity (Wouters 2003: 261).

The reasons for this different interpretation could lie in the ICJ's role as a court that primarily deals with disputes between states. In terms of its mandate and jurisdiction, it is not a specialized human rights court but reflects the 'old' vision of international law as law mainly concerned with regulating relations between states rather than between individuals. This limitation reflects the traditional state-centred view of international law which was predominant at the time the ICJ was set up.

The ICJ's decision to grant immunity to an *acting* Foreign Minister was not disputed by any of the judges. Yet, their reluctance to take a clear position on what should happen once that Minister had left office, and whether the nature of the crimes in question made any difference, is problematic because it does not lead to clear guidelines on the availability of state immunity for international core crimes.[7] Arguably, the ICJ's ruling is out of sync with developments in international law and politics where a greater recognition for human rights and individual justice has emerged since the Second World War. Norms have emerged through the first stage of the norm life cycle that need to be taken into consideration in international relations.

The overall judgment by the ICJ should not be seen as a 'backward' step in the norm life cycle's development of international human rights law, but much rather as a 'faltering' step. It confirms the need for further progress and also shows the dynamic of the norm development process. Further developments are necessary in order to incorporate consistent and universal enforcement of already established norms and to take account of new challenges faced by international law. The ICJ judgment did not question the existence of universal justice norms *per se*, but the possibility of enforcing them in national courts through judicial intervention. The ICJ decision and the separate opinions suggest that international law needs to develop further before universal jurisdiction can be fully incorporated. However, the fact that established justice norms were taken into consideration in the final judgment and also the separate opinions, and that a struggle between the two norms of order and justice is discernible, is already a change in international law in line with the underlying norm life cycle.

The main issue of controversy in both the cases of Pinochet and Yerodia, lies in the claim of universal jurisdiction by individual states which is problematic because it ultimately constitutes a political decision about international law's application.

Universal jurisdiction in Belgium's national law

The exercise of universal jurisdiction exposes the difficulties attached to the role of politics in international law. Universal jurisdiction places obligations on states to enforce universal values, but since no independent enforcement mechanism is attached to this provision, decisions on whether or not a particular situation can be regarded as a crisis that warrants external intervention are based on political considerations of individual states. This normalizes and legitimizes all conduct that falls short of being called an atrocity and also makes the application of universal norms very selective and dependent on politics. Developments in international society at the time both judgments were made had not progressed in a way that made the enforcement of such human rights norms universal and consistent. The exercise of universal jurisdiction in both cases constituted unilateral attempts by individual states (UK, Spain and Belgium) to enforce these principles. The interpretation of these international law principles which eventually led to claims of universal jurisdiction against Pinochet and Yerodia was ultimately political, which inevitably raises the question – why these two and not others?

Belgium tried to overcome the difficulties attached to the universal enforcement of international legal standards by establishing universal jurisdiction with regard to crimes with *jus cogens* character into its *national* laws. This strengthened the possibility of their enforcement and gave Belgium the authority to exercise jurisdiction over crimes against humanity, genocide, and war crimes regardless of where and by whom they were committed. By incorporating universal jurisdiction into its domestic laws, Belgium aimed to exercise its rights set out in the Geneva Conventions and other Conventions which place a duty on states to prosecute perpetrators in the interest of humanity as a whole. It took the provisions set out in these Conventions seriously by making them enforceable in its domestic legislation.

Belgium's law had been used successfully to prosecute crimes committed in Rwanda, a former Belgian colony, but other groups tried to take advantage of it as well. For instance, complaints were made against the former US President George Bush and others for their involvement in US action in Iraq in 1991. Belgium's Foreign Minister Louis Michel criticized such use of the law in what he saw as a political way. He argued that the law was 'being abused by opportunists' which made changes to its wide interpretation necessary. He also emphasized that 'Belgium must not impose itself as the moral conscience of the world.'[8]

Threats by the US to sanction Belgium, and pressure exerted by other states, eventually forced Belgium to amend its law to narrow the scope of its powers. The latest amendment in August 2003 resulted in abolishing the principle of extraterritorial jurisdiction over crimes so that it can only apply to cases in which a direct link is made between the alleged crime and Belgium. This 're-imposition of a nationality tie in effect negates the whole point of universal jurisdiction' (Roht-Arriaza 2005: 191) because jurisdiction is then based on nationality and territoriality principles rather than universality. This suggests that Belgium's law came at a stage where the justice norms (of enforcing crimes with *jus cogens* character through universal jurisdiction) had not been accepted by all members of international society unequivocally, making their institutionalization in national law problematic. Differing interpretations of the role of national courts and their role in the application of international human rights law still exist. Human rights norms that attract universal jurisdiction need to develop further in line with the life cycle to make their actual enforcement part of the rules of international society, accepted by all its members. This is necessary in order for these norms to become part of the normative structure and also part of states' identities as members of international society, thereby affecting their behaviour.

Even though Belgium aimed to exercise jurisdiction over *jus cogens* crimes universally by incorporating universal jurisdiction into its domestic law, it is doubtful whether this would have happened in reality. Cases brought under the Belgian Law only dealt with crimes committed in Africa, not Western or other powerful states. To end situations of severe human rights abuses or to initiate court proceedings, some form of agency is required to bring those abuses to a court's attention. Prosecutions are very costly and involve a number of other factors that need to be considered and it is therefore likely that enforcement through a national court is always going to be selective. Unilateral action always involves the potential for selectivity in the interpretation of international legal provisions and can lead to politicized prosecutions.

A number of international treaties explicitly include obligations for states to prosecute individuals who are accused of having committed such crimes of universal concern. In some situations, such as the cases discussed here, a domestic failing to prosecute a former head of state for international crimes required other states to act to enforce international law in the name of universal human rights (Bianchi 1999: 249–254). Even though such occurrences of states exercising universal jurisdiction are rare, they are nevertheless very important, because they indicate that some states take the provisions in international human rights agreements seriously. In accordance with the life cycle model, these can be seen as instances of norm entrepreneurs applying newly codified rules and engaging in norm affirming action because they consider them to be part of their identity as members of international society. This application of new norms is based on the understanding that the rules of international society can supersede any other rules and that they provide a normative environment that enables and constrains states' actions.

However, it is also debateable whether national courts can ever be appropriate fora for prosecuting crimes of international law. By definition, crimes of international law constitute an attack on the international community as a whole and therefore every state has the responsibility to prosecute them. In order to ensure that human rights provisions are not only enforced selectively whenever one state decides to act, an alternative judicial structure is necessary. International courts seem to provide one such alternative. The Yerodia case and the dissenting opinions in the Pinochet decisions both highlighted the necessity of prosecuting international crimes in international courts. Resistance to developments in the norm life cycle were predominantly based on arguments against national and unilateral application of international law rather than disagreement over the *content* of justice norms.

Conclusion

The two case studies of Pinochet and Yerodia illustrate unilateral attempts to enforce universal values, but they also show that these values are still dependent on differing interpretations. In the Pinochet decisions the judges took an overall solidarist approach by trying to find a balance to reconcile order and justice values through qualifying immunities for international crimes. The House of Lords recognized developments in the norm life cycle and based their decisions on norms established in its first stage. The ICJ, in contrast, took a more pluralist position and in trying to find a balance, established a presumption in favour of immunities, unless removed by express act. It thereby emphasized the importance of 'proper orderly conduct' between states. This demonstrates a different view of the nature and the role of international law – primarily understood to regulate relations between *states* rather than individuals – and also a resistance to norm development. The two cases illustrate that the dynamic of norm development is not a neat progression through various stages, but one which involves regress as well as progress.

The ICJ decision shows that ambiguities still exist when it comes to unilateral attempts to exercise universal jurisdiction. Universal jurisdiction is recognized as a principle of international law and incorporated as such into a number of treaties and conventions, but its enforcement is still selective and inconsistent. No clear rules or institutional frameworks exist that make the consistent application of universal jurisdiction possible, which leads to different interpretations of its position in the structure of international society. Even though some of the judges that argued against Belgium's application of universal jurisdiction acknowledged that it was an important principle of international law, they did not agree that rules existed to make its application in national courts possible. The main disagreement therefore seemed to lie in the question of *how far* these norms of justice and their enforcement have developed in the norm life cycle and whether they could be applied in these particular cases.

If the aim is to ensure that human rights norms are enforced consistently, universal jurisdiction as a mechanism for their enforcement is problematic – it can only function as a normative means to pressure states to comply with norms that are part of international society. It does so by including at least a theoretical possibility that non-compliance can lead to external intervention. Even though precedent-setting through unilateral action is important in facilitating change, in the long term it is not sustainable because it is too dependent on individual states' political will. In order for the norm life cycle to develop further, other solutions and mechanisms need to be found in order to enforce the principles that are incorporated in international law. Arguably, international courts that are established multilaterally, and which involve a greater number of states, can overcome some of the problems of unilateral action. In particular, they reduce the element of an individual state's national agenda in interpreting international law in its efforts to deal with international crimes. Enforcement on a multilateral basis through international courts will be explored in the subsequent chapters on the creation of the *ad hoc* International Criminal Tribunal for the Former Yugoslavia and the permanent International Criminal Court.

Notes

1 In November 2000, a governmental reshuffle took place in which Yerodia's role changed from Foreign Minister to Minister for Education. He ceased to hold any ministerial position when a new government was formed on 15 April 2001.
2 Yerodia even visited Belgium twice after the warrant had been issued.
3 The ICJ usually consists of fifteen judges that are elected by the UN General Assembly for a period of nine years. The judges do not represent their countries, but if there are no judges of the contesting parties on the bench, each country to the dispute can appoint an '*ad hoc* judge' to support their case. Judge Van Den Wyngaert was appointed as *ad hoc* judge by Belgium, Judge Bula-Bula by the Congo. Judges that voted in favour of cancelling the arrest warrant: President Guillaume; Vice President Shi; Judges Ranjeva, Herczegh, Fleischhauer, Koroma, Vereshchetin, Parra-Aranguren, Rezek; Judge *ad hoc*

Bula-Bula. Judges that voted against: Oda, Higgins, Kooijmans, Al-Khasawneh, Buergenthal, and Judge *ad hoc* van den Wyngaert.

4 '*Ultra vires* [Latin: beyond the powers]: Describing an act by a public authority, company, or other body that goes beyond the limits of the powers conferred on it. *Ultra vires* acts are invalid' (Martin 2002: 513).

5 Judge Oda voted against *all* provisions on the basis that he believed the ICJ lacked jurisdiction in this particular case. He argued that the case did not constitute a legal dispute between the two states but much rather a request by the Congo to receive a legal opinion from the ICJ. This issue is not relevant in the context of this analysis and will therefore not be discussed further.

6 In her argumentation, Judge Van Den Wyngaert referred to Lord Steyn's example of Hitler's final solution as an example that could clearly not be seen as part of an official act that attracts state immunity.

7 'Core crimes' are the most serious rights violations that are of concern to the international community as a whole, such as genocide and crimes against humanity.

8 'Belgian War Crimes Law Undone by Its Global Reach', *Washington Post*, 30 September 2003.

5   The creation of the *ad hoc* International War Crimes Tribunal for the Former Yugoslavia

In 1993, the UN Security Council decided to establish an *ad hoc* criminal court to investigate and prosecute the most serious human rights abuses committed on the territory of the Former Yugoslavia since 1991. This decision was based on Chapter VII of the UN Charter and constituted a response to the threat to international peace and security posed by those crimes. Similar to humanitarian interventions that are also based on Chapter VII and human rights concerns, the International Criminal Tribunal for the Former Yugoslavia (ICTY) constituted a judicial multilateral intervention – intervention with legal means, without the use of force.

The ICTY is another case in which the struggle between order and justice in international law and politics becomes apparent at a concrete level: the Former Yugoslavia's sovereign right[1] to exercise territorial jurisdiction was compromised in favour of an international mechanism for enforcing human rights norms. This chapter analyses how order and justice were deliberated in the argumentation surrounding the institution's establishment and how they were included in the ultimate decision to create the *ad hoc* Court.[2]

Unlike the unilateral attempts by individual states to enforce justice principles set out in the previous chapters, the establishment of the ICTY constituted a multilateral intervention – through the UN as an international institution – in a sovereign state's internal affairs in the pursuit of justice. The Court was imposed on the Former Yugoslavia with reference to Chapter VII of the UN Charter which made it binding on all UN member states. The decision to single out this particular crisis had involved political decisions by the Security Council members and the limited and *ad hoc* nature of the Court makes it a rather problematic international institution which suffers from a number of serious short-falls. The chapter argues, however, that the establishment of the ICTY constituted an important precedent for multilateral action by states in international society to enforce principles of justice. It suggests that these norms are being taken increasingly seriously and are given priority over other fundamental principles of order (sovereignty and non-intervention). The court's establishment constitutes a significant development in international politics and law and is a valuable example of the increased incorporation of justice norms in accordance with the second stage of the norm life cycle model.

The chapter starts with a very brief sketch of the historical and political background to the decision to establish the ICTY. This is followed by an analysis of various documents issued by the UN and by different states surrounding the tribunal's creation. Studying justifications and the public reasoning processes of the actors involved provides the basis for an analysis of underlying norm developments; in this context the progression of 'new' human rights and justice norms and states' compliance with them. This chapter also looks at a challenge to the ICTY's jurisdiction through the perspective of the *Prosecutor v. Tadić* decision, which questioned the ICTY's right to exercise jurisdiction and its primacy over national courts. The chapter concludes with an assessment of the main problems and achievements surrounding the ICTY's creation and examines how its creation contributed to the further institutionalization of new norms into international relations in line with the norm life cycle.

Background to the ICTY's creation

The end of the Cold War resulted in the disintegration of Yugoslavia and the onset of yet another violent conflict in the area. Serbian leader Slobodan Milosević encouraged Serb nationalism through his vision of the 'Great Serbian Project' aimed at creating an ethnically homogenous Serbian state.[3] In 1991, he orchestrated military action against Slovenia and Croatia after they had declared their independence, followed in 1992 by a similar offensive against Bosnia with devastating 'ethnic cleansing' of Bosnian Muslims and Croats. Despite widespread reports of grave human rights abuses and of Serb-run concentration camps, the international community was reluctant to act decisively and deploy troops to end the violence.

However, high media pressure and lobbying from various non-governmental organizations made it increasingly difficult to ignore the conflict and states were pressured 'to do something' to stop the conflict. The UN decided to establish the UN Protection Force (UNPROFOR), which was initially deployed in January 1992 in areas of conflict inside Croatia, as an interim measure with a restricted mandate to act as a peacekeeping force.

In March 1992, Bosnia declared itself an independent nation, a move that was opposed by the Bosnian Serb nationalist militia and which was followed by their rebellion under the leadership of Radovan Karadzic. It is alleged that during the ensuing invasion, 'Serb leaders carried out a policy of ethnic cleansing to rid the occupied territories of Bosnian Muslims' (Maogoto 2004: 150). In June 1992, the UN extended UNPROFOR's mandate to protect the delivery of humanitarian aid. States were reluctant, however, to expand UNPROFOR's remit further to allow action to put an end to the fighting, as to do so would have meant taking sides[4] and putting their soldiers' lives at risk. Yet, not extending the force's remit allowed a continued deterioration of the human rights situation.

On 6 October 1992, the UN Security Council unanimously adopted Resolution 780 which called for the establishment of an impartial 'Commission of Experts' to examine and analyse information related to 'the violations of humanitarian law, including grave breaches of the Geneva Conventions being committed in the territory of the former Yugoslavia.' The Commission faced a number of difficulties including lack of funding and states' reluctance to co-operate, but it nevertheless produced a report outlining the situation in the region, in which it

> concluded that grave breaches and other violations of international humanitarian law had been committed in the territory of the former Yugoslavia, including wilful killing, 'ethnic cleansing', mass killings, torture, rape, pillage and destruction of civilian property, destruction of cultural and religious property and arbitrary arrests (Secretary-General 1993: at 9).

The Commission also suggested the establishment of an *ad hoc* international tribunal to deal with these crimes, arguing that 'such a decision would be consistent with the direction of its work' (Commission of Experts 1993: at 74). The Commission argued that jurisdiction for war crimes was governed by the universality principle which could also be applied to genocide and crimes against humanity and that these could therefore be governed by the international community. The Commission conferred the responsibility for setting up a tribunal to the Security Council as part of its mandate to deal with threats to international peace and security. This echoed similar recommendations made by various other bodies, such as the UN Human Rights Commission and the Commission on Security and Cooperation in Europe (CSCE) (Morris and Scharf 1995: 29).

On 22 February 1993, the Security Council unanimously adopted Resolution 808, deciding in principle to establish the ICTY. The Resolution requested the Secretary-General to report on all aspects relating to this matter and to take into account suggestions put forward by member states to this effect. On 25 May 1993, the Security Council unanimously adopted Resolution 827 which contained the Statute of the ICTY. The Statute grants the Court subject matter jurisdiction over grave breaches of the Geneva Conventions, genocide, crimes against humanity and war crimes. In considering the establishment of the ICTY, the Security Council had to make a complex choice between upholding the inviolability of state sovereignty (accepting as a consequence that the crimes committed would go unpunished) and undermining state sovereignty through the creation of an international tribunal to prosecute the most serious human rights abuses (Maogoto 2004: 155). It eventually decided to do the latter.

The reasons *why* the Security Council decided to act this way are subject to speculation and a matter of great debate. It became clear that the 'war had spun out of control' (Fletcher and Weinstein 2004: 35) and the conflicting parties were unwilling and/or unable to bring to justice persons responsible for the serious human rights violations that were being committed. The end of the Cold War meant that the UN Security Council was not paralyzed by Great Power rivalry anymore and that there was 'new willpower, as well as the ability to effect political change' (Bodley 1999: 431). The Security Council may also have hoped to deflect criticism for its reluctance to get involved militarily to end the bloodshed (Maogoto 2004: 143–144) and it eventually opted for a non-military intervention based on established international legal norms.

Concerns regarding the ICTY's creation process

The establishment process of the ICTY involved numerous negotiations and meetings between a number of states and also the involvement of the UN Secretary-General. These negotiations brought out the underlying conflict between order and justice on a concrete level. Agreement had to be reached on whether the UN could infringe the Former Yugoslavia's sovereign right to exercise national jurisdiction over universal human rights norms. These norms are already established in international law and included universal jurisdiction provisions, thereby placing an obligation on all states to enforce them.

Report of the UN Secretary-General

In his report, the Secretary-General explained that the Security Council established the ICTY as an enforcement measure under Chapter VII of the UN Charter. He emphasized that this measure was judicial in nature and that the ICTY needed to function independently of political considerations and must not be controlled by the Security Council. He also underlined the Court's spatial and temporal limits, arguing that the Court's life span would be 'limited to the restoration and maintenance of international peace and security in the territory of the Former Yugoslavia, and the Security Council decisions related thereto' (Secretary-General 1993: at 28).

The Secretary-General set out that the principle of *nullum crimen sine lege* 'requires that the international tribunal should apply rules of international humanitarian law which are beyond doubt part of customary law' (Secretary-General 1993: at 34). This was important in order to avoid possible accusations of victors' justice and also to stay within clear limits of existing laws regarding justice and individual accountability. The Secretary-General also pointed out that because the ICTY was established under Chapter VII 'all states would be under an obligation to cooperate with the International Tribunal and to assist it in all stages of the proceedings (…)' (Secretary-General 1993: at 125).

The conflict between order and justice becomes apparent in the Secretary-General's report because he argued that compromising state sovereignty to enforce principles of justice was necessary in this case. He also emphasized, however, that this could only be done in a limited way with regard for other order principles, and only for universally agreed justice norms. The justification for compromising the most fundamental principles of international order (sovereignty and non-intervention) was based on the understanding that, by signing the UN Charter, states had accepted the primacy of the Security Council with regard to issues of international peace and security, and that this could 'trump' concerns for sovereignty. For the Secretary-General, the creation of the *ad hoc* tribunal was therefore already a possibility within provisions of the existing international order and did not constitute an unlawful violation of its basic principles. Emphasizing that crimes needed to be 'beyond doubt' part of existing legal principles underlined the importance of not creating *new* norms, but rather of enforcing already established ones and thereby staying within the scope of existing provisions. This is in line with the process of the norm life cycle whereby the norm cascade builds on developments in stage one that include codifications of new norms to integrate them further into the rules of international society.

The majority opinion – solidarist justifications

Before the ICTY was fully established, several states issued letters, reports and statements addressed to the UN in which they outlined their opinions and suggestions on the proposed tribunal. In a number of these statements states considered how sovereignty might be affected by enforcing justice principles through such an international judicial intervention. The majority of states were generally supportive of the establishment of the court, stressing the need for the UN to act in face of alleged violations of human rights in the territory of the Former Yugoslavia. The rhetoric used by states shows their support for the notion that some human rights are seen as universal and the responsibility of *all* states. States referred to such established norms in their arguments in support for the ICTY to justify the tribunal's creation.[5] Brazil, for instance, condemned the crimes against human rights that were allegedly committed and argued that these acts 'call for strong action by the international community, including through the United Nations, to uphold the fundamental values of justice and the dignity of the human person' (Brazil 1995: 435).

States placed great importance on the multilateral and international nature of the ICTY. They asserted that offences included in the Statute should be defined and interpreted in accordance with international conventions and customs 'as evidence of a general practice accepted as law and the general principles of law recognized by civilized nations' (Canada 1995: 460).

The majority of states agreed that emphasising the *ad hoc* nature of the ICTY was necessary because it could not and should not be seen as a precedent which could lead to similar action in other situations and conflicts. The UK, for instance, called the ICTY 'an exceptional step needed to deal with exceptional circumstances' (United Nations Security Council 1995: 189). Several states argued that this meant that the ICTY did not establish new norms or precedents of international law but 'simply applies existing international humanitarian law' (United Nations Security Council 1995: 182). States therefore argued that judicial intervention could only be justified in exceptional circumstances for the purpose of upholding universally agreed principles which are firmly established in international law.

By emphasising the importance of the *ad hoc* nature of the Court and the 'special' and 'extraordinary' circumstances of the conflict, these states demonstrated their concern about the effect of establishing the ICTY on the principle of state sovereignty. They emphasized the importance of limiting the competences of the Court to this particular conflict and of not creating a precedent with regard to the method of the court's establishment.[6] States argued that the ICTY should not be perceived as a unilateral attempt by a state to intervene in the Former Yugoslavia's internal affairs, but rather a multilateral action by an international institution to enforce agreed and established justice principles. States asserted the need to protect universal human rights as values of mankind and their belief that creating a tribunal

> would constitute a very important step towards building an international society more concerned about the respect for law. (…) and [that] its creation would, in the long term, constitute an invaluable symbol of the genuine will of the international community to uphold the rule of law (France 1995: 360–361).

The majority of states expressed an overall solidarist view of the solution of the order and justice conflict, aimed at creating a new enforcement mechanism for already existing international legal provisions. States tried to reconcile justice and order by referring to existing laws and treaties that are part of the international order, but have no independent means of enforcement attached to them. The protection of such universal justice norms was seen to be more important than preserving the inviolability of state sovereignty and non-intervention that are also principles of order. The approach taken by states acknowledges that the norm life cycle's first stage has been progressed towards codifying universal norms into international law that are then enforced through the ICTY. However, it is also evident that because states stressed the extraordinariness of the situation, further developments need to take place to make their enforcement permanent and universal.

Yugoslavia's opposition – a pluralist response

Not surprisingly, the government of Yugoslavia (Serbia and Montenegro) did not support the establishment of an *ad hoc* tribunal concerning crimes committed on its territory. It argued that alleged perpetrators should be prosecuted by national courts and under national laws that were harmonized with international laws. Yugoslavia supported the idea of a permanent international tribunal, but maintained that this should be established with 'respect for the principle of equality of States and universality and [Yugoslavia] considers, therefore, the attempts to establish an *ad hoc* tribunal discriminatory' (Yugoslavia 1995: 479).

Yugoslavia argued that crimes against international humanitarian law had also been committed in a number of other states, but that the international community had not interfered there with equal measure, 'so that the selective approach to the former Yugoslavia is all the more difficult to understand and is contrary to the principle of universality' (Yugoslavia 1995: 480). It doubted that the tribunal could be impartial and also questioned the legal basis for its establishment. It argued that the international tribunal was based on political motivations rather than international legal practice and that the 'proposed statute of the international tribunal is inconsistent and replete with legal lacunae to the extent that it makes it unacceptable to any State cherishing its sovereignty and dignity' (Yugoslavia 1995: 480).

Yugoslavia's position also highlights the underlying order and justice conflict, but it came to a different solution of the tension between the two values from other states, namely that the UN had no right to intervene in its internal affairs. Yugoslavia argued that it already subscribed to and had incorporated international justice principles into its national laws and that it was therefore not justifiable to infringe its sovereign right to exercise jurisdiction over the alleged perpetrators itself.[7] This illustrates a moderate pluralist view because even though Yugoslavia placed great emphasis on its sovereignty, at the same time it acknowledged the existence of international justice norms established in international law. It opposed the specific method of enforcement of these values through judicial intervention without its expressed consent because it perceived the selectivity of this approach to primarily be a result of political decisions rather than one based on international law.

Issues arising from the ICTY's establishment

The *ad hoc* court was built on the principal idea of providing justice through the enforcement of established principles of international law. This is based on the recognition of universal human rights that are of concern to all states and humanity as a whole. The emphasis is on rectifying injustice through the application of general, pre-existing rules through a formal system that adheres to principles of legal proceedings with respect to the rights of victims as well as the accused (Minow 1998: 25).

The conflict between order and justice

The main difficulty states faced in their struggle between order and justice lay in the efforts to reconcile two different values that are both incorporated into the international order and which they saw as irreconcilable and incommensurable. On the one hand, states were concerned about the value of the Former Yugoslavia's sovereignty and its right to non-intervention as fundamental principles of the existing order while on the other, they aimed to uphold legally codified human rights norms that were also part of the international order, but had not been given priority in the past.

The majority of states were reluctant to agree to external interference by a small number of states in the Security Council to uphold universal norms of justice, i.e. human rights that are agreed to be so fundamental that they affect humanity as a whole (and not just one state). These norms are recognized as such in international law and are incorporated in line with the norm life cycle's first stage. States solved the conflict they saw between the different values by stressing the 'extraordinary' and 'unique' nature of the situation. They also emphasized the importance of staying within existing international legal provisions and established norms regarding the ICTY's subject matter jurisdiction. The ICTY's jurisdiction is limited to the most serious human rights violations which are seen to be important not only as norms of international law, but 'quite simply our human concepts of morality and humanity.' (Russia 1995: 206) In the argumentation process surrounding the Court's creation primary emphasis was therefore not placed on states' interests, but the interests of humanity as a whole. References were made to existing international, universally recognized justice norms already part of international order.

Ad hoc *nature of the Court*

States were clearly concerned about the possibility that the ICTY would set a precedent that could lead to the Security Council deciding to intervene in similar situations in other states. They therefore repeatedly emphasized that the ICTY was an *ad hoc* court established in an extraordinary situation. This raises the question of how serious states' ambitions were for a more just order to ensure established norms of human rights violations that 'shock the conscience of mankind' are not left unpunished. The fact that states emphasized the *ad hoc* and unique nature of the ICTY suggests that they were ready to accept action which would compromise the sovereignty of other states, but that they remained very protective of their own. Even though states used solidarist rhetoric in favour of enforcing justice at the expense of compromising other principles of order, it is questionable whether they would have done so had it been their own sovereignty that was at stake. The arguments put forward by states represent attempts to rationalize the tension between order and justice, but is nevertheless problematic because the very function of law (that is being applied by states here) is to institutionalize ideas and norms into order to make the 'extraordinary' ordinary. A situation in which international law is applied cannot stay 'extraordinary'; this would be unjustifiable and unworkable.

The *ad hoc* nature of the ICTY makes it appear arbitrary and selective and, as Yugoslavia rightly pointed out, the question remains why the Security Council decided to act in this particular conflict and not in others. The decision by the Security Council to declare a situation a 'threat to international peace and security' is a political one and it is doubtful, for instance, that such an assessment would be made against any of the permanent members of the Security Council. There are no independent enforcement mechanisms attached to international law, but it still needs to be applied equally and in a non-discriminatory manner to all states that sign up to it and not just whenever a small group of states decides that a situation is 'extraordinary' and requires external interference. The ICTY should therefore only be seen as a step in the norm life cycle's second stage; further developments need to take place in international politics and law to achieve a more universal, less discriminatory enforcement of existing norms.

Chapter VII action

Some states questioned whether the Security Council had the right to establish the ICTY through a resolution based on Chapter VII of the UN Charter. A legal obligation to act in this conflict existed because the Commission of Experts' report into the situation in the Former Yugoslavia characterized the human rights atrocities as breaches of the Genocide and the Geneva Conventions (Williams and Scharf 2002: 97). By declaring the situation a threat to international peace and security, the Security Council claimed to act as the representative of international society as a whole. This mode of action ensured the ICTY's swift creation because it avoided lengthy negotiations between a large number of states that would inevitably have involved numerous compromises before an agreement could be reached. It also meant, however, that only a very small number of states, namely the members of the Security Council, were involved in the actual decision to set up an international tribunal that would be binding on all UN member states. Thus state sovereignty was compromised by externally imposing a judicial mechanism on states to deal with a particular situation of serious human rights abuses. However, by becoming a UN member, states accept the possibility that their state sovereignty can be affected by the Security Council on matters related to international peace and security.

The way the ICTY was established led to criticisms that a very conservative approach had been taken with regard to its subject matter jurisdiction, i.e. the crimes included in its statute (see for instance Bodley 1999; Kerr 2004; Williams and Scharf 2002). Only rules that were 'beyond doubt' part of international humanitarian law could be included. The Security Council did not set out to create new law, but to enforce already existing international rules that have no independent enforcement mechanisms. By creating an *ad hoc* international criminal court, it set a precedent of intervention with judicial means within the limits of existing provisions of the international order. This action can be seen as 'groundbreaking' (Maogoto 2004: 144) in political and legal terms, because the Council saw the creation of the ICTY as a worthy precedent even if that meant subjugating the sovereignty of states involved.

Another criticism levied at the Security Council was that establishing the ICTY was seen to be a less expensive and easier option than military intervention to stop the human rights atrocities in the Former Yugoslavia (Forsythe 2000: 94). Some (see for instance Bass 2002: 283) even argue that the ICTY can be seen as testimony to the *failure* of the West not to get involved militarily: if state leaders had managed to summon up the political will to stop atrocities when they occurred, there would have been no need for a war crimes tribunal to deal with the conflict's aftermath.

Arguably, establishing an international tribunal to deal with crimes committed during the conflict provided a way of getting involved without having to commit military troops. It thus required fewer resources from states which in turn made it easier to gain broader agreement for such action. Even though the ICTY's creation was a genuine implementation of international humanitarian law, it was also a by-product of international Realpolitik, 'born out of a political desire to redeem the international community's conscience rather than the primary commitment of the international community to guarantee international justice' (Maogoto 2004: 145).

Even if states could not summon enough political will to intervene militarily in the conflict, and establishing an enforcement mechanism to deal with human rights abuses in this particular situation was seen as the 'easier' option, it was nevertheless important in terms of its overall normative potential. The ICTY's establishment affected the overall development of human rights norms towards ending the culture of impunity to prevent human rights abuses from going unpunished. This progress is in line with the norm life cycle's development of creating a normative environment in which these human rights norms are increasingly seen as part of the international order. The establishment of the ICTY is a norm affirming action that cascades expectations of appropriate behaviour in the context of international society.

Normative impact

The ICTY can be seen as part of a more general development process of emerging norms of international justice that are becoming increasingly important in international law and politics (Kerr 2004; Peskin 2000; Robertson 2002; Rudolph 2001; Scheffer 1996). The creation of the ICTY was followed in 1994 by the establishment of the *ad hoc* tribunal for Rwanda (ICTR), a number of hybrid courts (such as in Sierra Leone), the arrest of Pinochet in London and the creation of the International Criminal Court (ICC) to name just a few.

Ad hoc courts as mechanisms for providing justice for crimes of a particular conflict have a long term normative impact on international society because they are 'fundamentally oriented toward delivering justice for the global community and establishing precedents for the further extension of international law' (Peskin 2000: 132). The establishment of the ICTY together with other cases of judicial intervention have normative importance for overall developments of the rules of international society and how they enable and constrain state action. They are based on emerging ideas and concerns for human rights that are already established in international law in accordance with the first stage of the norm life cycle. The

> increasing frequency of calls for investigations into war crimes and crimes against humanity is a strong indicator of changing norms and sensibilities. (…) In addition the emergent atrocities regime itself may be seen as a norm entrepreneur. Once established, the tribunal articulates and reinforces norms of state conduct and may also apply direct pressure to states through calls for investigations or by releasing information to the media (Rudolph 2001: 681).

This suggests that the ICTY can be seen as an important step in the norm life cycle towards increased incorporation of new norms into the international order. The fact that human rights abuses were regarded in this particular instance as threats to international peace and security is significant because it confirms the recognition that individuals have rights beyond their state borders. It also reinforces the notion that individuals as well as states are understood to be subjects of international law. Some human rights abuses are seen to be so serious that they affect humanity as a whole, regardless of state borders. The ICTY as an *ad hoc* court can lead as an intermittent step towards furthering the norm life cycle by affirming established norms in particular instances. Such a court is not part of the final stage of the norm life cycle because norms are not fully internalized, but it contributes to enforcing norms and thereby affirms their existence and their incorporation into what is regarded appropriate behaviour in international society.

Challenge to the ICTY's jurisdiction – the Tadić case

The first case that was tried before the ICTY was that of Dusko Tadić, who was initially arrested by German authorities in 1994 on suspicion of having committed offences that constituted crimes under German law. Following a formal request for deferral, Tadić was transferred to the ICTY's detention unit in The Hague in 1995, where he was charged (together with a co-accused) with numerous counts of human rights abuses involving grave breaches of the Geneva Conventions, violations of the law or customs of war, and crimes against humanity. The indictment alleged that between late May 1992 and 31 December 1992, Dusko Tadić participated in attacks on and the seizure, murder and maltreatment of Bosnian Muslims and Croats in the Prijedor municipality, both within and outside a number of prison camps. On 7 May 1997, Tadić was found guilty on eleven of thirty-one counts and on 14 July 1997 was sentenced to twenty years imprisonment.

Tadić questioned the legality of the creation of the ICTY and the decision to intervene in the Former Yugoslavia's internal affairs through the UN Security Council with judicial means. He challenged the jurisdiction of the ICTY on three grounds: 'the alleged improper establishment of the International Tribunal; the improper grant of primacy to the International Tribunal; and (...) the subject-matter jurisdiction' (Trial Chamber 1995: at 1). Tadić's challenge was dismissed by the ICTY Trial Chamber and also its Appeals Chamber.[8]

The case is significant in the context of this analysis because it was the first case tried before the ICTY in which its validity and method of establishment were challenged by the accused. The order and justice conflict is thereby played out on a very concrete level: the principles of non-intervention and state sovereignty were held to be prior to human rights and justice norms. The case also established important new case law by ruling that crimes that are established in international law can also be prosecuted if they take place in internal conflicts. This extended the reach of international society with regard to the universal protection of human rights that are seen as fundamental to all states. It confirmed the recognition of the possibility of norms transcending state borders and that no *international* link needs to exist to make the protection of individual justice possible.

The Trial Chamber's and the Appeals Chamber's decisions

The defence for Tadić argued that the Security Council had acted beyond its powers and that the ICTY should have been created either by treaty or by amendment of the UN Charter, rather than by Security Council resolution. The defence asserted that the Security Council had acted inconsistently and selectively in focussing on the Former Yugoslavia and not on other conflicts occurring at the same time in other parts of the world. Tadić's defence also challenged the ICTY's primacy over national courts. It argued that the UN was based on the principles of 'sovereign equality of all its members' and that therefore 'no State can assume jurisdiction to prosecute crimes committed on the territory of another State, barring a universal interest justified by a treaty or customary international law or an *opinio juris* on the issue' (Tadić Case Appeal 1995: at 55).

In their judgments, the ICTY's Trial and the Appeal's Chamber countered that the ICTY was established within the scope of Chapter VII and that the competence of the tribunal was clearly defined with spatial and temporal limits based on existing international law. They argued that the Security Council had not acted arbitrarily, but that it had recognized the violations of international law that were occurring in the Former Yugoslavia as threats to international peace and security and had therefore acted in accordance with Article 39 of the UN Charter. The Trial Chamber conceded that Security Council action under Chapter VII, imposing its decision on the Former Yugoslavia, meant 'some surrender of sovereignty by the member nations of the United Nations but that [this was] precisely what was achieved by the adoption of the Charter' (Trial Chamber 1995: at 37).

Both Chambers rejected Tadic's challenge to the ICTY's primacy because they considered the crimes he was accused of to be internationally significant, 'offences which, if proven, do not affect the interests of one State alone but shock the conscience of mankind' (Tadić Case Appeal, 1995: at 57). They argued that some principles of justice were so important that it was sometimes necessary to compromise other principles of order to protect them. The Chambers maintained that the principles of sovereignty and non-intervention should never be used as 'shields' behind which states could hide whenever issues of justice were at stake.

The conflict between order and justice is apparent in the judgements through the notion of 'sovereign rights of states' versus crimes that 'affect the whole of mankind and shock the conscience of all nations of the world'. Both Chambers recognized that the nature of the crimes Tadić was accused of was important because they attract universal jurisdiction and are therefore the responsibility of the international community as a whole and not just of one individual state. They both saw multilateral action through an international institution like the UN Security Council as justified and necessary in such cases.

The Chambers argued from solidarist points of view that state sovereignty could not and should not take precedence over the protection of human rights, especially in relation to serious international crimes that are recognized as affecting humanity as a whole. The Appeals Chamber called the failure to give priority to justice over order in cases that included such serious human rights abuses a 'travesty of law' and a 'betrayal of the universal need for justice' (Tadić Case Appeal 1995: at 58). The judgments were based on firmly established international law that developed towards increased recognition of the position of individuals regardless of state borders. It also confirmed progress towards a redefinition of order principles such as state sovereignty to include notions of human rights and justice.

In line with a constructivist view, the concept of sovereignty changed to reflect new circumstances and a modified understanding of what this principle should entail. This places greater emphasis on enforcing human rights and justice norms over the necessity to maintain the rights of sovereign states to deal with these crimes purely on a national basis. It suggests an acceptance of developments in the norm life cycle that justice norms exist that affect all states and therefore need to be enforced universally.

Creating new case law –the internal and international nature of conflicts

An important precedent was established through the Appeals Chamber's decision that charges could be brought against Tadić for acts committed in the course of an internal conflict. Tadić's defence had challenged the very existence of an *international* armed conflict, arguing that the ICTY lacked subject matter jurisdiction over the alleged crimes because they were committed in the context of an *internal* conflict (Tadić Case Appeal 1995: at 65). In the initial decision of the Trial Chamber, the judges did not consider the nature of the conflict but argued that the ICTY had jurisdiction regardless. The Appeals Chamber, in contrast deliberated at length whether the conflict was internal or international in character. It eventually concluded that the conflict had both characteristics and that questions about the ICTY's jurisdiction should be considered in this context.

The Appeals Chamber recognized that the distinction between internal and international conflicts with regard to serious human rights violations had become increasingly blurred and meaningless and that internal conflicts were more and more affected by international legal rules. The Chamber argued that

> in the area of armed conflict the distinction between interstate wars and civil wars is losing its value as far as human beings are concerned. Why protect civilians from belligerent violence, or ban rape, torture or the wanton destruction of hospitals, churches, museums or private property, as well as proscribe weapons causing unnecessary suffering when two sovereign States are engaged in war, and yet refrain from enacting the same bans or providing the same protection when armed violence has erupted 'only' within the territory of a sovereign State? If international law, while of course duly safeguarding the legitimate interests of States, must gradually turn to the protection of human beings, it is only natural that the aforementioned dichotomy should gradually lose its weight (Tadić Case Appeal 1995: at 97).

This recognition emphasizes the increasing importance of universal human rights norms that are seen as transcending state borders and are accepted as part of international society, established and codified in international laws. The Appeals Chamber argued that new laws on internal wars have emerged, designed to protect individuals and also to regulate methods of warfare, in a move away from a very state-oriented to a more human being-oriented approach. The Chamber's decision to advance human rights and individual justice regardless of the nature of the conflict showed an increased willingness to intervene in matters that were traditionally seen to be 'essentially within the domestic jurisdiction of any state' (Article 2(7) UN Charter). As Alvarez argues, 'for many, the grandest legacy of the Tadic trial might be the Tribunal's jurisdictional holding: its finding that charges can be brought against Tadic even for acts committed in the course of an 'internal' conflict' (1996: 19–20). This also sets a precedent for increasing the possibility for intervention in domestic conflicts, because enforcing these particular human rights norms is no longer linked to the existence of an international conflict.

Human rights law enforcement is increasingly attached to the notion of humanity, rather than states.

Silencing the accused – the ICTY as 'show trial'?

Tadic's challenge to the ICTY's jurisdiction also raises more general issues on a very fundamental level. It poses questions of the context in which the Court was established and how the Court could make sense of its own jurisdiction. The fact that Tadić could only challenge the ICTY on jurisdiction through its own Appeals Chamber (and did not have recourse to a third, independent, party) is problematic because it represents the

> limits of legal possibility: to challenge the jurisdiction of the court challenges its ability to pronounce judgment and thus say anything at all about the challenge itself, in the same way that to challenge the constitutional process challenges the capacity of the system to express the 'will of the people' since that will is bound – constitutively – to the processes that yield it (Christodoulidis 2004: 201).

Even though it is necessary to reduce the complexity of the legal process by establishing codified rules and norms, this process by its very nature can have serious costs in terms of what is contestable, and the result causes a 'silencing that finds no representation in law' (Christodoulidis 2004: 186). It is therefore difficult to determine whether the ICTY did have jurisdiction in this case to decide on its own jurisdiction.

One of the aims of criminal tribunals is to uncover 'truth' and to establish an accurate historical record of conflict which can enable victims to start their healing process.[9] The ICTY, however, already embodies a certain understanding of what constitutes the 'truth', because it is based on *one* particular understanding of the Yugoslav conflict in which context it was established. The tribunal assumed universal legitimacy of the international community as a whole whereas in fact it was imposed externally by only a few states in the Security Council. This makes the Tadić decision that much more difficult to justify, because the judges were part of the very context he tried to challenge. As Koskenniemi argues: 'To accept the terms in which the trial is conducted – what deeds are singled out, who is being accused – is already to accept one interpretation of the context among those between which the political struggle has been waged' (2002: 17).

At the beginning of his trial in 2001, Slobodan Milosević similarly challenged the trial's jurisdiction: 'I consider this Tribunal a false Tribunal and the indictment a false indictment. It is illegal being not appointed by the UN General Assembly, so I have no need to appoint counsel to illegal organ'. And further: 'I don't see why I have to defend myself in front of false Tribunal from false indictments' (Milosević Transcript 3 July 2001: at 3–6 & 23–25).[10]

It is difficult to see how the aim of an international criminal tribunal to hold individuals accountable for their deeds can be accomplished if the accused does not recognize the validity of the tribunal. The accused should be given an opportunity to challenge the very context that provides the basis for the tribunal, because as Koskenniemi argues:

> If individual criminality always presumes some context, and it is the context which is at dispute, than it is necessary for an accused such as Milosevic to attack the context his adversaries offer to him. (...) The fact that Milosevic is on trial, and not Western leaders, presumes the correctness of the Western view of the political and historical context (2002: 17).[11]

This lack of objectivity and the contextual constraints lead to the ICTY running the danger of becoming a 'show trial' in which the accused is being silenced. This illustrates a difficulty attached to an international court that is created in response to a particular crisis situation. Determining a 'crisis' that warrants external intervention is selective and involves the politicized use of international legal provisions. Koskenniemi calls this a 'paradox' attached to *ad hoc* courts that are established to deal with particular situations:

> In order for the trial to be legitimate, the accused must be entitled to speak. But in this case, he will be able to challenge the version of truth represented by the prosecutor and relativise the guilt that is thrust upon him by the powers on whose strength the Tribunal stands. His will be the truth of the revolution and he himself a martyr for the revolutionary cause (2002: 35).

The Court thereby cannot fulfil its goal of enforcing universal justice principles in the international order consistently and unambiguously. This is a shortcoming resulting from the limitations of the way the ICTY had been set up and also from its *ad hoc* nature. Nevertheless, the ICTY constituted a valuable precedent for the ICC as an international and permanent court. It set important precedents in its case law and also elucidated issues attached to the enforcement of international criminal justice on a universal level.

Conclusion

The ICTY was borne out of a desire to 'do something' in response to the human rights violations taking place in the Former Yugoslavia. Despite a number of limitations associated with the ICTY and the way it was established, the court has great importance for the institutionalization of norm enforcement in international society in the long term. The ICTY is a means rather than an end in itself, making the enforcement of universal justice norms possible on an international basis. The court's establishment process brought out the underlying tension between order and justice that are both incorporated in the rules of international society: fundamental, state-centred principles of state sovereignty and non-intervention conflict with justice based ones of universal human rights that are 'beyond doubt' part of international law. In the end a predominantly solidarist approach was taken to reconcile the two values. It made compromising Yugoslavia's sovereign right to exercise jurisdiction on its territory necessary to make possible the creation of an international mechanism to deal with serious human rights abuses allegedly committed.

The UN Charter sets out the principle of non-intervention which can only be infringed in cases of 'threats to international peace and security'. That serious human rights abuses are regarded to constitute such a threat, demonstrates that rights of individuals are taken more and more seriously in international politics and law. The principle of non-intervention is increasingly qualified to include universal justice norms. The growing practice of declaring human rights abuses 'threats to international peace and security' could become a '*de facto* norm that trumps Article 2(7) in certain circumstances' (Holsti 2004: 160). This is an important development and is taken up in the final report of the International Commission on Intervention and State Sovereignty (ICISS)[12], which argues that if a state is unable or unwilling to stop serious harm of its population, the 'principle of non-intervention yields to international responsibility to protect' (ICISS 2001: xi). This does not mean that states in international society have an automatic right to intervene, but much rather that they have a responsibility to act to protect individual justice if the state in question has not fulfilled its sovereign responsibility to protect its own people.

The question of when intervention based on human rights motives is justified continues to be problematic particularly because of the selectivity in its application. Norms of human rights law enforcement have not developed enough to include clear guidelines that make it possible to avoid political decisions about individual conflicts. A starting point needs to be found to challenge existing practice – in this case of letting serious human rights abuses go unpunished – to further the norm life cycle and integrate justice norms into international society. The precedent set through the ICTY is rooted in existing international law and is in line with developments that have taken place over time. Its establishment can therefore be seen as expressing acceptance that norms have developed and are now part of international society's rules. It reflects changes that have taken place with regard to the understanding what the principle of state sovereignty and what 'appropriate behaviour' in international society entail. States' general support for the creation of the court can be seen as part of the socialisation process of the norm life cycle's second stage which includes norm affirming action of already codified international norms.

The fact that states emphasized the 'extraordinary' nature of the Court shows that there is some reluctance to establishing a precedent that can lead to similar interventions. This demonstrates the dynamic of the norm life cycle in which progress as well as resistance to norm developments become obvious. Even though states were reluctant to see the ICTY as a precedent, its set-up and new case law were influential in the creation of the permanent International Criminal Court which is the focus of the next chapter. The ICC seeks to overcome problems associated with the ICTY as a limited, *ad hoc* measure by building on its achievements and avoiding its shortfalls as a court imposed on states without expressed consent. Unlike the ICTY, the ICC was established through negotiations in a treaty-based approach and not imposed externally by only a few states that were members of the Security Council. It is an independent court that was not created as a response to a particular conflict and does therefore not include a pre-existing understanding of what the 'truth' in individual cases entails. Despite its problems, however, the ICTY was an important step towards further progress of the norm life cycle aimed at creating a more solidarist international society.

Notes

1 At the time the ICTY was created, the Socialist Federal Republic of Yugoslavia (SFRY) had ceased to exist. 'Former Yugoslavia' in the context of this book therefore refers to the governments on the territory following the state's break-up.

2 The ICTY was the first *ad hoc* court established by the UN Security Council followed in 1994 by the creation of the International Criminal Tribunal for Rwanda (ICTR). The ICTR was established to deal with human rights abuses committed in Rwanda during 1994 and built on a number of precedents set by the ICTY. Even though the ICTY is not exceptional and unique, this chapter only deals with the creation of the ICTY as the first *ad hoc* court established by invoking Chapter VII of the UN Charter.

3 The history and the origins of the conflict in the Former Yugoslavia are very complex and it is not the intention of this study to explore them in great detail. Only a very brief summary is given to provide the context for the subsequent analysis. It should also be noted that the way this conflict was perceived by the different parties involved was influenced by how the mass media reported the events at the time. Distinguishing between what the mass media claimed to be the 'reality' and the 'real' reality, however, is not pertinent in the context of this study. The focus is on the way the conflict was *perceived* by the actors involved that led to the decision to create the ICTY.

4 Even though most of the atrocities were being committed by Serb forces, it is important to bear in mind that Croats and Bosnian Serbs also committed serious crimes and that 'all parties to the conflict had committed abuses against other ethnic groups' (Morris and Scharf 1995: 22).

5 It is not the objective of this present analysis to study in-depth the *national* interests of individual states behind their rhetoric. In the context of this analysis it is important that states referred to established norms to justify their action, which can set precedents for future international judicial intervention and also furthers the norm life cycle.

6 It is noteworthy that the concerns over creating a 'precedent' were only linked to the procedure of setting up the ICTY – by resolution rather than through negotiation – and not to the nature of an international court as a tool for enforcing universal justice norms.

7 Interestingly, the government linked its concerns of 'sovereignty' with 'dignity', arguing that infringing a state's sovereignty has far reaching effects on the state. In contrast, Brazil and Spain had noted in their submissions to the UN that the ICTY was necessary in order to restore the 'dignity' of human beings.

8 The ICTY is composed of fourteen judges that sit in three trial chambers each with three judges and one appeals chamber with five judges. The judges are elected by the General Assembly selected from a shortlist provided by the Security Council.

9 See for instance Goldstone and Bass (2000) who argue that participants of war crimes tribunals often express their desire for the trial to provide a full historical record of the atrocities committed. Robert Jackson, for example, chief prosecutor of the Nuremberg tribunals, 'wanted the evidence prepared for the trials to stand as a massive documentary record of Nazi criminality' (2000: 54).

10 The trial against Milosevic ended when he was found dead in his cell in The Hague in March 2006. The trial was often criticized for taking too long and giving Milosevic too

much freedom in disrupting the proceedings. He repeatedly refused to enter a plea, and attempted to denounce the legitimacy of the Court. The Court recorded a not guilty plea to all the charges on his behalf.

11 This is also evidenced by the fact that the ICTY decided against prosecuting NATO soldiers for war crimes and crimes against humanity during the war in Kosovo. An initial investigation was conducted, but an Expert Commission's report led to the Prosecutor's decision not to further investigate claims against NATO soldiers.

12 This Commission of Experts was established by the General Assembly in 2000 in response to 'the increasing number of systematic abuse of populations by their governments (…) to weigh the alternatives among the competing views about the limits of sovereignty' (Holsti 2004: 158).

6 Judicial intervention coming of age? The International Criminal Court and US opposition

> As long as there is a breath in me, the United States will never – and I repeat never, never – allow its national security decisions to be judged by an international criminal court.
>
> *(Senator Jesse Helms before a Senate Hearing on the ICC)*

The establishment of the International Criminal Court (ICC) in 1998 can be seen as the latest development in enforcing human rights, closely related to the third stage of the norm life cycle in which norms that have cascaded have become increasingly institutionalized. States' sovereign right to exercise national jurisdiction over the most serious human rights abuses is challenged in favour of creating an international mechanism charged with enforcing universal justice norms. The primary focus of a number of states during the ICC's creation process was on attempts to preserve state sovereignty as far as possible. This was reflected in disagreements about the scope of the Court's jurisdiction, its relationship to the UN, and the powers given to the Court's prosecutor. Most of these issues can be linked back to matters discussed in preceding chapters, such as questions of universal jurisdiction and state immunity arising in the Pinochet and Yerodia cases and multilateral enforcement of universal values through international courts like the International Criminal Tribunal for the Former Yugoslavia (ICTY).

The ICC can be seen as an attempt to incorporate justice norms and their enforcement more fully into provisions of the international order through an independent supranational institution. The creation of the Court ties in with a solidarist understanding of international society that aims to build a more 'just' order in which norms are fully internalized and are seen as an integral part. A number of innovations were incorporated into the ICC's Statute that express both solidarist as well as pluralist aspects to arrive at a compromise acceptable to a large number of states. The ICC is not accepted by *all* states and opposition to its creation still exists. Most importantly, the US – the only remaining great power – opposes the ICC and has launched a number of counter-attacks aimed at undermining the effective functioning of the Court.

The establishment of the ICC can be seen as an example of the third stage of norm development in which already existing and universally agreed upon international norms are partially institutionalized. It builds on the norm cascade and preceding stages of the norm life cycle by providing clearer guidance on universal application to institutionalize the norms permanently into the rules of international society in a way that they will achieve a taken-for-granted quality. As argued previously, norms do not enter a normative vacuum, but need to be tied in with existing values to gain acceptance by international society. This means that developments in the third stage of the norm life cycle must include a re-evaluation of other norms to achieve a 'fit' between these and the emerging norms. This process was already evident in the cases discussed in earlier chapters. A reassessment of the sovereignty principle to include recognition of states' duties to enforce universal human rights is necessary to make further norm internalization possible. A number of concessions and compromises with regard to more traditional understandings of the principles of the international order had to be incorporated into the ICC in an attempt to reconcile these concerns for sovereignty with demands for universal enforcement of existing justice norms.

The way the ICC is set up means that the primary responsibility for the enforce-ment of justice norms lies with states themselves; the ICC is only a safety net that acts if the state in question is unable or unwilling to do so itself. This indirect effect of the ICC is central because it leads to a normative environment in which states are expected to comply with norms that are increasingly taken for granted and are seen as integral part of the rules of international society. US opposition to the ICC arguably demonstrates resistance to such developments in the norm life cycle and in particular to the attempt to incorporate norms permanently into international society through an independent court. US opposition thereby illustrates the dynamic of the norm life cycle and the fact that norm development is not a neat progression but one which is also characterized by resistance.

This chapter starts with an outline of the background to the ICC's creation and a discussion of the main issues arising from the negotiations which were mainly based on concerns for state sovereignty. The chapter then analyses US opposition to the Court. The opposition can be seen as a pluralist response to the mainly solidarist achievements of the compromises, based on considerations for national interest and the principle of non-intervention. Questions remain as to whether long-term US opposition has the potential to seriously hamper the ICC's contribution towards the creation of a more just order. It is argued here, however, that even though US opposition is difficult for the ICC, it is not strong enough to constitute an insurmountable obstacle for the Court's effective functioning. The Court is built on strong foundations that have developed in line with the norm life cycle and it also enjoys widespread support from a large number of states. In addition, the US has recently changed its position from initial hostility to an overall more pragmatic approach towards the Court.

Background to the ICC's creation

Developments towards a permanent international criminal court started in the 1950s, but concrete attempts to establish such a court were not made until after the end of the Cold War. The project of establishing a permanent court gained renewed momentum after the creation of *ad hoc* courts (such as the ICTY) by the Security Council, which had indicated both that a permanent court was needed, and that states might be willing to support its creation. In 1994, the UN General Assembly established an *Ad Hoc* Committee

> open to all States Members of the United Nations or members of specialized agencies, to review the major substantive and administrative issues arising out of the draft statute prepared by the International Law Commission and, in the light of that review, to consider arrangements for the convening of an international conference of plenipotentiaries[1] (United Nations General Assembly 1994: Note 3).

In September 1995, the Committee issued a report outlining the progress made during two meetings that had taken place earlier that year. The Committee argued that establishing a single, permanent court could make future *ad hoc* courts unnecessary, 'thereby ensuring stability and consistency in international criminal jurisdiction' (*Ad Hoc* Committee 1995: 3). The report of the *Ad Hoc* Committee formed the basis for further meetings held by the Preparatory Committee (PrepCom), which had been created by a General Assembly Resolution in 1995.

The PrepCom had a more specific, goal-oriented mandate than the *Ad Hoc* Committee, which included the task of preparing a text that could be used as a basis for negotiations towards a final compromise on the establishment of a permanent international criminal court. Numerous proposals were submitted by states during the six meetings of the PrepCom held between March 1996 and April 1998. The range and complexity of the submissions made the creation of a consolidated text very difficult, but in the end, a draft statute was created that formed the basis for the final negotiations that were to take place in Rome. The text comprised 173 pages, included 116 articles and 1400 words in brackets, i.e. points of disagreement between states.

The *United Nations Diplomatic Conference of Plenipotentiaries on the Establishment of an International Criminal Court* (Rome Conference) took place in Rome from 15 June to 17 July 1998. Nearly 160 states met to negotiate a 'Final Act' for the proposed ICC. The negotiations were very complex and by the end of the Conference, some of the key issues were still not resolved to everyone's satisfaction. However, a 'package deal' was put to the vote on 17 July 1998 with 120 states voting in favour, seven against and twenty-one abstaining.[2] The ICC eventually came into being on 1 July 2002, six months after the sixtieth state ratified the Court's Statute into their national laws.[3]

Main issues arising from the negotiations

The main issues of debate related to states' concerns about the ICC's effect on state sovereignty as one of the fundamental principles of international order. In general, states were very supportive of the Court in terms of its potential to enforce the most fundamental human rights but argued that this needed to be done with respect for other provisions of the existing international order. The Republic of Korea, for instance, argued that the establishment of the Court 'should not conflict with but reinforce the judicial sovereignty of States' (Rome Proceedings 1998: 69). Kazakhstan similarly asserted that 'maximum account must be taken of universal human rights and also of the sovereignty and independence of each State' (Rome Proceedings 1998: 72). The tension between fundamental principles of sovereignty and non-intervention on the one hand and considerations for enforcing individual justice values already established in that order on the other, were evident during the whole negotiation processes.

Numerous compromises integrated into the Statute demonstrate that the ICC aims to combine both values, which could be achieved (among other things) through changes in states' understanding of the principle of sovereignty. Some states pointed out that the principle of state sovereignty had transformed over the years to incorporate new norms and that its value therefore needed to be considered in this changed light. Germany, for instance, argued that 'in an interdependent, globalized world, states must accept the Court's jurisdiction over core crimes; sovereignty would be better served by cooperation than by futile attempts to stand alone' (Rome Proceedings 1998: 83). Croatia also argued that conditions for 'just and equal treatment of all individuals and states' needed to be met and 'to a certain extent that meant abandoning the traditional concept of sovereignty of states (…)' (Rome Proceedings 1998: 94).

One of the key objectives at the Rome Conference was to reconcile states' concerns to preserve sovereignty with the aim of creating a functioning institution that would enforce existing justice norms effectively. This was achieved in the Statute, which 'proposed (at least) three important ways in which State sovereignty was buttressed within the regime established: complementarity, content and consent' (Simpson 2004: 55).

The principle of complementarity

The principle of complementarity reflects the jurisdictional relationship between the ICC and national courts. The Court complements national jurisdiction and can only act if the state in question is genuinely unable or unwilling to investigate or prosecute itself. This places the primary responsibility for investigation and prosecution on national authorities. The principle of complementarity aims to strengthen rather than replace national courts in matters of enforcing international laws by reinforcing states' existing obligations. Yet, it also fills a gap when states either cannot or will not act to ensure the global enforcement of human rights. The principle thereby preserves state sovereignty in two respects: states can be sure of non-interference in their internal affairs if they act in accordance with their obligations, and they also continue to have the primary responsibility towards their own people to enforce existing international legal obligations themselves.

The *Ad Hoc* Committee's report had already emphasized the significance of the complementary nature of the Court, stressing the importance of retaining existing judicial procedures and of not unduly interfering in states' national matters. It was argued that states needed to remain primarily responsible and accountable for prosecuting violations of their laws and that this would serve 'the interest of the international community, inasmuch as national systems would be expected to maintain and enforce adherence to international standards of behaviour within their own jurisdiction' (*Ad Hoc* Committee 1995: 6). The aim was to restrict the Court's ability to intervene in internal affairs and to infringe the sovereign right of states to exercise jurisdiction nationally. At the same time, the report demonstrated that states recognized that sovereignty not only involves rights but also obligations – most importantly the responsibility to protect the most fundamental human rights – and that it was necessary to create an institution that would ensure states adhered to those obligations.

Complementarity with national courts means that the ICC functions as an *indirect* enforcement mechanism, because the 'very knowledge that the ICC may act (…) is intended to prod governments into the more energetic primary enforcement of human rights' (Mayerfeld 2003: 96). This underlines the ICC's nature as a Court of 'last resort'; a safety net designed to act in case the commission of core crimes is ignored by the state that has the primary responsibility to act. Strengthening national compliance in this way is important in order to create a permanent enforcement mechanism for international norms with the long term effect of internalizing those norms into the international order in line with the norm life cycle. It leads to a process of socialization between states by creating an environment in which states are expected to observe norms or face the possibility of sanctions if they fail to comply. The ICC thereby does not relieve states of their treaty obligations and responsibilities but on the contrary requires them to act in accordance with them. The ICC's indirect effect is significant and

> provoking states to incorporate and apply the Statute's principles in their national courts might even be greater than direct applications of its jurisdiction against indicted persons in The Hague. Ideally, the ICC will be redundant, as war criminals are genuinely prosecuted in national courts in all countries of the world (Popovski 2000: 405–406).

Giving the ICC complementarity with rather than primacy over national courts[4] was seen to be necessary to preserve the most fundamental principles of non-intervention and states' sovereign right to exercise jurisdiction on their own territory. In terms of the underlying order and justice debate, complementarity includes both pluralist as well as solidarist elements: state sovereignty is protected by giving national courts primary responsibility to exercise jurisdiction, international judicial intervention through the ICC can only occur under very specific circumstances. This constitutes a compromise whereby universally agreed upon international norms of justice can still be protected if the state in question fails to do so. Sovereignty is seen as the primary concern (pluralist element), but it does not have primacy over justice principles. If states are not able or willing to enforce these principles themselves, the ICC can intervene (solidarist element). To give the ICC primacy over national courts would have incorporated a stronger solidarist element, but it is unlikely that states would have agreed to such a considerable and permanent compromise of their sovereignty.

The aspect of complementarity that raised most controversy was the question of how to determine the trigger which would give the ICC the right to exercise jurisdiction. Article 17(1) negotiated in Rome sets out that the Court can only act if the state in question is 'unwilling or unable genuinely to carry out the investigation or prosecution'. The Statute also includes provisions as to how the Court should determine a state's 'unwillingness' or 'inability' to investigate cases. It was generally agreed that it was necessary to include the notion of 'unwillingness' in this Article to avoid 'show trials' and to ensure that crimes were prosecuted properly. However, this provision was at the same time seen as problematic on the grounds that it would open up the possibility of using the ICC as a form of 'appeals court' that passes judgment on national proceedings. China, for instance, was critical that criteria for determining what constituted a 'fair' trial were very subjective and ambiguous. It criticized that 'the Statute authorized the Court to judge the judicial system and legal proceedings of a State and negate the decision of the national court' (Lee 1999: 585).

The term 'genuinely' includes a good faith element that can create ambiguities and therefore lead to inconsistent application. Good faith assumes that the investigation or prosecution is carried out honestly and complies with standards of decency, which is a very subjective assessment of a situation. The Statute's failure to provide unambiguous standards to judge its own terms is arguably a weakness of the complementarity principle. Even though it is necessary to establishing criteria in international law they are always prone to be either over- or under-inclusive. This can lead to difficulties in their consistent and universal application, because their exact meaning is always dependent on individual interpretation (Koskenniemi 2002: 167).

Content – the ICC's subject-matter jurisdiction

The second compromise that had to be reached in ICC provisions in order to reconcile sovereignty with universal enforcement of justice norms was related to the subject-matter jurisdiction – or content – of the Statute. The *Ad Hoc* Committee agreed that the Court's jurisdiction should be limited to

> the most serious crimes of concern to the international community as a whole (…) to promote broad acceptance of the court by States and thereby enhance its effectiveness; to enhance the credibility and moral authority of the court; to avoid overloading the court with cases that could be dealt with adequately by national courts; and to limit the financial burden imposed on the international community (*Ad Hoc* Committee 1995: 11).

Agreement was eventually reached in Rome that the ICC should have jurisdiction over three clearly defined core crimes: genocide, war crimes and crimes against humanity (Articles 6–8). A fourth crime, the crime of aggression, was added to the Statute subject to further negotiations regarding its precise definition.[5] The aim of limiting the Court's subject-matter jurisdiction in this way was to include only crimes 'whose criminality was thought to be beyond dispute' (Simpson 2004: 56). These crimes were seen to be reflective of customary international law and of universal concern, established in Conventions and other legal instruments. States did not want to create new legal provisions for international crimes, but much rather strengthen the enforcement of already existing international laws and norms. These norms have already cascaded through the first two stages of the norm life cycle – they are universally recognized norms incorporated into international law.

A number of states were dissatisfied with the limited nature of the Court's jurisdiction and there was also disagreement over what the 'most serious' crimes of concern for humanity were. Trinidad and Tobago, for instance, proposed to include drug trafficking as a crime in the Statute, because they regarded it as one of the 'most serious crimes of international concern' (Rome Proceedings 1998: 66). The majority of states, however, saw too many practical difficulties attached to investigating and prosecuting crimes such as drug trafficking in an international court as to do so would require extensive fieldwork and access to classified information. It was argued that the inclusion of such crimes would lay the Court open to abuse by national courts using it to avoid expensive trials by shifting responsibility to the international level (McGoldrick 2004: 41). This could result in the Court being overburdened and unable to work effectively. The majority of states therefore agreed that limiting the subject-matter jurisdiction of the Court was necessary in order to be able to arrive at a consensus in the 'Final Act'. This compromise also protects the principle of sovereignty because limiting the ICC's jurisdiction means that a vast array of international crimes remains solely within the national jurisdiction of states.[6]

Agreement on the definition of core crimes reflected developments in international law which suggests progress of these norms in line with the norm life cycle. Based on precedents set by the ICTY, the crimes in the Statute included internal as well as international armed conflicts. The definition of 'crimes against humanity' furthermore includes the notion that these crimes do not necessarily need to be linked to armed conflicts at all. With regard to the definition of genocide, the International Law Commission (ILC) 'did not articulate a definition for the crime, but observed in its commentary that this crime is 'clearly and authoritatively defined' in the 1948 Convention on the Prevention and Punishment of the Crime of Genocide' (Hebel and Robinson 1999: 89).

One concrete example that illustrates considerable progress in line with the norm life cycle and builds on precedents discussed in the context of the present analysis is the Statute's provision that states cannot claim immunity for their state officials. The extent of norm acceptance is evident from the fact that the issue was not contested during the negotiation process 'and there were no problems reaching agreement on an acceptable text' (Schabas 2001: 92). It demonstrates that developments have already contributed to the institutionalization of certain norms in line with the norm life cycle and that these have been further internalized in the ICC Statute. Article 27 sets out that the Statute shall 'apply equally to all persons without any distinction based on official capacity' and that states cannot claim immunity for their state officials. The question of whether the official position of alleged perpetrators of core crimes could be used as a valid defence had been a key issue in Nuremberg and later during the Pinochet and Yerodia cases. The latter two cases held that state officials enjoyed immunity *ratione personae* for all acts as long as they were in office and continued to be immune for official acts after that. In the Pinochet case it was further decided that serious international crimes could not be regarded as 'official' acts and that immunity was therefore not available in any such cases. The ICC provision to rule out *any* availability for state immunity with regard to the specific crimes (irrespective of whether they were committed as part of official functions) builds on these two decisions. It also follows the precedent set in the ICTY Statute that equally excludes the availability of immunity for the crimes included in the Statute.

States agreed without opposition on the necessity to exclude immunity from the Statute, even though it meant that a large number of states had to amend their national constitutions in order to make their own laws compatible with the ICC Statute. South Africa, for example, had to modify its own laws in order to ratify the Statute, which 'is a significant aspect of the ICC Act and one which is to be welcomed insofar as it signals South Africa's intention of acting hand-in-hand with the International Criminal Court to bring government officials, whatever their standing, to justice' (Du Plessis 2003: 11). This demonstrates not only that the ICC Statute incorporates developments that have taken place over a long period of time by providing further clarifications and new laws, but also that it has instigated additional changes at the national level to conform with them. The fact that states did not contest the inclusion of this provision in the Statute, even if that meant amending their national, sovereign laws, confirms that progress has occurred in the norm life cycle. The cycle has advanced with regard to state immunity far enough for this norm to be accepted in a way that institutionalizing it into international law was not seen as a major shift in the international order, but much rather only a formality.

Consent – the treaty-based approach and the ICC's automatic jurisdiction

Another issue related to states' concerns about sovereignty was the question of whether states needed to consent to the ICC's powers of jurisdiction or whether such consent could be seen as implied in the Statute. The majority of states in the *Ad Hoc* Committee agreed that the best method of establishing the Court would be to take a treaty-based approach, because 'such an approach based on the express consent of States was considered consistent with the principle of State sovereignty and with the goal of ensuring legal authority of the court' (*Ad Hoc* Committee 1995). By arguing for a treaty-based approach, states wanted to ensure that the Court was not imposed as an external force on states and that it would not be perceived as dramatically eroding state sovereignty (Durham 2000: 184). This approach ensured that the Court was based on the principle of reciprocity, which means that 'any state that joins the Court, and thereby shapes its direction through the selection of judges and prosecutors, understands that it makes its own citizens and leaders vulnerable to the Court's prosecution' (Mayerfeld 2003: 124). However, the treaty-based approach also meant that any state could refuse to ratify the Statute and thereby evade membership. This weakens the impact of the Court because the international prosecution of war crimes is still dependent on states willingness to co-operate with the ICC by signing up to it and assisting in its workings by surrendering indicted persons or retrieving documentary evidence (Tomuschat 2003: 283).

A treaty-based approach was nevertheless seen as necessary to avoid the criticisms which had been made of the Security Council's decisions to create *ad hoc* courts for particular conflicts and to impose these courts on states without their consent. Such an approach has often been criticized for being selective and 'in a sense, the International Criminal Court was meant to transcend the political. Correspondingly, its trials would resist the appellation, 'political trials'. These trials would be international, impartial, non-selective' (Simpson 2004: 51).

Another key question debated by states was whether the Court should be given inherent jurisdiction over the crimes included in the Statute. 'Inherent' jurisdiction means that states do not have to issue separate declarations that they accept the jurisdiction of the ICC over certain crimes. By ratifying the Statute all states automatically concede to the ICC's jurisdiction over the crimes set out in that Statute.[7] During the PrepCom meetings, states expressed their support for including inherent jurisdiction for the three core crimes in the Statute with respect to states parties, i.e. states that ratified the Statute. This was 'fully compatible with respect for State sovereignty, since States would have expressed their consent at the time of ratification of the Statute as opposed to having to express it in respect of every single crime listed in the Statute at different stages' (Preparatory Committee 1996: at 117).

During the Rome proceedings individual states expressed very different views on the Court's powers to exercise jurisdiction. Some argued in favour of universal jurisdiction covering all states, others were in favour of letting states opt in and out of the ICC's provisions. Kazakhstan, for instance, argued that 'each state should be able to decide on the degree to which it should participate in the Court' (Rome Proceedings 1998: 86). A number of states made different proposals to find ways of solving this issue. Germany made the most far-reaching suggestion by arguing that as the crimes in the Statute already carried universal jurisdiction under international law, states already had an obligation to act with regard to them. It argued that the Court should therefore have automatic jurisdiction over the crimes in the Statute, a position which would give the ICC the power to prosecute the core crimes regardless of the nationality of the accused, even when the accused was a national of a state that was not party to the ICC. A further, slightly more restricted compromise proposal came from South Korea which suggested that the ICC should have automatic jurisdiction over states parties, but non-states parties, i.e. states that had not ratified the Statute, would have to consent to make investigations involving their nationals possible.

In the end a compromise similar to the Korean proposal was agreed in Article 12 giving the ICC jurisdiction over crimes committed on a state party's territory or by one of its nationals. The ICC has automatic jurisdiction for state parties over crimes against humanity and genocide,[8] but with regard to non-state parties, consent from either the territorial state or the state of nationality of the accused is required. This means that if a national of a non-state party were accused of committing a crime covered by the Statute while on the territory of a member state, and if this member state consented to the ICC taking action, the accused could be subjected to the ICC's jurisdiction without a need for the non-state party to give its consent.

Article 12 has been a major bone of contention for a number of states and has been cited by the US as one of the main reasons for its opposition to the ICC. The US has argued that the Court's powers are too wide and that it should not be able to exercise jurisdiction over non-state party nationals without the state's consent.[9] The US voted against the Statute on the final day of the Conference because it 'did not accept the concept of universal jurisdiction as reflected in the Statute of the International Criminal Court, or the application of the treaty to non-parties, their nationals or officials, or to acts committed in their territory' (Rome Proceedings 1998: 123). China similarly explained that it felt 'obliged' to vote against the Statute, because it 'granted universal jurisdiction to the Court over three core crimes. (...) That imposed an obligation upon non-parties and constituted interference in the judicial independence or sovereignty of States (...)' (Rome Proceedings 1998: 123–124). However, Article 12 does not set out new obligations for states that are not party to the Statute, but only provides for jurisdiction over their nationals. These obligations are not 'new' because the crimes included in the ICC are already established as crimes carrying universal jurisdiction provisions in international law, giving every state the right (and also the duty) to act in order to protect them. These norms have developed in line with the norm life cycle; they have become increasingly accepted by states in the international society and institutionalized in international law. The enforcement powers given to the ICC built upon these developments.

These discussions surrounding the Court's jurisdiction demonstrate the reluctance of states to give a supranational body the ability to exercise jurisdiction on their own territory, in effect giving it the right to interfere in their sovereignty with regard to the three core crimes. Germany was (legally) right in arguing that all crimes contained in the Statute already carry universal jurisdiction provisions, and that the ICC in fact therefore only enforces norms that are already agreed and established in the international order. However, as outlined in previous chapters, states are often reluctant to agree to the exercise of universal jurisdiction. In the case of the ICC, states were concerned that by giving the Court inherent jurisdiction, they would lose an element of control over their own sovereign right to exercise national jurisdiction. However, without this inherent jurisdiction, the ICC would essentially be meaningless. Giving states the opportunity to opt in and out of the Court's provisions with regard to their own nationals increases the Court's selectivity in its application and introduces double standards. It would be possible for states to shield their own nationals from jurisdiction but still impose the Court's standards on other states and their nationals.

The ICC aims to be a universal enforcement mechanism for crimes that already carry universal jurisdiction provisions. If states could exclude their own nationals by opting out of the Court's jurisdiction, there would be no reason to agree on crimes in the Court's subject-matter jurisdiction in the first place. It would increase the political element in the ICC as a legal institution because decisions on whether or not to agree to parts of its jurisdiction would be based on political and subjective criteria. To overcome at least some of these concerns, states made considerable efforts to define the crimes in the Statute in minute detail so that compromises to state sovereignty were kept to a 'predictable' minimum. Once agreement had been found regarding the exact definition of the crimes, the ICC was given powers to exercise jurisdiction with regard to these crimes on an almost universal basis.

A large number of states wanted to include provisions in the Statute to the effect that the consent of an alleged criminal's state would not be necessary in order to prevent suspected criminals from continuing to have immunity from jurisdiction. The majority of the states saw a need to 'close a gap' that, if left, would allow alleged perpetrators of the most serious crimes to escape prosecution. This gap would remain open if only states that ratified the Statute were exposed to the ICC's jurisdiction. Article 12 of the Statute aimed to address some of these issues by allowing for the possibility of jurisdiction based on the territoriality principle without the consent of the state to which the alleged perpetrator belonged. Some loopholes continue to exist, because the ICC cannot exercise jurisdiction in cases in which no state parties are involved in the alleged offence, as is for instance the case in internal conflicts. This is a pluralist element of the ICC that restricts the exercise of universal jurisdiction in that – when no state party is involved – states still have the sovereign right to decide whether or not to agree to the ICC taking action. This means that order principles of sovereignty and non-intervention can take precedence over universal justice norms. The ICC therefore does not administer universal jurisdiction, but continues to be based on state consent. Once a state accepts the Statute provisions, however, it is bound by them and the Court's solidarist element takes over whereby justice norms can be given priority over order principles because no further consent is necessary for the ICC to act.

The relationship to the UN and the role of the Security Council

During the Rome Conference, states disagreed over what role the Security Council should play and whether it should be given powers to instigate and/or to halt ongoing investigations by the ICC. It was argued that giving the Security Council powers to refer a situation to the prosecutor when acting under Chapter VII of the UN Charter would have the advantage of making the establishment of any further *ad hoc* tribunals unnecessary. The Security Council could thereby still intervene judicially in a situation it deemed a threat to international peace and security, but would be able to make use of the ICC as a standing court. However, some delegations were opposed to giving the Security Council any powers to initiate proceedings, arguing that 'this would subject the functioning of the Court to the decisions of a political body and therefore undermine the Court's independence and credibility' (Yee 1999: 146–147). This argument was based on concerns that the Security Council would be unlikely to ever use this trigger against its permanent members and their allies.

Not surprisingly, the permanent members of the Security Council strongly argued in favour of such powers, claiming that the Security Council's position of having primary responsibility for maintaining international peace and security in the international community had been firmly established in the international order. China argued that the ICC 'should not compromise the principal role of the United Nations, and in particular of the Security Council, in safeguarding world peace and security' (Rome Proceedings 1998: 75). The US similarly argued that it was not prepared to agree to considerable changes to the existing international order by reducing the Security Council's powers and that the ICC needed to fit into existing provisions.

It was clear that although states wanted the ICC to be independent from the UN as a political body, the Security Council's powers under Chapter VII could not be ignored and needed to be incorporated into the Statute's provisions. Sidelining the Security Council would have meant a major change of the existing international order, a step most states were not prepared to take. It was therefore decided to negotiate a compromise that would allow the ICC to exist alongside the Security Council.[10] Article 13(b) reflects the agreement that was eventually reached in Rome whereby the Security Council was given the power to instigate investigations, but is not the only body that can do so; states parties and the international prosecutor can refer cases to the Court too.

The main issue of controversy regarding the role of the Security Council, however, was the question of whether the Security Council should be given the power to halt proceedings taking place before the ICC. In the initial draft of the ILC it was proposed that the ICC should not be able to act in situations already dealt with by the Security Council unless the Council decided otherwise. A large number of states were concerned about the judicial independence of the Court and that 'the Court could, in effect, be deprived of jurisdiction by the mere placement of a situation on the agenda of the Security Council, where it could remain under consideration for a potentially indefinite period of time' (Yee 1999: 150).

During the Rome Conference, the so-called 'Singapore compromise'[11] became increasingly popular, which in effect reversed the provision of the ILC draft. The ILC Draft Statute had envisaged that an investigation into a situation which the Security Council had identified as falling under Chapter VII would not be able to commence unless the Security Council specifically stated otherwise. This would mean that any one of the permanent members would be able to unilaterally veto any proposal instructing the ICC to act in a particular situation and thereby block investigations, as a vote in the Security Council to allow the investigation would have to be passed unanimously. The 'Singapore compromise' on the other hand proposed that the Court should be able to proceed with its actions unless the Security Council took a formal decision to halt the process. This meant that the

Council had to adopt a positive declaration to stop proceedings. Such a declaration would require a minimum of nine affirmative votes and would thus prevent the possibility of unilateral veto by any one of the Security Council's permanent members. This compromise was essentially included in Article 16 of the Statute with the additional provision that the Security Council could only defer (but not terminate) an investigation or prosecution for a period of twelve months (with the possibility of renewal).

Article 16 represents a significant innovation integrated into the Statute because it means that no one state (including the five permanent members of the Security Council) has more power than any of the others or the authority to act unilaterally to control ICC proceedings. The role of the Security Council in maintaining international peace and security is still integrated in the Statute, but the Council is awarded only limited powers. The Statute only gives the Security Council the power to defer (but not to terminate) ICC proceedings. This compromise makes it more feasible for the ICC to function independently from the UN as a political body than under the initial proposal which would have included the possibility of unilateral veto. This removal of direct Security Council control over the Court is an 'innovative aspect' (Edgar 2002: 141) of the Statute. The compromise was necessary because of the different natures of the two institutions: the UN is a state-centred institution, primarily concerned with protecting the inviolability of state sovereignty, whereas the ICC, in contrast, aims to enforce justice for individuals universally, independent from different states' national interests. Even though the permanent members of the Security Council continue to have a special role in international relations, Article 16 ensures that the ICC cannot be dominated by one state acting unilaterally by exercising its power of veto in the Security Council and that all states are treated as equals. [12]

The role of the prosecutor

By far the most extensive and surprising innovation in the Statute was made by giving the ICC's prosecutor independent powers to refer a situation to the Court and thereby instigate investigations independently from states parties and the Security Council. This was very controversial during the negotiations and still remains so because states fear that the prosecutor could abuse his/her powers and launch politicized investigations – thereby undermining the Court's impartiality and independence.

Proponents of a strong prosecutor argued that it would enhance the Court's credibility as a whole, because the prosecutor would 'be able to function on behalf of the international community rather than on behalf of a particular complainant State or the Security Council' (Gurmendi 1999: 178). They also pointed out that the ICTY's prosecutor already had such powers and that there was therefore no reason to deny the ICC's prosecutor the same rights. Some states emphasized the need for victims (as individuals) to be given the possibility of submitting their case to the ICC without having to rely on state parties or a Security Council referral. Giving the prosecutor such far-reaching independent powers is a fundamental aspect of the ICC's aim to achieve greater respect for individual justice, independent from states and their national interests.

States that opposed giving the prosecutor such extensive powers, on the other hand, 'feared an overzealous or politically motivated prosecutor targeting, unfairly or in bad faith, highly sensitive political situations' (Gurmendi 1999: 181). The US argued that giving the prosecutor independent powers 'would be unwise' and further that it 'would overload the Court, causing confusion and controversy, and weaken rather than strengthen it' (Rome Proceedings 1998: 95). Turkey also argued that this 'risked submerging [the Prosecutor] with information concerning charges of a political, rather than a juridical nature' (Rome Proceedings 1998: 124).

It was generally agreed by states that appropriate safeguards and checks and balances needed to be incorporated into the Statute in order to prevent such arbitrary actions. These were included in Article 15[13] of the Statute.

> This decision of far-reaching consequences, both from the legal and political perspective, surprised many of the participants of the Conference. Even some of the firm proponents for an independent Prosecutor had doubted that States would be willing to share their power to control the initiation of investigations and prosecutions with an independent individual (Gurmendi 1999: 176).

The disagreement surrounding the role of the prosecutor highlights the reluctance of states to subject themselves to the control of an individual rather than a state. In the context of a society comprised of states and an international order that incorporates state sovereignty as one of its fundamental principles, it is indeed surprising that states agreed to give an individual person powers to instigate investigations or prosecutions concerning states. This can be seen as a strong solidarist expression of the aspiration to build an independent institution primarily dominated by considerations of established norms of individual justice rather than order principles between states. Giving the prosecutor independent powers means that he/she has the ability to act to protect individual justice, regardless of states' national interests.[14]

Ultimately, this decision also gives individual citizens the chance to utilize the ICC even when the state in question (or any other state) or the Security Council would not be willing to act on their behalf. States attempted to build enough safeguards into the Statute so that the prosecutor cannot abuse these powers, but it remains to be seen whether this will lead to politicized investigations. This is an unprecedented and important compromise of sovereignty states agreed to when signing the Rome Statute, which has opened up 'international justice to a society beyond that dominated by powerful states' (Ralph 2003: 206).

US opposition to the ICC

Even though the ICC enjoys broad support from a large number of states, the US has so far refused to join the Court. This opposition is problematic because the ICC ultimately depends on state co-operation and would benefit from great power support. The US took a number of actions to undermine the Court which can be seen as a pluralist response that emphasizes state sovereignty to the predominantly solidarist achievements incorporated into the Statute. The US opposition demonstrates resistance to changes in the international order and also to developments in the norm life cycle's third stage of norm internalization.

Historically, the US has been a strong supporter of international criminal courts, it supported the Nuremberg trials and the UN *ad hoc* courts. The US was also in favour of the idea of a permanent international court demonstrated by its active engagement in the Rome Conference and various other related meetings. It always maintained, however, that it was important for the right protection measures to be built into the Statute and was not satisfied with the compromises reached in Rome.

The US stance towards the ICC shifted with different governments. The Clinton administration was generally more supportive of international law and multilateralism than its successor and engaged cautiously, but nevertheless constructively, in negotiations regarding the ICC. The administration was restrained in its overall support for these treaties particularly because of concerns over the potential effect on the US and its national interests. Domestic constituencies on the federal and state level, and a strong Republican Senate, posed further constraints on the US's multilateral engagements. The Bush administration that took over in 2001 was hostile to multilateralism from the start and set out a foreign policy agenda that places primary importance on national interests and US security, best achieved through unilateral action. The previous constructive engagement with the ICC gave way to active opposition aimed at undermining the Court.

Signing the treaty

Despite its opposition to the ICC Statute as it emerged from the Rome conference, the US delegation continued to engage in the Preparatory Commission meetings that followed the Conference, which aimed at negotiating further details of the Statute, such as 'Elements of Crimes' and the 'Rules of Procedure and Evidence'. David Scheffer, head of the US delegation, believed that enough progress had been made in the negotiations after Rome to reconsider the US position on whether or not to sign the Statute. He was convinced that the US delegation had achieved

> the most that pragmatically could be achieved in light of all that we confronted, both internally and externally: a sophisticated matrix of safeguards that provided a high degree of protection for U.S. interests and (…) additional safeguards that would achieve the best possible relationship for the United States with the ICC (Scheffer 2002: 63).

He argued that some compromises were necessary to achieve a greater good of enforcing universal norms globally and he also believed that the US could gain from membership of the Court.

On 31 December 2000, the last possible day for signatures, President Clinton eventually decided to sign the Statute and expressed the US's 'strong support for international accountability and for bringing to justice perpetrators of genocide, war crimes, and crimes against humanity' (Clinton 2000). He argued that the US signed the treaty in order to 'remain engaged in making the ICC an instrument of impartial and effective justice in the years to come' and to sustain the tradition of US 'moral leadership' in its commitment to individual accountability. The President also made clear that the US was still not satisfied with the Rome Statute in its present form and that 'in signing, however, we are not abandoning our concerns about significant flaws[15] in the Treaty'. He would therefore 'not recommend my successor submit the Treaty to the Senate for advice and consent until our fundamental concerns are satisfied.' He concluded on a positive note that the ICC could make a 'profound contribution in deterring egregious human rights abuses worldwide' (Clinton 2000) and that by signing, the US wanted to continue to engage in discussion with other governments in order to advance these goals.

'Un-signing' the treaty

The Bush administration did not take a favourable approach to the ICC from the start and did not engage constructively in further Preparatory Commission meetings once it took over from its predecessors in 2001. Scheffer criticized the 'short-sighted and anaemic approach' (Scheffer 2002: 63) of the Bush administration and believed that it resulted in forfeiting opportunities his delegation had initiated in preceding meetings.

On 6 May 2002, President Bush decided to formally withdraw from the Rome treaty and to effectively 'un-sign' it.[16] Under-Secretary for Political Affairs Marc Grossman emphasized the US's resolve not to co-operate with the ICC on the grounds that 'states, not international institutions are primarily responsible for ensuring justice in the international system' (Grossman 2002). This action under-lines the US's state-centred view that realising justice is part of individual states' sovereignty and not the task of an international institution with the right to interfere in internal affairs.

The move to 'un-sign' the treaty was in line with a general shift of the Bush administration away from multilateralism, during which it similarly 'un-signed' the Kyoto Protocol and outlined its unilateral approach towards national security. The National Security Strategy of the Bush administration sets out a clear agenda of possible unilateral and also pre-emptive action and adapts interpretations of international law to justify such conduct.[17] The Strategy aims to create an international order supportive of US security, prosperity and principles and holds back support for international laws that are not in line with these aims or at least tries to ensure that they are not applicable to the US.

Un-signing the treaty was condemned by a number of different groups. A group of Members of Congress sent a letter to President Bush in which they criticized the action because it 'has damaged the moral credibility of the United States and serves as a U.S. repudiation of the notion that war criminals and perpetrators of genocide should be brought to justice' (Letter to President George W. Bush 22 May 2002). They argued that the US had the same values as those intended by the ICC and that rejecting the institution 'now places the United States in the company of notorious human rights abusers like Iraq, North Korea, China, Cuba, Libya, and Burma.' The EU also formally issued a declaration on behalf of its member states criticising the US position and stating its 'disappointment and regret'. It argued that it respected the sovereign right of the US not to sign the treaty, but also believed that 'this unilateral action may have undesirable consequences on multilateral Treaty-making and generally on the rule of law in international relations' (Declaration by the EU 13 May 2002).

US opposition to the ICC focuses on two main areas: firstly the Court's jurisdiction as set out in Article 12, and secondly criticisms about the role afforded to the US in the ICC's provisions. The US was dissatisfied that the ICC did not recognize the 'special' role the US played as major superpower in international relations which was demonstrated by the fact that the US could not constrain the ICC through its power of veto in the Security Council. The US position therefore constituted a pluralist response aimed at strengthening order principles of sovereignty and non-intervention at the expense of establishing universal enforcement of justice norms.

Article 12 and the ICC's jurisdiction

The US opposes Article 12 of the Statute which gives the ICC jurisdiction over alleged criminals if the offence is committed on a state party's territory or if the accused is a national of an ICC member state. This means that – at least in theory – the ICC could exercise jurisdiction over US nationals if they were accused of committing an ICC crime on a state party's territory, without the need for US consent.[18] The US claims that Article 12 provisions mean that the ICC is effectively exercising universal jurisdiction which the US does not see as customary international law. Article 12, however, does not give the ICC universal jurisdiction, it sets out the preconditions under which the ICC can act. The Court's jurisdiction is based on the principles of nationality and territoriality which are well established in customary international law. Complete universal jurisdiction would mean that the ICC could act regardless of whether any of the states involved are party to the Statute or not.

The fact that the ICC can exercise jurisdiction over third parties without the need for additional express consent is part of the Court's fundamental set-up. It empowers the Court to investigate and prosecute individuals for the most serious crimes that are already established in international law, independent from states. The US agreed to such provisions in different treaties, such as the Torture Convention, which allows (and even requires) prosecution or extradition of alleged criminals regardless of their nationality. The ICC is based on the precedents set by such Conventions and also the *ad hoc* courts established by the UN Security Council. These courts similarly do not require express state consent and given that they enjoy US support, it is evident 'that there is no objection in principle to the idea of international courts' (Sands 2005: 51), but that the objection is only related to an international court exercising criminal jurisdiction over Americans.

The crimes in the ICC's Statute are already established as such in treaties and Conventions and carry universal jurisdiction provisions which means that they are not new crimes, but are recognized as being of universal concern to all states in international society. States do not only have the right, but also the obligation to act in cases when such core crimes are committed – regardless of where and by whom. The Rome Statute therefore does not create new laws but a new collective enforcement mechanism for already accepted universal norms. The ICC's primary focus is not on states but on universal justice norms and their enforcement. This is the point where the ICC adds to existing provisions and where it aims to fill a gap: it constitutes a global enforcement mechanism for universal values aimed to be largely independent from states. This means that 'the failure of the US to become a party to the ICC does not exempt its citizens from the universality already established' (Weller 2002: 700). The essence of the doctrine of universality lies in the fact that it can be applied by any state over any national of any other states without the requirement of having to obtain additional express consent from the latter. The Rome Statute creates a new collective enforcement mechanism which builds on normative developments in the norm life cycle with the aim of closing the enforcement gap in existing international law with regard to human rights norms.

The US claims that Article 12 contravenes international law as it poses new obligations on states that have not signed the Statute. This is not the case, because Article 12 only has implications for nationals of these states and it also only covers crimes that are already established in international law. Even without the ICC, if an individual committed an offence in another state's territory, they would be subject to that state's jurisdiction which could choose to extradite or prosecute. It could even be argued that the ICC can afford better protection than some states' national judicial systems because it leaves the primary jurisdiction with national states, operates with international standards, is treaty-bound and involves due process protections (Leigh 2001: 127).

During the Rome Conference it became clear that most states wanted to include provisions in the Statute that meant that consent of an alleged criminal's state was not necessary in order to close a gap for alleged perpetrators of the most serious crimes (which would have been left if only states that ratified the Statute were exposed to the ICC's jurisdiction). Article 12 aims to close this gap, but some loopholes continue to exist, because the ICC cannot exercise jurisdiction in cases in which no state parties are involved in the offence, as for instance is the case in internal conflicts. This is an element of the ICC that restricts the exercise of universal jurisdiction because states still have the sovereign right to decide whether or not to agree to the ICC. The ICC thereby does not administer universal jurisdiction, but is based on state consent and continues to emphasize the principles of non-intervention and state sovereignty.

Article 12 was seen as necessary by the majority of states during the Rome negotiations to ensure that universal human rights and justice concerns are protected consistently even if that means compromising a particular state's sovereign right to decide whether or not to exercise jurisdiction or to consent to ICC action.

Changing Article 12 to accommodate US concerns would have meant restricting the ICC's jurisdiction even further, thereby leaving more alleged criminals out of possible prosecutions. Numerous safeguards exist in the Statute that make politicized investigations against any state (not just the US) highly unlikely which suggests that US fears are exaggerated. The principle of complementarity, for instance, means that the US can investigate alleged crimes itself in order to avoid ICC interference.

Great power responsibility and the Security Council veto

The US claims that it supports the overall aims of the ICC, but is concerned that the ICC could threaten the independence and flexibility of US military forces. Some argue that the US should be given special protection, because it 'shoulders responsibilities worldwide that no other nation comes even close to undertaking' (Scheffer 2002: 70) and that it cannot support a Court that fails to recognize these unique global responsibilities (see for instance Lietzau 2001: 138; Wedgwood 1999). Others, however, point out that even though the US has unique responsibilities as a great power, 'when it claims to act for the common good of international society (…) it also has a democratic duty to be accountable to international society for the way it fulfils those responsibilities' (Ralph 2003: 208). The US is accountable for its actions to the international community in whose name it claims to act, but this does not mean that the US can impose double standards, exempting its personnel from acting in accordance with universal justice norms others have to adhere to.

The US, as the only remaining great power, might face special responsibilities and greater risks because its personnel are engaged in a large number of states, but it is not acting in a vacuum. It is not solely responsible for deciding when a 'crisis' situation arises that warrants external intervention in the pursuit of global justice. Such use of 'crisis' language to justify interventions can lead to distortions of international law if states claim to act in the interest of universal values that are in fact only based on their own interests. Individual states' interpretations of existing criteria of what constitutes a 'crisis' can lead to inconsistent application of international law. Decisions on whether or not to intervene are based on political considerations and some argue that the US determines 'humanitarian necessity' for armed interventions 'haphazardly (ignoring genocide in Rwanda but not in Serbia) and without clear or objective criteria other than a precondition that it should serve (or at least do no disservice to) US national interests' (Robertson 2002: 530). The Statute of the ICC and its meticulously defined subject-matter jurisdiction aims to provide such 'clear and objective' criteria which can be used to justify external intervention in another state's affairs. Human rights are always going to be vague and subject to interpretation, but some form of codification is necessary to establish at least some criteria to reduce the political element in international law enforcement.

International law provides minimum standards of acceptable behaviour based on universal norms and it provides an independent measure for judging the legitimacy of international action by *all* states – regardless of their size and power. Granting a permanent exemption to its jurisdiction would undermine the ICC's authority, because a court that focuses primarily on universal enforcement of human rights (rather than power relations between states and national interests) cannot justify an exemption without becoming essentially meaningless. Such an exemption would sacrifice the Court's underlying premise of non-discriminatory and non-selective enforcement of justice. Where would one draw the line if one exemption were to be granted? Other states would then equally be justified in applying for exemptions based on, for instance, their population size or economic power. The ICC is based on the idea of non-selective enforcement of universal norms which 'vexes the United States because all individuals (and, by extension, states) stand before it as equals' (Sewall and Kaysen 2000: 3). The US has not been given a special role in the ICC's provisions, like it has in the UN, which is in line with the ICC's objective of discontinuing the existing hierarchy between states by focussing primarily on individual justice norms.

During the Rome conference states had to weigh up these considerations against the difficulties the ICC faces if it does not have US support. The very nature of the issues negotiated in Rome and afterwards reduced the influence of the US on other states because the 'principle of equal justice and accountability for serious international crimes may not be particularly susceptible to compromise.' (Brown 2002: 335) The decision was eventually made that even though the Court would be weakened by US opposition, further concessions in order to incorporate the US demands would harm the ICC and eventually render the whole institution meaningless.

The US argued that integrating the possibility of Security Council control into the ICC Statute was necessary because US soldiers were required in a large number of UN missions to restore or maintain international peace and security. These soldiers would then be uniquely vulnerable to possible ICC jurisdiction. However, other permanent members of the Security Council, such as the UK and France (and to a degree Russia[19]) who also commit peacekeeping forces to UN missions were satisfied with the safeguards incorporated into the Statute. This opens the question why they were not sufficient for the US. The answer might lie in the fact that even though the ICC was created to work alongside the UN and not to undermine it, it also attempted to do indirectly what could not be done directly; namely to reform the UN and amend its Charter. This challenge to the Security Council can be seen on the one hand as a reason for the US opposition, but on the other as a cause for the enthusiasm and support of such a large number of states that support the idea of equal treatment (Schabas 2004: 720). By not giving in to US pressure, states supporting the ICC accept that US opposition is a price that needs to be paid in order to achieve a move away from existing power hierarchies towards equal standing of states in international society.

US opposition to the ICC is in line with the current administration's general critical approach to multilateralism and 'the Court has become a useful stalking horse for a broader attack on international law and the constraints which it may place on hegemonic power' (Sands 2005: 60). Ever since taking office, the Bush administration has stressed the rights and responsibilities of national sovereignty and has seen multilateralism and global governance as being in conflict with the

US Constitution.[20] Previous administrations had been more sympathetic to the ICC and multilateralism in general, but once in power,

> very quickly, the [Bush] administration sought to reverse what it perceived as a creeping American acquiescence towards global governance (Joseph 2005: 375).

The events of 9/11 further underlined this trend of focusing primarily on US citizens and national interests. This demonstrates the government's pluralist approach of focusing primarily on principles of international order to maintain its powerful position.

US actions in opposition to the ICC

Since the US could not prevent the ICC from being established and coming into force, it undertook a number of actions to undermine the workings of the Court and to exempt US citizens from its reach. In an attempt to exempt UN peacekeeping forces from possible ICC jurisdiction, the US proposed adopting a Security Council resolution in accordance with Article 16 of the Statute which allows the Security Council to defer an ICC investigation for twelve months (renewable). Resolution 1422 was adopted by the Security Council on 12 July 2002 and renewed as Resolution 1487 a year later. In 2004, however, the US faced too much opposition to propose a further renewal of the resolution in the Security Council mainly in response to allegations of prisoner abuses in the Iraqi Abu Ghraib prison and had to withdraw its request for another extension.

UN resolutions

In 2002, after the ICC had come into existence, the US vetoed the extension of the UN peacekeeping mission in Bosnia and Herzegovina and threatened to withdraw all its other UN peacekeeping forces because, it claimed, that its soldiers were at risk of possible ICC jurisdiction in that territory. Justifying this action, the US ambassador to the UN, John Negroponte, argued that even though it was unfortunate that the US had to veto the extension of the mission, it was not prepared to ask its peacekeepers 'to accept the additional risk of politicized prosecutions before a court whose jurisdiction over our people the Government of the United States does not accept' (UN Security Council 2002: 2). He maintained that the US was still committed to contributing to UN peacekeeping missions, but because it was not prepared to accept the ICC's jurisdiction, a compromise to solve this problem needed to be found. The US proposed complete immunity for UN peacekeepers by adopting a Resolution in line with Article 16 of the Statute with the prospect of renewing it after 12 months. The US Ambassador to the UN argued that 'with our global responsibilities, we are and will remain a special target and cannot have our decisions secondguessed by a court whose jurisdiction we do not recognize' (UN Security Council 2002: 2).

UN Secretary-General Kofi Annan expressed his anger over the US actions and argued that 'the whole system of United Nations peacekeeping operations is being put at risk' (Annan 2002). He argued that the US had misinterpreted Article 16 of the Rome Statute, which was meant for completely different circumstances, namely particular and specified situations whenever they arose and not blanket immunity expressed in advance. He acknowledged, however, that a compromise needed to be found, and argued that 'there might be other solutions to avoid that the Council precipitated into adopting a resolution, the effects of which may soon be deeply regretted by all' (Annan 2002).

Despite criticisms expressed by a number of states (most of which were not allowed to vote), Resolution 1422 was adopted unanimously by the members of the Security Council, exempting peacekeeping personnel from the ICC's jurisdiction for a period of twelve months with the option of renewal of the resolution as long as it was deemed necessary. The resolution was renewed for another twelve months in 2003.[21]

In May 2004, the US sought to renew Resolution 1422 for a second time, but faced stiff opposition from a number of states and eventually decided to withdraw the request. One major argument of the opposition were the growing concerns about allegations of abuse by US troops against prisoners at Abu Ghraib prison in Iraq. Kofi Annan believed that requesting an exemption for the US in this situation would seem hypocritical and would impose double standards since the US was accused of having violated universal standards of justice in the way it treated Iraqi prisoners.[22]

US officials interpreted the situation to the contrary, arguing Abu Ghraib proved that

> the United States does stand for justice and will itself impose justice on any members of our services who might undertake things that constitute international crimes. (...) But it's a matter for us to take care of and not for some court with some jurisdiction that we're not party to (US Department of State 2004, 23 June).

The US thereby emphasized that even though it proclaimed to be committed to protecting and enforcing justice norms, this could only be achieved through national courts without external intervention. The US favoured national enforcement of these international norms rather than enforcement through an international court, which illustrates the US's pluralist approach whereby order principles of state sovereignty and non-intervention cannot be compromised in favour of justice.

However, Colin Powell admitted that Abu Ghraib had affected the way people looked at the ICC and acknowledged that it was less likely the US would be able to achieve another renewal of the resolution under these circumstances. The US eventually decided to withdraw its request, arguing that it did not want to engage the Security Council in a 'prolonged and divisive debate'.[23] The US issued a statement to the UN, in which it argued that it would have preferred to retain the compromise achieved in Resolutions 1422 and 1487 and that this failure to renew them would mean that the US 'will need to take into account the risk of ICC review when determining contributions to UN authorized or established operations.' A few days later, the Defense Department announced that it would withdraw personnel from peacekeeping missions in Ethiopia and Eritrea and also Kosovo (nine people altogether), because they were perceived to be at risk of possible ICC jurisdiction.

Additional measures to exempt US nationals

Since the UN Resolutions only protected US personnel acting as part of UN peacekeeping missions and only for a limited period of time, additional measures were created to exempt *all* US nationals from the ICC permanently. The two most important measures implemented by the Bush administration were bilateral agreements with individual states to prevent US citizens from being handed over to the ICC and the American Servicemembers' Protection Act (ASPA).

The bilateral so-called 'Article 98 agreements'[24] between the US and individual states stipulate that US personnel and nationals cannot be detained, arrested or sent to the ICC. The original intent of Article 98 was to cover so-called Status of Force Agreements (SOFAs) between the US and other countries (mainly NATO states) that give the US primacy in exercising jurisdiction over US personnel acting on foreign soil. The Bush administration, however, used this provision to seek exemptions from a number of different states, exerting strong diplomatic and financial pressure if states refused to sign with 'many of the states approached (...) too weak to resist' (McGoldrick 2004: 424). In October 2004, the US government also signed the so-called Nethercutt Amendment to the Foreign Operations Appropriation Bill into law that suspends economic aid to ICC states parties that have not signed Article 98 agreements.

At the time of writing, over 100 states have signed such agreements, including forty-six ICC member states. Larger and more influential states, such as Canada and states in the EU, have refused to sign these bilateral agreements, arguing that doing so would be inconsistent with their obligations as ICC state parties. The European Parliament even issued an official position in which it not only outlines its opposition to these agreements, but argues that 'ratifying such an agreement is incompatible with membership of the EU' (European Parliament 2002).

In addition to these agreements with individual states, the Bush administration signed the American Servicemembers' Protection Act into law[25], which authorizes the US to use 'all means necessary, including military force, to rescue a US citizen taken into the court's custody'. This provision led the ASPA to be called 'The Hague Invasion Act'. It limits US cooperation with the ICC, including the ability to collaborate, extradite, support, fund, and share classified information. The ASPA also imposes prohibition of military aid to states parties to the ICC but allows waivers if it is in the US national interest, if states signed Article 98 agreements and also for NATO states and major NATO allies. All these measures are designed to circumvent and undermine the ICC and to avoid any possibility of it being able to act against US nationals.

Changing US perceptions

Since the ICC's first actions in 2004, however, the US seems to have adopted a more pragmatic approach towards the Court. A shift is discernible from the Bush administration's initial firm opposition to a fresh assessment of the Court. In March 2005, the UN Security Council adopted a resolution to refer the situation in Darfur to the ICC. The US did not veto this resolution (it abstained) and even declared to be prepared to assist the Court if asked. John Bellinger, State Department Chief Lawyer, admitted that the US could not delegitimize a Court that has more that 100 member states including a number of major US allies (such as the UK, Canada and Australia). He further argued that even though the Bush administration will never allow US nationals to be tried by the ICC, 'we do acknowledge that it has a role to play in the overall system of international justice' (Bravin 14 June 2006).

A number of influential US politicians admitted that the bilateral Article 98 agreements and the ASPA are actually harmful to US interests. Cuts in military assistance to certain countries mean lost opportunities of military training provided by US troops which is aimed at strengthening US links to other countries and their fight against terrorism abroad. The US Defense Department severely criticized the effects these measures have, especially on military operations and co-operation in strategically important regions (such as Latin America and Africa). One US commander argued that the restrictions placed on US assistance in such countries has given China the opportunity to fill a void and step up its efforts to gain influence. Condoleezza Rice admitted that the Article 98 agreements are like 'shooting ourselves in the foot' (Rice 10 March 2006). In September 2006, the US House of Representatives and Senate passed an amendment that repeals the section of the ASPA that restricts International Military Education and Training (IMET) funds to ICC states parties. This, however, does not include other funding cuts (including non-military aid) that are still in place.

The initial active opposition of the Bush administration has gradually given way to a more pragmatic approach towards the ICC: the US has not opposed ICC action in its first three cases. Admittedly, these action are against states in Africa and do not involve major US allies, which raises the question of whether the US might be willing to only selectively support the Court. This selectivity is problematic, but a starting point needs to be found for the ICC to take action and to prove that it is not primarily created as an instrument to undermine US hegemony but to enforce justice norms on a universal basis. Philippe Kirsch, president of the Court, is optimistic that the ICC will prove to doubters that it is not a political instrument, but acts 'exclusively judicially'. He is sure that opponents of the Court will join at some point, arguing that 'To me, it is not a matter of whether: it's a matter of when'[26].

Conclusion

The creation of the ICC represents the latest in a number of developments towards increased recognition of justice norms and their enforcement in an increasingly solidarist international society that combines considerations for justice with principles of international order. It builds on precedents set in cases such as Pinochet's arrest and the ICTY and also progress that has taken place in line with the first two stages of the norm life cycle. The ICC combines two competing values existent in the international order, one based on states and their sovereignty and the other based on individual justice. The long term aim of the ICC is not only to carry out international law by enforcing existing human rights provisions but also to enhance the 'international normative framework' (Sewall and Kaysen 2000: 2–3) by setting norms and standards of acceptable behaviour.

The ICC aims to institutionalize enforcement of already established norms that have been codified in international law and are part of the rules of international society. The fact that the ICC only includes already well established norms means that it starts at a point where agreement on universal values and norms has already been reached and developments in the norm life cycle have taken place. The creation of the ICC is an example of the cycle's third stage in which norms that have emerged during the first two stages and that have cascaded into the rules of international society become further internalized. The third stage of the model leads to further changes in the norm's progression as demonstrated by the creation of the ICC, which

> has the potential to change the proscriptive norms against genocide, crimes against humanity, and war crimes into *instrumental* norms; that is, norms that not only reflect social expectations (intrinsic norms) but also encourages compliance through repeated and consistent application (Nel 2002: 152).

The US launched a strong pluralist response to the ICC because it was concerned that changes in the international order would lead to an erosion of the existing hierarchy between states, thereby challenging its own unique and powerful position. The ICC aims to overcome the hierarchy that has existed over decades to achieve equality between all its member states. All states are seen as equal in the ICC and no one state (or group of states) is given more powers than any others. This constitutes a problem for the US as a great power that claims to have unique standing in international relations that it wants to be reflected in the Court's set-up. The ICC's main focus, however, is on justice norms rather than power politics and this makes equality between its members necessary.

US actions in opposition to the ICC were based on the understanding that universal justice can only be achieved by sovereign states and that fundamental principles of international order should not be changed to accommodate values of justice. The US is predominantly concerned about maintaining its unique and powerful position in the existing international order and fears that changes in this order lead to an erosion of the existing hierarchy between states. The US is inconsistent in its approach to international justice dispensed through international courts: on the one hand, it was instrumental in setting up the Nuremberg and Tokyo trials and also acted in a leading position during the establishment of the ICTY and the ICTR, but on the other it is hostile towards the ICC. It opposes the

ICC because it is an independent institution not controlled by the UN Security Council, which means that there is at least a theoretical possibility that the ICC can compromise the US's sovereignty on issues related to universally recognized human rights norms.

The initial assumption of ICC opponents that the Court was going to be weak and would not be able to survive without US support has so far proven to be wrong.

> Since adoption, the Statute has exceeded the expectations of even its most unconditional supporters and enthusiasts. Faced with an accelerated pace of ratification and entry into force, the United States took several aggressive measures directed against the Court. None have been particularly successful, and while both annoying and humiliating, none pose a serious threat to the success of the institution (Schabas 2004: 720).

This is also based on the fact that the ICC builds on a number of precedents in international law that developed over a long period of time.

US opposition is unfortunate for the ICC, because the Court's enforcement powers ultimately depend on state co-operation and it would greatly benefit if the US, as great power, would express its general willingness to assist the ICC. However, not all states have given in to US pressures and some have expressed disapproval at US actions. These states thereby confirm their resolve to create an effective global enforcement mechanism for justice norms regardless of whether the US participates or not. Such a development has been made possible through changes in human rights and justice norms that are increasingly incorporated in international law. The ICC is the latest step towards the full internalisation of these norms to become an integral part of the rules of international society. Even though it is strongly contested by the US, it is at least a starting point from which the international system can develop further. US opposition demonstrates that it takes time to create a universal mechanism but the innovations and compromises included in the ICC have put procedures in place from which the universal enforcement of justice can develop further.

ICC supporters have come to the conclusion that the institution will be viable without the support from the US and even though it would be desirable, no reasonable price for winning its approval has yet emerged.

> The judgement to date has been that, while the ICC might be weaker without the United States' involvement, it enjoys sufficient support not to fall victim to the same fate as the League of Nations, and that the legitimacy the ICC gains through maintaining the integrity of the Statute compensates for the loss of U.S. backing (Broomhall 2003: 182–183).

The actions taken in opposition to the ICC (in form of the Article 98 agreements and the ASPA) are harmful to the Court because other states are being prevented from co-operating and assisting the Court in its operations.

The initial hostility and actions taken to undermine the ICC were based on a belief that the US could prevent the Court from coming into being. The threatening statements and actions undertaken by the US government were aimed at intimidating the Court's supporters with the aim of achieving further concessions and exclusions from the ICC's jurisdiction. However, the ICC has so far proved to be too strong. A large number of developments preceded the creation of the Court that provided strong foundations on which the ICC could build. The *ad hoc* tribunals, for example, were the last in a line of developments towards increased international criminal justice and developments in international law. International politics has developed further towards the global enforcement of human rights and also changes in the understanding of state sovereignty. Agreement on some of the most basic human rights exists which also led to the desire to establish a working enforcement mechanism. The majority of states see the ICC as such an institution that includes enough safeguards to not erode state sovereignty dramatically.

Ideally, the ICC will never have to act and only exists as a safety net if states fail to act themselves to enforce international human rights laws. This is also in the US's interests because by creating a more 'just' and stable order with greater respect for human rights, external interventions that compromise state sovereignty become increasingly unnecessary. Maybe in the years to come the US will see that the ICC is only a court of last resort, it is not aimed at undermining the predominant position of the US, but focuses on the protection of human rights. The fact that the US abstained from the Security Council resolution that referred the situation in Darfur to the prosecutor is evidence that the US is trying to find a practical way to work with the ICC and its supporters, rather than continuing its active opposition. The US government even started to co-operate with the ICC in calling the government of Sudan to enforce the ICC's arrest warrant and in acknowledging the ICC's role in the overall system of justice. This is an important step because in the post-9/11 world it is important to be consistent with existing and fundamental principles of the liberal democratic order that includes multilateral action and recognizes the importance of universal principles, human rights and international law. As Held argues, 'what is needed is a movement of global, not American or French or British, justice and legitimacy' (2005: 13).

Notes

1 The Committee was comprised of delegates of a large number of different states. For instance, the Chairman of the Committee was Adrian Bos (Netherlands); Vice-Chairmen: Cherif Bassiouni (Egypt), Silvia A. Fernandez de Gurmendi (Argentina), Markek Madej (Poland), Rapporteur: Kuniko Saeki (Japan). The Working Group, established to prepare the meeting schedules, was chaired by Gerhard Hafner (Austria).
2 Although the voting records have never been made public, it is widely believed that the states voting against the statute were: the USA, China, Israel, Libya, Iraq, Yemen, and Qatar. Among those abstaining were believed to be India, Japan, and Mexico (Edgar 2002: Note 3).
3 As of 18 July 2008, the ICC has 139 signatories and 108 states parties, i.e. states that have ratified the Statute into their national laws.

4 In contrast, the International Criminal Tribunals for the Former Yugoslavia and for Rwanda both have primacy over national courts.

5 Article 5: 'Crimes within the jurisdiction of the Court: (…) 2. The Court shall exercise jurisdiction over the crime of aggression once a provision is adopted in accordance with articles 121 and 123 defining the crime and setting out the conditions under which the Court shall exercise jurisdiction with respect to this crime. Such a provision shall be consistent with the relevant provisions of the Charter of the United Nations.'

6 Article 123 of the ICC Statute sets out that seven years after entry into force, a Review Conference shall be convened to consider any amendments to the Statute which may include, but is not limited to, the list of crimes contained in Article 5.

7 This is contrary to the ICJ's Statute, for instance, where states need to 'opt-in' to jurisdiction on specific crimes and jurisdiction is not conferred automatically with a state's ratification of the Statute. Additional declarations to accept jurisdiction are necessary.

8 An opt-out provision was included for war crimes. Article 124 of the Statute sets out that states that ratify the Statute can opt-out of the Court's jurisdiction for the period of seven years. This compromise was included to secure the support of France and a few other states for the ICC (Schabas 2001: 159).

9 Article 12 and the controversy surrounding it will be further explored in the following section on US opposition.

10 The Statute sets out its relationship to the UN in its Preamble: it reaffirms 'the Purposes and Principles of the Charter of the United Nations, and in particular that all States shall refrain from the threat or use of force against the territorial integrity or political independence of any State, or in any other manner inconsistent with the Purposes of the United Nations' and further in Article 2, that: 'The Court shall be brought into relationship with the United Nations through an agreement to be approved by the Assembly of States Parties to this Statute and thereafter concluded by the President of the Court on its behalf.'

11 This compromise derived from a proposal made by Singapore during the August 1996 PrepCom meeting.

12 At the time of writing, the UK and France, as two of the permanent Security Council members have ratified the ICC Statute. Russia has signed it, but has not ratified its provisions into its national laws. China and the US stand opposed to the ICC and have no immediate plans to sign the Statute.

13 Article 15: 'Prosecutor: (…) 3. If the Prosecutor concludes that there is a reasonable basis to proceed with an investigation, he or she shall submit to the Pre-Trial Chamber a request for authorization of an investigation, together with any supporting material collected. Victims may make representations to the Pre-Trial Chamber, in accordance with the Rules of Procedure and Evidence. 4. If the Pre-Trial Chamber, upon examination of the request and the supporting material, considers that there is a reasonable basis to proceed with an investigation, and that the case appears to fall within the jurisdiction of the Court, it shall authorize the commencement of the investigation, without prejudice to subsequent determinations by the Court with regard to the jurisdiction and admissibility of a case. (…)'

14 This aspect of the ICC can be seen as a very strong solidarist element integrated into the Statute. It can be seen as moving the ICC towards an approximation of what Linklater (1998) calls a solidarist society of peoples, independent from states and their sovereignty considerations.

15 David Scheffer criticized the use of the words 'significant flaws' because he believed that even though the Rome Statute had its problems, describing its flaws as 'significant' was not 'accurate and would [not] improve our leverage as a signatory' (Scheffer 2002: 64). He was furthermore concerned that this wording would give the opponents of the ICC further ammunition.

16 According to Article 18 of the Vienna Convention on the Law of Treaties, a signatory to a treaty is 'obliged to refrain from acts which would defeat the object and the purpose' of

the treaty. The Bush administration therefore had to formally 'un-sign' the Rome Statute in order to be able to take action that effectively undermined the functioning of the ICC.

17 With regard to the ICC, the National Security Strategy sets out the following: 'We will take the actions necessary to ensure that our efforts to meet our global security commitments and protect Americans are not impaired by the potential for investigations, inquiry, or prosecution by the International Criminal Court (ICC), whose jurisdiction does not extend to Americans and which we do not accept' (US Government 2002: 31). It further sets out the possibility of negotiating bilateral and multilateral agreements to protect US nationals from the ICC.

18 Such action would only be possible in accordance with the complementarity principle which means that the US was itself unwilling or unable to launch an investigation.

19 Russia signed the Statute but has not ratified it.

20 The US Constitution cannot be superseded by any international agreement or institution.

21 Resolution 1487 (2003) was adopted with twelve votes in favour and three abstentions from Germany, France and the Syrian Arab Republic.

22 In a brief press encounter in June 2004 he expressed the following: 'Q: In light of the prisoner abuses in Iraq, should the US get another exemption on ICC at the Council, for peacekeepers? SG: As you know, for the past two years, I have spoken quite strongly against the exemption, and I think it would be unfortunate for one to press for such an exemption, given the prisoner abuse in Iraq. I think in this circumstance it would be unwise to press for an exemption, and it would be even more unwise on the part of the Security Council to grant it. It would discredit the Council and the United Nations that stands for rule of law and the primacy of rule of law.' (Secretary-General 2004)

23 Daily Press Briefing, US Department of State, Richard Boucher, Spokesman.

24 The US claims that these agreements are in line with Article 98(2) of the ICC's Statute, which states that 'the Court may not proceed with a request for surrender which would require the requested State to act inconsistently with its obligations under international agreements pursuant to which the consent of a sending State is required to surrender a person of that State to the Court, unless the Court can first obtain the cooperation of the sending State for the giving of consent for the surrender.'

25 The ASPA was already proposed in 2000, but only a heavily modified version that included a number of exemptions allowing for presidential discretion was eventually adopted in August 2002.

26 'The court that tries America's patience', *Daily Telegraph,* 12 January 2006.

Conclusion – a more 'just' order?

At the time of writing, 108 states have ratified the Rome Statute. They had to adjust their national laws to incorporate the ICC's provisions and thereby incorporate the enforcement of universal values on the domestic level. Since its coming into force on 1 July 2002, the ICC has already shown notable indirect and direct effects on states in international society.

The ICC's indirect effects

British soldiers in Iraq

One of the first examples of the ICC's *indirect* influence came in July 2005 when three British soldiers faced war crimes charges over incidents that took place in Iraq in September 2003. These charges were brought under the International Criminal Court Act 2001, the law with which the ICC Statute was ratified into UK law. Even though the crimes existed in UK law before the Act came into force, the ratification of the ICC Statute clarified the definition of the crimes and made it possible to investigate them as war crimes. The UK exercised its right of primary jurisdiction by showing that it was 'willing' and 'able' to investigate the charges itself, preventing the ICC from taking action. This demonstrates the ICC's indirect effect on the national level; the UK had to take action to avoid ICC intervention. It is likely that the UK would have launched an investigation into these cases even without the ICC's existence, but its ratification of the ICC Statute and the definition of war crimes into its national laws provided an additional impetus for action.

The ICC's direct actions

The ICC has also begun its first *direct* actions in four different situations: the Security Council referred the situation in Darfur to the ICC and the governments of Uganda, the Democratic Republic of the Congo (DRC) and the Central African Republic (CAR) referred their situations to the ICC themselves.

Security Council action in Darfur

The Security Council referred the situation in Sudan's Dafur region to the prosecutor in March 2005[1] to start investigations into cases of alleged war crimes and genocide. This was the first time that the Security Council made such a decision.[2] As a consequence of this referral, the ICC prosecutor Luis Moreno Ocampo received access to the document archives of the UN International Commission of Inquiry on Darfur as well as a sealed list of names of individuals suspected of grave international human rights crimes. Following the examination of documents from a variety of sources and interviews with over fifty independent experts, the prosecutor decided that there was a reasonable basis to initiate an investigation on Darfur. On 6 June 2006, Ocampo officially opened the investigation and in May 2007 issued the first arrest warrants against two individuals: Ahmad Harun, the former Minister of State for the Interior, and Ali Kushayb, a militia/Janjaweed leader. These warrants were issued because there are 'reasonable grounds' (International Criminal Court 2 May 2007) to believe that the two suspects bear criminal responsibility for crimes against humanity and war crimes committed in Darfur in 2003 and 2004.

The Sudanese government has so far done little to assist the ICC in its working. It resisted the investigations into human rights violations committed by government-sponsored militias in the region and vowed never to surrender any of its citizens to The Hague. In October 2007, Sudan officially refused to hand over the two suspects that are sought by the ICC. The prosecutor has called upon the international community to help apprehend the accused and bring them before the ICC.

Sudan is not a state party to the ICC and is creating its own court in order to avoid ICC interference which shows that the threat of ICC judicial intervention can pressure a state into taking action to avoid external interference. However, these local justice initiatives are widely believed to be 'show trials' that do little to hold actual perpetrators accountable for the atrocities committed. The ICC's complementarity principle means that such show trials are not sufficient to prevent the ICC from taking action.

ICC action in Uganda

The government of Uganda asked the ICC to investigate crimes allegedly committed by the Lord's Resistance Army (LRA). Over the course of its existence, the LRA is alleged to have killed thousands of civilians and abducted an estimated 20,000 children, forcing them to be child soldiers. In January 2004, the Ugandan President became the first head of state to refer a situation in his own country to the ICC. The ICC has issued arrest warrants against members of the LRA including its leader Joseph Kony. This was a historic moment for the Court, but the continuation of violence in Uganda has complicated the proceedings. ICC investigators have been slowed by ongoing debates over the merits of seeking justice in a society where peace still does not exist and also whether the country should rather rely on its own methods of achieving 'justice' rather than taking matters to an international court. The ICC is also at odds with the same government that first referred the case to it. The Ugandan government has offered amnesties to Kony and his followers if they abandon their 'criminal activities'. Amnesties are not possible under the ICC Statute and it remains to be seen how this situation will be resolved. This case is nevertheless an important example where a state that did not have the resources and ability to deal with the most serious of human rights offences itself used the ICC as a court of last resort to hold individuals accountable for their actions.

The ICC and the Democratic Republic of the Congo

The first major breakthrough for the ICC came in March 2006 when the first suspect of international crimes under the ICC Statute was arrested and transferred into ICC custody. Thomas Lubanga, a Congolese militia leader, is alleged to have been involved in the commission of war crimes, specifically by using child soldiers in the Congo's armed conflict. The Democratic Republic of the Congo formally referred the situation to the prosecutor in April 2004. It requested the prosecutor to investigate if crimes under the Court's jurisdiction were committed in the territory of the DRC since the entry into force of the Rome Statute. The DRC noted that thousands of deaths by mass murder and summary execution had been reported in the country since that date. In June 2004, after thorough analysis of the situation in the DRC and especially in the Eastern region of Ituri, the prosecutor announced his decision to open investigations. The pre-trial chamber examined the evidence and found it met the criteria set out in the Rome Statute, enabling the prosecutor to issue an arrest warrant. The investigation into the situation in the Congo is ongoing at the time of writing and according to the ICC, this initial arrest is the 'first in a series' (International Criminal Court 17 March 2006).

ICC action in the Central African Republic

The third referral by a state party came from the government of the Central African Republic in December 2004. The CAR's highest court, the Cour de Cassation, confirmed that the national justice system was unable to carry out the complex proceedings involved in investigating and prosecuting the alleged crimes and therefore decided to refer the situation to the ICC. In May 2006, the prosecutor officially announced that he would conduct an investigation into the situation based on preliminary analysis of alleged crimes that fall within the ICC's jurisdiction. The crimes were committed in the context of an armed conflict between the government and rebel forces in 2002 and 2003. The worst allegations are related to killing, looting, sexual violence and attacks against civilians by armed individuals. The ICC's investigations are currently not targeting individual suspects but the situation in CAR in general. Even though the main focus is on crimes committed in 2002–2003, the ICC also monitors the current situation in the state which is still troubled by widespread violence and worsening humanitarian conditions. Underlining the role criminal justice plays in situations like these, the prosecutor stated: 'In the interests of deterring future violence and promoting enduring peace in the region, we have a duty to show that massive crimes cannot be committed with impunity. We will do our part, working through our judicial mandate.'(International Criminal Court 22 May 2007).

Human rights and their enforcement

The road towards creating the ICC as an instrument to institutionalize human rights and to encourage their increased enforcement has not been a straightforward one. This book dealt with a number of developments since the end of the Second World War that provide strong foundations on which the ICC is built. International law has changed considerably; the traditional notion of international law as the law between nations is no longer valid and individuals have emerged as subjects and objects of international law. The Holocaust and its aftermath led to a recognition of rights and duties for individuals under international law. The Nuremberg trials set a precedent in which individuals were held accountable for crimes they committed and also affirmed that international law included the 'right' of individuals to be treated with a minimum of civility by their own governments. A shift has taken place away from a predominantly state-centric view of international law towards an increased recognition of the rights of human beings.

Numerous laws, treaties, and Conventions aimed at protecting human rights emerged after the end of the Second World War but the problem of international law continued to lie in the lack of independent enforcement mechanisms. States signed treaty after treaty on human rights protection, but for a long time no meaningful enforcement action could be taken. This changed with the end of the Cold War which led to a revival of the Nuremberg precedent: with the end of great power rivalry came a real possibility of actually *enforcing* some of the provisions states signed up for. Yet, as was discussed throughout this book, a conflict exists between order and justice principles that are both part of the rules of international society.

Agreements exist in international law on a very limited number of crimes that are seen to belong to a special category of rights that affect *all* states and therefore place an obligation on all states to ensure their enforcement. The main challenge therefore does not lie in finding agreement on at least some universal norms and values, but in the lack of political will to enforce them. Since international law operates without overarching enforcement authority it is dependent on states' political will to enforce its provisions. This lack of authority makes its application selective and can lead to a politicized use of international law.

As discussed in this book, unilateral and multilateral judicial interventions aim to enforce existing standards of international law by breaking with customary state practice and setting precedents in the enforcement of existing laws. These interventions aim to internalize the consistent enforcement of norms into international society with long term effects, making them part of states' identities and thereby affecting their behaviour. 'If we had reliable criminal justice on a global scale we could punish individual criminals with more certainty, bring some catharsis to victims and/or relatives, try to break the vicious circle of group violence, and hope to deter future acts' (Forsythe 2006: 89). This is not to say that judicial intervention is always the only option nor is it necessarily the best, but it nevertheless puts institutional frameworks in place that lead to the creation of an overall normative environment in which the most serious of human rights abuses are not ignored.

The case studies in this book were chosen to reflect different stages of the norm life cycle to examine how norms emerge and are internalized in the rules of international society. They illustrate normative developments particularly through the norm cascade which leads to broad norm acceptance by states and changes in the overall normative context. The case studies demonstrate acceptance as well as resistance to such changes in the cycle which suggest that norm development is a dynamic process and not a neat progression. Progress is followed by setbacks which demonstrates that norm internalisation is almost inevitably a lengthy and a contested process. Nevertheless, it can be argued that an overall progression has taken place in international society towards increased recognition of human rights norms and their institutionalization in the international order, thereby reconciling order with justice to establish a more 'just order' in the solidarist sense.

The Pinochet and Yerodia cases were two instances of unilateral action by individual states based on universal jurisdiction claims to challenge states' right to grant state immunity. In the Pinochet decisions, an overall solidarist view was taken on existing legal provisions and developments in international law to allow his extradition. The case of Yerodia showed that the life cycle had not progressed far enough with regard to universal jurisdiction in national courts and led to an opposing outcome. The result was thus an outcome in which an overall pluralist view was taken that emphasized the importance of maintaining order principles over considerations for particular justice norms. This did not constitute a backward step in the overall development of the norm life cycle but much rather showed that further progress needed to take place to make justice norm enforcement universal. A number of judges in the Yerodia decision clarified that they did not question the justice norms themselves or the fact that they are part of international law. Rather, they objected to the way they were being enforced through unilateral action and in national courts.

The two cases also brought out more general questions regarding the suitability of national courts and the principle of universal jurisdiction to investigate international crimes. Unilateral action is bound to be selective because it is based on one particular state's interpretation of the law in certain circumstances. It is not sustainable in the long term because it leads to an inconsistent and politicized use of international law. States refer to international law to legitimize their actions but they are more likely to be motivated by national interests as well and not exclusively by concerns for universal justice. One effect is that other instances that would equally benefit from external intervention and selectivity in the application of international law are ignored.

International law needs some form of agency to be enforced. Situations that are identified by states as a crisis provide important focal points that call for normative change based on already established legal provisions. A difficulty of such 'crisis' language is, however, that it can be used by individual states in an inconsistent and self-serving way. It also normalizes all conduct that falls short of being called a crisis even though some of it would, arguably, equally warrant external intervention. However, a starting point needs to be found somewhere to make the further integration of justice norm enforcement along the norm life cycle possible. Unilateral actions are therefore necessary to break with customary state practice and to facilitate the norm cascade, but they are not suitable as a long term solution to the conflict and are not the only way to enforce justice.

The creation of the ICTY was presented in this book as one example of multilateral action by a number of states to enforce justice norms through an international court. International courts are better suited to applying international law because they are less dependent on individual states' national agendas and represent more than just one state. However, by using the UN Security Council to create the court, this approach was still selective because it was only based on a limited number of states. It was imposed on states without their consent, which leads to a number of additional problems. Most of all it can lead to states not accepting the legitimacy of the court which makes it difficult to fulfil its objectives of breaking with the past and creating a new normative environment in which individuals are held accountable for their actions. States that created the ICTY emphasized the extraordinary nature of the court which is problematic because international law aims to make the extraordinary ordinary. A situation in which international law is applied cannot stay extraordinary because its provisions are devised for *all* to follow and not just particular states and in certain circumstances. Nevertheless, the ICTY created a powerful precedent for multilateral action through an international court and also provided renewed impetus for the creation of the ICC as a permanent court.

The ICC includes solidarist as well as pluralist elements. It incorporates a number of innovations and compromises, such as the limited role of the Security Council and the extensive powers given to its prosecutor. The most important aspect of the ICC is its indirect effect because it does not aim to relieve states of their national responsibility to enforce justice. Instead it seeks to create an environment in which norms achieve a taken-for-granted quality and become an integral part of international society. It is a court of last resort that creates expectations about what states perceive to be appropriate behaviour in line with their membership of international society. The creation of the ICC as an example of the norm life cycle's third stage of norm internalization is strongly contested by the US which launched a pluralist counter-attack to the Court. The US emphasized state sovereignty and the importance of non-intervention with regard to matters concerning the dispensing of justice through criminal courts. This opposition shows that norms need to develop further to make it possible to create an enforcement mechanism acceptable to all. More recent events suggest that the US is scaling down its initial active hostility and is moving towards a more pragmatic approach to the Court. Rather than opposing it, the US started to work with the ICC, accepting that it is an independent institution that enjoys large scale support from 108 states in the world. This acceptance is arguably selective and the US has no immediate plans to become a state party to its Statute, but it allows the Court to work without having to fight off challenges from the great power.

The norm life cycle is a dynamic process characterized by progress as well as setbacks, but it can be argued that an overall progression has taken place towards an increasing institutionalization of justice norms and their enforcement into international society. This general trend has faced significant resistance which shows that the process is difficult and contested. Norms do not enter a vacuum, but need to fit with other already existing norms which makes the redefinition of the contents of these pre-existing norms necessary. Sovereignty and the principle of non-intervention have changed to incorporate notions of human rights and the recognition that individuals are subjects of international law and have rights independent from states. Normative changes in the attitudes to human rights and their increased recognition has led to a reconstitution of what it means to be a state.

Critics could argue that the cases chosen for the present analysis could be dismissed as 'freak' occurrences without lasting impact. Unilateral attempts to exercise universal jurisdiction could be dismissed by realists, for instance, as only being a disguise for the pursuit of state's own interests. The creation of *ad hoc* courts could be criticized as constituting an 'easy way out' to not get involved militarily in the conflict and to deflect attention from the failure to act more decisively. Critics could also point to a number of occasions, such as East Timor and Cambodia, in which criminal justice did not take place or was very slow in coming. However, the fact that a number of cases can be found that support the idea of norm progression in the norm life cycle in the first place, suggests an underlying trend that cannot be ignored. Even twenty years ago it would have been nearly impossible to find as many examples that illustrate an underlying progress in which human rights norms become increasingly prominent in international politics and law. Criminal justice is not the only instrument to influence policy and respect for human rights. The failure to establish courts or to act unilaterally should therefore not be seen as a failure to act or as a revival of the culture of impunity, but as acknowledging the limits of the power of criminal justice. Considerations of how criminal justice affects a peace process, for instance need to be taken into account. This point was evident during the Balkan conflict where the ICTY did not indict Milosević for a number of years in order not to jeopardize peace negotiations.

The cases outlined in the present analysis have a cumulative impact and build and expand on each other. Resistance to the norm life cycle is acknowledged as evidence that human rights norms are taken seriously by states, but that there is also the need for additional developments to make their enforcement universal. The cases analysed identify a number of difficulties attached to human rights law enforcement, but much rather than dismissing them as extraordinary occurrences without meaning, these cases are presented here as evidence that the creation of a permanent mechanism (such as the ICC) is necessary to establish an effective regime in which agreed upon justice norms can be enforced consistently. The cases show a revival of the Nuremberg precedent that the most serious human rights abuses are unforgivable and that the culture of impunity needs to be replaced with one of accountability. Criminal justice is seen as a way of protecting human rights and as a means to create a normative context in which those norms become self-enforcing. The case studies focus on a number of events that occurred within a very short space of time that have taken place after years of inaction and foot-dragging, particularly during the Cold War. Thus, a general movement towards global justice is taking place. It faces hard resistance in the form of traditional notions of sovereignty, but the emerging regime is a good starting point from which further developments can take place.

Notes

1 UN Security Council Resolution 1593.
2 This move was not opposed by the US that could have exercised its veto to prevent the ICC from taking action in this case.

Bibliography

Al-Khasawneh, A. S. (2002) *Separate Opinion in Case Concerning the Arrest Warrant of 11 April 2000 (Democratic Republic of the Congo v. Belgium)*: International Court of Justice.

Adler, E. (1997) 'Seizing the Middle Ground: Constructivism and World Politics'. *European Journal of International Relations*, 3(3): 319–363.

Alexy, R. (1999) 'A Defence of Radbruch's Formula'. In D. Dyzenhaus (ed.), *Recrafting the Rule of Law: the Limits of Legal Order*. 15–39. Oxford: Hart.

Alston, P. (1998) 'The UN's Human Rights Record: From San Francisco to Vienna and Beyond'. In C. Ku, and P. F. Diehl (eds), *International Law: Classic and Contemporary Readings*. 355–368. Boulder and London: Lynne Rienner.

Alvarez, J. E. (1996) 'Nuremberg Revisited: The *Tadic* Case'. *European Journal of International Law*, 7(2): 245–264.

Annan, K. (2002) 'Letter to Secretary of State Colin Powell, 3 July 2002'.

Arendt, H. (1994) *Eichmann in Jerusalem: A Report on the Banality of Evil*. Harmondsworth: Penguin.

Arrest Warrant Case (2002) 'Case Concerning the Arrest Warrant of 11 April 2000 (Democratic Republic of the Congo v. Belgium)': International Court of Justice.

Bass, G. J. (2002) *Stay the Hand of Vengeance: The Politics of War Crimes Tribunals*. Princeton: Princeton University Press.

Bellamy, A. J. (2003) 'Humanitarian Responsibilities and Interventionist Claims in International Society'. *Review of International Studies*, 29(3): 321–340.

Bellamy, A. J. (2005) 'Introduction: International Society and the English School'. In A. J. Bellamy (ed.), *International Society and its Critics*. 1–26. Oxford and New York: Oxford University Press.

Best, G. (1990) 'Whatever Happened to Human Rights?' *Review of International Studies*, 16(1): 3–18.

Bianchi, A. (1999) 'Immunity Versus Human Rights: The Pinochet Case'. *European Journal of International Law*, 10(2): 237–277.

Bindman, G. (2002) 'Bringing International Criminals to Justice'. In N. Owen (ed.), *Human Rights, Human Wrongs: The Oxford Amnesty Lectures 2001*. 145–163. Oxford: Oxford University Press.

Bodley, A. (1999) 'Weakening the Principle of Sovereignty in International Law: The International Criminal Tribunal for the Former Yugoslavia'. *New York University Journal of Law and Politics*, 31(2): 417–471.

Bosch, W. J. (1970) *Judgment on Nuremberg: American Attitudes Toward the Major German War-Crimes Trials*. Chapel Hill: University of North Carolina Press.

Bravin, J. (14 June 2006) 'US Warms to Hague Tribunal', *The Wall Street Journal*.

Brazil (1995) 'Letter Dated 6 April 1993 From the Permanent Representative of Brazil to the United Nations Addressed to the Secretary-General'. In V. Morris, and M. P. Scharf (eds), *An Insider's Guide to the International Criminal Tribunal for the*

Former Yugoslavia: A Documentary History and Analysis. Vol. 2. 435–437. Irvington-on-Hudson, New York: Transnational Publishers.

Broomhall, B. (2003) *International Justice and the International Criminal Court: Between Sovereignty and the Rule of Law.* Oxford: Oxford University Press.

Brown, B. S. (2002) 'Unilateralism, Multilateralism, and the International Criminal Court'. In S. Patrick, and S. Forman (eds), *Multilateralism and US Foreign Policy.* 323–344. Boulder: Lynne Rienner.

Brown, C. (2002) *Sovereignty, Rights and Justice: International Political Theory Today.* Cambridge: Polity Press.

Bull, H. (1966) 'The Grotian Conception of International Society'. In H. Butterfield, and M. Wight (eds), *Diplomatic Investigations: Essays in the Theory of International Politics.* 51–73. London: George Allen & Unwin Ltd.

Bull, H. (1984) *Justice in International Relations: The Hagey Lectures.* Waterloo, Ontario: University of Waterloo.

Bull, H. (1995) *The Anarchical Society: A Study of Order in World Politics.* Basingstoke and London: Macmillan.

Buzan, B. (2004) *From International to World Society? English School Theory and the Social Structure of Globalisation.* Cambridge: Cambridge University Press.

Byers, M. (2000) 'The Law and Politics of the Pinochet Case'. *Duke Journal of Comparative and International Law,* 10(2): 415–441.

Canada (1995) 'Letter Dated 13 April 1993 From the Permanent Representative of Canada to the United Nations Addressed to the Secretary-General'. In V. Morris, and M. P. Scharf (eds), *An Insider's Guide to the International Criminal Tribunal for the Former Yugoslavia: A Documentary History and Analysis.* Vol. 2. 459–461. Irvington-on-Hudson, New York: Transnational Publishers.

Cassese, A. (1990) *Human Rights in a Changing World.* Cambridge: Polity Press.

Cassese, A. (1999) 'Ex iniuria ius oritur: Are We Moving Towards International Legitimation of Forcible Humanitarian Countermeasures in the World Community?' *European Journal of International Law,* 10(1): 23–30.

Cassese, A. (2001) *International Law.* New York: Oxford University Press.

Cassese, A. (2002) 'When May Senior State Officials Be Tried for International Crimes? Some Comments on the Congo v. Belgium Case'. *European Journal of International Law,* 13(4): 853–875.

Cassese, A. (2003) 'The Belgian Court of Cassation v. the International Court of Justice: the Sharon and Others Case'. *Journal of International Criminal Justice,* 1(2): 437–452.

Checkel, J. T. (1998) 'The Constructivist Turn in International Relations Theory'. *World Politics,* 50(2): 324–348.

Chigara, B. (2000) 'Pinochet and the Administration of International Criminal Justice'. In D. Woodhouse (ed.), *The Pinochet Case: A Legal and Constitutional Analysis.* 115–131. Oxford and Portland, Oregon: Hart Publishing.

Chinkin, C. (1998) 'International Law and International Human Rights'. In T. Evans (ed.), *Human Rights Fifty Years On: A Reappraisal.* 105–129. Manchester and New York: Manchester University Press.

Christodoulidis, E. A. (2004) 'The Objection that Cannot Be Heard: Communication and Legitimacy in the Courtroom'. In A. Duff (ed.), *The Trial on Trial.* 179–202. Oxford and Portland, Oregon: Hart Publishing.

Clapham, A. (2003) 'National Action Challenged: Sovereignty, Immunity and Universal Jurisdiction Before the International Court of Justice'. In M. Lattimer, and P. Sands (eds), *Justice for Crimes Against Humanity.* 303–332. Oxford and Portland, Oregon: Hart Publishing.

Clark, I. (2005) *Legitimacy in International Society.* Oxford and New York: Oxford University Press.

Clinton, B. (2000) 'Statement by the President: Signature of the International Criminal Court Treaty', *31 December 2000.* Camp David, Maryland: Office of the Press Secretary.

Commission of Experts (1993) 'Interim Report of the Commission of Experts Established Pursuant to Security Council Resolution 780 (1992)'.

Daily Telegraph (12 January 2006). 'The Court that tries America's Patience.'

Donnelly, J. (1999) 'The Social Construction of International Human Rights'. In T. Dunne, and N. J. Wheeler (eds), *Human Rights in Global Politics*. 71–102. Cambridge: Cambridge University Press.

Du Plessis, M. (2003) 'The Creation of the ICC: Implications for Africa's Despots, Crackpots and Hotspots'. *African Security Review*, 12(4): 5–15.

Dunne, T. (2005) 'The New Agenda'. In A. J. Bellamy (ed.), *International Society and its Critics*. 65–79. Oxford and New York: Oxford University Press.

Durham, H. (2000) 'The International Criminal Court and State Sovereignty'. In L. Hancock, and C. O'Brien (eds), *Rewriting Rights in Europe*. 169–190. Aldershot, Burlington, Singapore, and Sydney: Ashgate.

Edgar, A. D. (2002) 'Peace, Justice, and Politics: The International Criminal Court, "New Diplomacy", and the UN System'. In A.F. Cooper, J. English, and R. Thakur (eds), *Enhancing Global Governance: Towards a New Diplomacy?* 133–151. Tokyo; New York; Paris: United Nations University Press.

European Parliament (26 September 2002). 'Resolution on the ICC regretting UN Security Council Resolution 1422 and asking Member States not to sign bilateral agreements with the US.' *http://www.derechos.org/nizkor/icc/ep26sep.html* Date of download: 21 August 2008.

European Union (13 May 2002) 'Declaration by the EU on the position of the US towards the International Criminal Court'. *http://www.amicc.org/docs/EUdec5_13_02.pdf* Date of download: 21 August 2008.

Farer, T. J., and Gaer, F. (1993) 'The UN and Human Rights: At the End of the Beginning'. In A. Roberts, and B. Kingsbury (eds), *United Nations, Divided World: The UN's Roles in International Relations*. 240–296. Oxford: Oxford University Press.

Finnemore, M. (2001) 'Exporting the English School?' *Review of International Studies*, 27(3): 509–513.

Finnemore, M. (2003) *The Purpose of Intervention: Changing Beliefs About the Use of Force*. Ithaca and London: Cornell University Press.

Finnemore, M., and Sikkink, K. (1998) 'International Norm Dynamics and Political Change'. *International Organization*, 52(4): 887–917.

Fletcher, L. E., and Weinstein, H. M. (2004) 'A World Unto Itself? The Application of International Justice in the Former Yugoslavia'. In E. Stover, and H. M. Weinstein (eds), *My Neighbor, My Enemy: Justice and Community in the Aftermath of Mass Atrocity*. 29–48. Cambridge: Cambridge University Press.

Forsythe, D. P. (2000) *Human Rights in International Relations*. Cambridge: Cambridge University Press.

Forsythe, D. P. (2006) *Human Rights in International Relations*. Cambridge: Cambridge University Press.

Fox, H. (1999) 'The First Pinochet Case: Immunity of a Former Head of State'. *International and Comparative Law Quarterly*, 48(3): 207–216.

France (1995) 'Letter Dated 10 February 1993 From the Permanent Representative of France to the United Nations Addressed to the Secretary-General'. In V. Morris, and M. P. Scharf (eds), *An Insider's Guide to the International Criminal Tribunal for the Former Yugoslavia: A Documentary History and Analysis*. Vol. 2. 327–385. Irvington-on-Hudson, New York: Transnational Publishers.

Franck, T. M. (1990) *The Power of Legitimacy Among Nations*. New York and Oxford: Oxford University Press.

Franck, T. M. (1992) 'The Emerging Right of Democratic Governance'. *American Journal of International Law*, 86(1): 46–91.

Franck, T. M. (1999) 'Sidelined in Kosovo?' *Foreign Affairs* (July/August).

Goldsmith, J., and Krasner, S. D. (2003) 'The Limits of Idealism'. *Daedalus*, 132(1): 47–63.

Goldstone, R. J., and Bass, G. J. (2000) 'Lessons from the International Criminal Tribunals'. In S. B. Sewall, and C. Kaysen (eds), *The United States and the International Criminal Court: National Security and International Law*. 51–60. Oxford: Rowman & Littlefield.

Grossman, M. (2002) 'American Foreign Policy and the International Criminal Court', *Remarks to the Center for Strategic and International Studies*. Washington D.C.

Guillaume, G. (2002) *Separate Opinion in Case Concerning the Arrest Warrant of 11 April 2000 (Democratic Republic of the Congo v. Belgium)*: International Court of Justice.

Gurmendi, S. A. F. d. (1999) 'The Role of the International Prosecutor'. In R. S. Lee (ed.), *The International Criminal Court: The Making of the Rome Statute: Issues, Negotiations, Results*. 175–188. The Hague, London, and Boston: Kluwer Law International.

Harris, D. J. (1998) *Cases and Materials on International Law*. London: Sweet & Maxwell.

Hawthorn, G. (1999) 'Pinochet: the Politics'. *International Affairs*, 75(2): 253–258.

Hebel, H. v., and Robinson, D. (1999) 'Crimes within the Jurisdiction of the Court'. In R. S. Lee (ed.), *The International Criminal Court: The Making of the Rome Statute: Issues, Negotiations, Results*. 79–126. The Hague, London, and Boston: Kluwer Law International.

Held, D. (2005) 'Globalization, International Law and Human Rights', *Human Rights Institute Research Papers*. University of Connecticut.

Higgins, R., Kooijmans, P. H. and Buergenthal, T. (2002) *Separate Opinion in Case Concerning the Arrest Warrant of 11 April 2000 (Democratic Republic of the Congo v. Belgium)*: International Court of Justice.

Holsti, K. J. (2004) *Taming the Sovereigns: Institutional Change in International Politics*. Cambridge: Cambridge University Press.

Hurrell, A. (2003) 'Order and Justice in International Relations: What is at Stake?' In R. Foot, J. Gaddis, and A. Hurrell (eds), *Order and Justice in International Relations*. 24–48. Oxford: Oxford University Press.

International Criminal Court (17 March 2006). 'Issuance of a Warrant of arrest against Thomas Lubanga Dyilo', *Press Release*.

International Criminal Court (2 May 2007). 'Warrants of Arrest for the Minister of State for Humanitarian Affairs of Sudan, and a leader of the Militia/Janjaweed', *Press Release*.

International Criminal Court (22 May 2007). 'Prosecutor Opens Investigation in the Central African Republic', *Press Release*.

ICISS (2001) 'The Responsibility to Protect'. Ottawa: International Commission on Intervention and State Sovereignty.

Joseph, J. (2005) 'The Exercise of National Sovereignty: The Bush Administration's Approach to Combating Weapons of Mass Destruction Proliferation'. *Nonproliferation Review*, 12(2): 373–387.

Keck, M. E., and Sikkink, K. (1998) *Activists Beyond Borders: Advocacy Networks in International Politics*. Ithaca and London: Cornell University Press.

Kennedy, D. (2004a) *The Dark Sides of Virtue: Reassessing International Humanitarianism*. Princeton and Oxford: Princeton University Press.

Kennedy, D. (2004b) 'International Humanitarianism: The Dark Sides'. *International Journal of Not-for-Profit Law*, 6(3).

Kerr, R. (2004) *The International Criminal Tribunal for the Former Yugoslavia: An Exercise in Law, Politics, and Diplomacy*. Oxford and New York: Oxford University Press.

Koroma, A. G. (2002) *Separate Opinion in Case Concerning the Arrest Warrant of 11 April 2000 (Democratic Republic of the Congo v. Belgium)*: International Court of Justice.

Koskenniemi, M. (2002a) 'Between Impunity and Show Trials'. In J. A. Frowein, and R. Wolfrum (eds), *Max Planck Yearbook of United Nations Law*. Vol. 6. 1–35: Kluwer Law International.

Koskenniemi, M. (2002b) ''The Lady Doth Protest Too Much' Kosovo, and the Turn to Ethics in International Law'. *The Modern Law Review*, 65(2): 159–175.

Koskenniemi, M. (2004) *International Law and Hegemony: A Reconfiguration*. http://www. valt.helsinki.fi/blogs/eci/Hegemony.pdf.

Lee, R. S., ed. (1999). *Views and Comments by Governments*. The Hague, London and Boston: Kluwer Law International.

Letter to President George W. Bush, Members of Congress (22 May 2002).

Leigh, M. (2001) 'The United States and the Statute of Rome'. *American Journal of International Law*, 95(1): 124–131.

Lietzau, W. K. (2001) 'International Criminal Law After Rome: Concerns from a U.S. Military Perspective'. *Law and Contemporary Problems*, 64(1): 119–140.

Linklater, A. (1998) *The Transformation of Political Community: Ethical Foundations of the Post-Westphalian Era*. Cambridge: Polity Press.

Lutz, E. L., and Sikkink, K. (2000) 'International Human Rights Law and Practice in Latin America'. *International Organization*, 54(3): 633–659.

Malanczuk, P. (1997) *Akehurst's Modern Introduction to International Law*. London and New York: Routledge.

Maogoto, J. N. (2004) *War Crimes and Realpolitik: International Justice from World War I to the 21st Century*. Boulder: Lynne Rienner.

Martin, E. A. (2002) *A Dictionary of Law*. Oxford: Oxford University Press.

Mayerfeld, J. (2003) 'Who Shall be Judge?: The United States, the International Criminal Court, and the Global Enforcement of Human Rights'. *Human Rights Quarterly*, 25(1): 93–129.

McGoldrick, D. (2004) 'Political and Legal Reponses to the ICC'. In D. McGoldrick, P. Rowe, and E. Donnelly (eds), *The Permanent International Criminal Court: Legal and Policy Issues*. 389–449. Oxford and Portland, Oregon: Hart Publishing.

Milosevic Transcript (2001) 'Transcript: Milosevic (IT-02-54) "Kosovo, Croatia and Bosnia-Herzegovina"', International Criminal Tribunal for the Former Yugoslavia, 3 July 2001.

Minow, M. (1998) *Between Vengeance and Forgiveness: Facing History After Genocide and Mass Violence*. Boston: Beacon Press.

Morris, V., and Scharf, M. P. (1995) *An Insider's Guide to the International Criminal Tribunal for the Former Yugoslavia: A Documentary History and Analysis*. Irvington-on-Hudson, New York: Transnational Publishers.

Nel, P. (2002) 'Between Counter-Hegemony and Post-Hegemony: The Rome Statute and Normative Innovation in World Politics'. In A. F. Cooper, J. English, and R. Thakur (eds), *Enhancing Global Governance: Towards a New Diplomacy?* 152–161. Tokyo, New York, and Paris: United Nations University Press.

Overy, R. (2003) 'The Nuremberg Trials: International Law in the Making'. In P. Sands (ed.), *From Nuremberg to The Hague: The Future of International Criminal Justice*. 1–29. Cambridge: Cambridge University Press.

Papadatos, P. (1964) *The Eichmann Trial*. London: Stevens & Son.

Peskin, V. (2000) 'Conflicts of Justice - An Analysis of the Role of the International Criminal Tribunal for Rwanda'. *International Peacekeeping*, 6(4–6): 128–137.

Pinochet I (1998) 'Regina v. Bartle and the Commissioner of Police for the Metropolis and Others Ex Parte Pinochet (On Appeal from a Divisional Court of the Queen's Bench Division); Regina v. Evans and Another and the Commissioner of Police for the Metropolis and Others Ex Parte Pinochet (On Appeal from a Divisional Court of the Queen's Bench Division)': House of Lords.

Pinochet III (1999) 'Regina v. Bartle and the Commissioner of Police for the Metropolis and Others Ex Parte Pinochet; Regina v. Evans and Another and the Commissioner of Police for the Metropolis and Others Ex Parte Pinochet (On Appeal from a Divisional Court of the Queen's Bench Division)': House of Lords.

Popovski, V. (2000) 'International Criminal Court: A Necessary Step Towards Global Justice'. *Security Dialogue*, 31(1): 405–419.

Ralph, J. (2003) 'Between Cosmopolitan and American Democracy: Understanding US Opposition to the International Criminal Court'. *International Relations*, 17(2): 195–212.

Report of the *Ad Hoc* Committee on the Establishment of an International Criminal Court (1995). New York: United Nations.

Report of the Preparatory Committee on the Establishment of an International Criminal Court: Proceedings of the Preparatory Committee during March–April and August 1996, Vol. I (1996). New York: United Nations.

Reus-Smit, C. (2001) 'Constructivism'. In S. Burchill, and A. Linklater (eds), *Theories of International Relations*. 209–230. Basingstoke: Macmillan.

Reus-Smit, C. (2004) 'Society, Power, and Ethics'. In C. Reus-Smit (ed.), *The Politics of International Law*. 272–290. Cambridge: Cambridge University Press.

Reydams, L. (2003) *Universal Jurisdiction: International and Municipal Legal Perspectives*. Oxford: Oxford University Press.

Rice, C. (10 March 2006) 'Trip Briefing – En Route to San Juan, Puerto Rico'. In U.S. Department of State (ed.).

Risse, T., and Sikkink, K. (1999) 'The Socialization of International Human Rights Norms into Domestic Practices: Introduction'. In T. Risse, S. C. Ropp, and K. Sikkink (eds), *The Power of Human Rights: International Norms and Domestic Change*. 1–38. Cambridge: Cambridge University Press.

Robertson, G. (2002) *Crimes Against Humanity: The Struggle for Global Justice*. London: Penguin.

Rodman, K. A. (2006) 'Compromising Justice: Why the Bush Administration and the NGOs Are Both Wrong About the ICC'. *Ethics and International Affairs*, 20(1): 25–53.

Roht-Arriaza, N. (2005) *The Pinochet Effect: Transnational Justice in the Age of Human Rights*. Philadelphia: University of Pennsylvannia Press.

Rome Proceedings (1998). *Official Records of the United Nations Diplomatic Conference of Plenipotentiaries on the Establishment of an International Criminal Court: Summary Records of the Plenary Meetings and of the Meetings of the Committee of the Whole*, Vol. II, Rome: United Nations.

Rudolph, C. (2001) 'Constructing an Atrocities Regime: The Politics of War Crimes Tribunals'. *International Organization*, 55(3): 655–691.

Russia (1995) 'Letter Dated 5 April 1993 From the Permanent Representative of the Russian Federation to the United Nations Addressed to the Secretary-General'. In V. Morris, and M. P. Scharf (eds), *An Insider's Guide to the International Criminal Tribunal for the Former Yugoslavia: A Documentary History and Analysis*. Vol. 2. 439–457. Irvington-on-Hudson, New York: Transnational Publishers.

Sands, P. (2003a) 'After Pinochet: the Role of National Courts'. In P. Sands (ed.), *From Nuremberg to The Hague: The Future of International Criminal Justice*. 68–81. Cambridge: Cambridge University Press.

Sands, P. (2003b) 'International Law Transformed? From Pinochet to Congo ...?' *Leiden Journal of International Law*, 16: 37–53.

Sands, P. (2005) *Lawless World: America and the Making and Breaking of Global Rules*. London: Penguin; Allen Lane.

Schabas, W. A. (2001) *An Introduction to the International Criminal Court*. Cambridge: Cambridge University Press.

Schabas, W. A. (2004) 'United States Hostility to the International Criminal Court: It's All About the Security Council'. *European Journal of International Law*, 15(4): 701–720.

Scheffer, D. (1996) 'International Judicial Intervention'. *Foreign Policy*(102): 34–51.

Scheffer, D. J. (2002) 'Staying the Course with the International Criminal Court'. *Cornell International Law Journal*, 35(1): 47–100.

Schmitz, H. P., and Sikkink, K. (2002) 'International Human Rights'. In W. Carlsnaes, T. Risse, and B. A. Simmons (eds), *Handbook of International Relations*. 517–537. London, Thousand Oaks, and New Delhi: Sage.

Secretary-General (1993) 'Report of the Secretary-General Pursuant to Paragraph 2 of Security Council Resolution 808'.

Secretary-General (2004) 'Secretary-General's Press Encounter upon Arrival at UNHQ (unofficial transcript)', *Off the cuff remarks to the press and public*. New York.

Sewall, S. B., and Kaysen, C. (2000) 'The United States and the International Criminal Court: An Overview'. In S. B. Sewall, and C. Kaysen (eds), *The United States and the International Criminal Court: National Security and International Law*. 1–27. London, Boulder, New York, and Oxford: Rowman & Littlefield.

Shklar, J. N. (1964) *Legalism*. Cambridge: Harvard University Press.

Simpson, G. (2004) 'Politics, Sovereignty, Remembrance'. In D. McGoldrick, P. Rowe, and E. Donnelly (eds), *The Permanent International Criminal Court: Legal and Policy Issues*. 47–61. Oxford and Portland, Oregon: Hart Publishing.

Stone, J. (1961) 'The Eichmann Trial and The Rule of Law'. Address at the Annual Meeting of International Commission of Jurists.

Summary of Opinions (2002) *Separate Opinion in Case Concerning the Arrest Warrant of 11 April 2000 (Democratic Republic of the Congo v. Belgium)*: International Court of Justice.

Tadić Case Appeal (1995) 'Prosecutor v. Dusko Tadić A/K/A "Dule" – Decision on the Defence Motion for Interlocutory Appeal on Jurisdiction': Appeals Chamber of the ICTY.

Tomuschat, C. (2003) *Human Rights: Between Idealism and Realism*. New York: Oxford University Press.

Trial Chamber, (1995) 'Prosecutor v. Dusko Tadić A/K/A "Dule" - Decision on the Defence Motion on Jurisdiction': Trial Chamber of the ICTY.

UN Security Council (1995) 'Record of Debate on Resolution 827, 25 May 1993'. In V. Morris, and M. P. Scharf (eds), *An Insider's Guide to the International Criminal Tribunal for the Former Yugoslavia: A Documentary History and Analysis*. Vol. 2. 179–208. Irvington-on-Hudson, New York: Transnational Publishers.

UN Security Council (2002) 'Record of 4563rd Security Council Meeting – 30 June 2002', *United Nations Security Council*.

US Department of State (23 June 2004), Daily Press Briefing, Richard Boucher, Spokesman.

US Government (2002) 'The National Security Strategy of the United States of America'. Washington D.C.

Van den Wyngaert, C. (2002) *Separate Opinion in Case Concerning the Arrest Warrant of 11 April 2000 (Democratic Republic of the Congo v. Belgium)*: International Court of Justice.

Vincent, R. J. (1974) *Nonintervention and International Order*. Princeton: Princeton University Press.

Washington Post (30 September 2003). 'Belgian War Crimes Law Undone by Its Global Reach.'

Wedgwood, R. (1999) 'The United States and the International Criminal Court: Achieving a Wider Consensus Through the "Ithaca Package"'. *Cornell International Law Journal*, 32(3).

Weller, M. (1999) 'On the Hazards of Foreign Travel for Dictators and Other International Criminals'. *International Affairs*, 75(3): 599–617.

Weller, M. (2002) 'Undoing the Global Constitution: UN Security Council Action on the International Criminal Court'. *International Affairs*, 78(4): 693–712.

Wendt, A. (1992) 'Anarchy is What States Make of it: the Social Construction of Power Politics'. *International Organization*, 46(2): 390–425.

Wheeler, N. J. (1992) 'Pluralist and Solidarist Conceptions of International Society: Bull and Vincent on Humanitarian Intervention'. *Millennium: Journal of International Politics*, 21(3): 463–487.

Wheeler, N. J. (2000) *Saving Strangers: Humanitarian Intervention in International Society*. Oxford: Oxford University Press.

Wheeler, N. J., and Dunne, T. (1996) 'Hedley Bull's Pluralism of the Intellect and Solidarism of the Will'. *International Affairs*, 72(1): 91–107.

White, N. D. (2002) *The United Nations System: Toward International Justice.* Boulder and London: Lynne Rienner.

Wight, M. (1994) *International Theory: The Three Traditions.* London: Leicester University Press.

Williams, P. R., and Scharf, M. P. (2002) *Peace with Justice? War Crimes and Accountability in the Former Yugoslavia.* Lanham, Boulder, New York, and Oxford: Rowman & Littlefield Publishers.

Winants, A. (2003) 'The *Yerodia* Ruling of the International Court of Justice and the 1993/1999 Belgian Law of Universal Jurisdiction'. *Leiden Journal of International Law*, 16(3): 491–509.

Wirth, S. (2002) 'Immunity for Core Crimes? The ICJ's Judgment in the Congo v. Belgium Case'. *European Journal of International Law*, 13(4): 877–893.

Woodhouse, D. (2000) 'Introduction: The Extradition of Pinochet: A Calendar of Events'. In D. Woodhouse (ed.), *The Pinochet Case: A Legal and Constitutional Analysis.* 1–14. Oxford and Portland, Oregon: Hart Publishing.

Woodhouse, D., ed. (2000). *The Pinochet Case: A Legal and Constitutional Analysis.* Oxford and Portland, Oregon: Hart Publishing.

Wouters, J. (2003) 'The Judgement of the International Court of Justice in the *Arrest Warrant* Case: Some Critical Remarks'. *Leiden Journal of International Law*, 16(2): 253–267.

Yee, L. (1999) 'The International Criminal Court and The Security Council: Articles 13(b) and 16'. In R. S. Lee (ed.), *The International Criminal Court: The Making of the Rome Statute: Issues, Negotiations, Results.* 143–152. The Hague, London, and Boston: Kluwer Law International.

Yugoslavia, Serbia and Montenegro (1995) 'Letter Dated 19 May 1993 From the Charge D'Affaires A.I. of the Permanent Mission of Yugoslavia (Serbia and Montenegro) to the United Nations Addressed to the Secretary-General'. In V. Morris, and M. P. Scharf (eds), *An Insider's Guide to the International Criminal Tribunal for the Former Yugoslavia: A Documentary History and Analysis.* Vol. 2. 479–480. Irvington-on-Hudson, New York: Transnational Publishers.

Index

Go further with Routledge. . .
Other titles on global politics and security
to further your studies

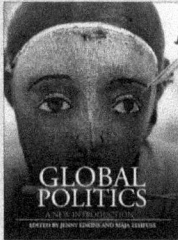

For Product Safety Concerns and Information please contact our EU
representative GPSR@taylorandfrancis.com
Taylor & Francis Verlag GmbH, Kaufingerstraße 24, 80331 München, Germany

www.ingramcontent.com/pod-product-compliance
Lightning Source LLC
Chambersburg PA
CBHW050511280326
41932CB00014B/2277